HOLLYWOOD 101

HOLLYWOOD 101

THE FILM INDUSTRY

Frederick Levy

RENAISSANCE BOOKS
Los Angeles

For my mom and dad,
who allowed me the latitude to move to Los Angeles to pursue
my dreams when I was only seventeen years old.

For my brother, David, who's about to embark
on his own journey into the world of entertainment.

And in loving memory of my papa, Harold, and my aunt, Lois.

Acknowledgments
Grateful acknowledgment is extended to the American Film Institute for its List of America's 100 Greatest Movies and to Breakdown Services, Ltd., for the sample breakdown.

Library of Congress Catalog Card Number: 99-69668
ISBN: 1-58063-123-1

10 9 8 7 6 5 4 3 2 1

Design by Tanya Maiboroda

Published by Renaissance Books
Distributed by St. Martin's Press
Manufactured in the United States of America
First Edition

CONTENTS

ACKNOWLEDGMENTS

Let's face it. This book wouldn't even exist if it weren't for the efforts of my agent, Andree Abecassis of the Ann Elmo Agency. She ran around town with merely an idea that I had pitched to her, and from that, got me a book deal. For starting me on my new literary career, I thank you.

Hand in hand with Andree, I have to give equal gratitude to my editor, Jim Parish, of Renaissance Books. Since my first lunch meeting with Jim, he has always gone above and beyond the call of duty with his personal attention and guidance. For taking a risk on a kid who had never written a book before, I thank you.

Certainly, without the time and cooperation of my colleagues, who let me interview them for this book, I could not have presented the in-depth look at the film business that this project required. In alphabetical order: Carl Bressler, Amy McIntyre Britt, Tom Bronson, Bonnie Bruckheimer, John Caglione Jr., Craig Cannold, Angela Cheng, Joel Dean, Debbie Deuble,

Jimmy Dobson, Ingrid Ferrin, Tim Garrick, Michael Green, KristieAnne Groelinger, Marshall Herskovitz, Debra Hill, Mark Indig, Christian Kaplan, David Katz, Marty Katz, Stephen M. Katz, Jonathan King, Mary Lambert, Maggie Martin, Karon May, Micheal McAlister, Mark McNabb, Bruce Mink, Andy Nelson, John Ottman, Dean Pitchford, Robert Ramos, Ira Shuman, Mary Ann Skweres, David Steinberg, Yvette Taylor, Jon Turteltaub, Michael Valeo, Gary Wissner, and Daniel Yost.

Additional information was provided by the following: Sarah Amundson, Kevin Brady, Jerry Bruckheimer, Andrew Carey, Pauline Cymet, Eric M. Davis, Callie de Quevedo, Dan Fitzgerald, Jeremy Garelick, Jeff Hare, Susan Ireland, Campbell Katz, Chris Skinner, and Jim Wills.

Those who helped me coordinate different aspects of the book: the American Film Institute (Shanna Bright, Tehya Kopp, Seth Oster), Lisa Fitzgerald, Joe Gatta, Terry Goldman, Gary Marsh, Beth Reiter, Laura Rhodes, Jessica Sitomer, Allan Taylor, and Vanessa Torres.

I had a fantastic crew of assistants and interns who helped me with a great deal of the administrative end of putting this book together. First and foremost, Andy Putschoegl, and Tiffany Tiesiera. Also: Aleigh Bracken, Jason Debose, Susie Fanslow, Andrew Friedman, Russell Kaplan, James Krisel, Fabrice Lachant, Lucien Lefcourt, Josh Lurie, Maria Pulera, Todd Roth, Troy Smith, Kevin Steinberg, Dan Tebo, Danielle Wright, and Patrick Young.

The people who encouraged me, inspired me, and gave me my own breaks along the way: Paula Freeman-Bert, Campbell Katz, Marty Katz, Teri Markowitz, and Andrea Newman.

Those friends who keep me most focused in life: Jonah Brown, Ellen Cleghorne, Robin Conkey, Julie Corcoran, Wesley Eure, Hilary Friedman, Melissa Harper, Noah Hathaway, Rick Joyce, Jayson Kalani, Susan Lenser, Robin Locke, Michael Polonsky, and Michelle Primack.

PREFACE

As a feature film development executive, part of my job is lunching with literary agents to discuss new material. Not long ago, I was dining in Los Angeles with an agent who represents several nonfiction writers. Kidding around, I asked her if anyone would be interested in someone such as me writing a guidebook about breaking into the film business. She thought it was a great idea.

Having never written a full-length book before, the agent sent me guidelines to help me prepare an outline for what would eventually become this volume. She submitted my outline to several publishers. I took meetings with various editors. An editor at Renaissance Books thought I was on to something and had me write sample pages so that he and the firm's editorial board could get a better idea of the book I envisioned.

A few weeks later, my literary representative called to say we had an offer on the proposal. I signed the contract, spent the advance, and blocked out the next year's worth of weekends so I would have time to write.

It dawned on me that getting a book deal is not unlike breaking into the Hollywood film industry. It's about having a good idea, knowing the correct people, being in the right place at the right time, and having a bit of luck. These are some of the same elements that helped me get my first break in Hollywood.

Getting a break and making something of it, however, are two very different things. Now that I had a book to prepare, it was time for me to reprioritize my life and focus a good deal of energy on writing every day. When I moved to Los Angeles, my energies were directed toward finding my niche within the film industry. Once I found it, my focus turned to doing a good job *and* getting noticed. By keeping both of these goals in mind, I have been able to make things happen. With similar vigor and enthusiasm, you can too. If a career in the movie business is what you *really* want, then direct your attention constructively and you will achieve it.

In this day and age, there is a great deal of interest in breaking into Hollywood. Books on the subject, therefore, are by no means uncommon. What I've tried to do with this guidebook is bring to it a unique perspective.

First and foremost, I came to Hollywood without knowing anyone in the entertainment business. Through many experiences, which I will share with you, I found my way into the mainstream of the film industry. In researching this project, I've asked many of my colleagues to share their stories about how they found success in the business. I hope their experiences and perspectives will inspire you as they did me.

I have organized this book as simply as possible. Read cover to cover, it serves as an accurate survey of the film industry. For those who already know where their particular career passion lies, this reference guide is organized to let you jump from section to section or chapter to chapter. Each segment is easy to understand both in and out of context.

Hollywood 101 describes the various career opportunities that exist in the moviemaking community. It outlines how to get started in each field. This information is combined with advice from professionals who are working in various areas of the film industry.

In several instances, I have listed contact information. For companies that you would be contacting but not visiting, I have omitted addresses. When available, toll-free telephone numbers are provided for companies located outside of the greater Los Angeles area. E-mail addresses are given only when no Web site exists.

I have tried my best to be politically correct when using pronouns in this guide. However, the film industry, steeped in tradition, has not yet changed to unisex names for many of its positions, such as best boy, cameraman, and so forth.

Two appendixes are included at the back of this book. Appendix A is a list of resources where you can find more information on a particular subject covered in a given chapter. Contact information for many of the resources mentioned in the text can be found here. Appendix B references salaries for many of the craft positions. All salaries listed are at union scale rates as of January 1999. Because rates change periodically, consult the appropriate union or guild for the most updated information. There is no difference between a union and a guild. The chart on pay reflects whether each job is union, and rates generally are organized from lowest to highest minimum in each category. Finally, the glossary defines terms with which you may be presently unfamiliar.

Although the film industry certainly exists outside of Los Angeles, this book focuses on Hollywood, as it is the film capital of the world. In all honesty, if you are starting out, Los Angeles is the place you need to be. I plan to detail the film business outside of Southern California in a future volume. Two additional, expansive subjects have been purposely omitted from this book, as each deserves full discussion on its own. These are the television industry and the acting profession. I plan to cover both of these subjects in future, separate guides as well.

PART ONE

PREPARING
FOR A
CAREER
IN THE
FILM INDUSTRY

REEL DREAMS

I still don't understand what it is you do.

LOIS LEVY, author's mother

Congratulations on your recent investment. Oh yes, that's what this book is—an investment in your future in the Hollywood film business.

In 1988, I migrated to Los Angeles from a small suburban Massachusetts town. I had always fantasized about moving west to pursue an entertainment career, but I hadn't a clue about how to make it really happen. With persistence and passion, I got my first industry break. With just a bit of luck, I got my foot in the door. With a lot of hard work, I found initial success. With each passing day, I continue to grow in my field.

The path I chose led me in many directions. My education was simply trial and error. As I learned more about the entertainment business, I soon discovered my professional objective. Throughout this journey, high points and low, I sought to stay true to my dreams and never to lose focus of my career goals. Along the way I met people who offered me professional advice. They showed me the ropes and taught me the importance of networking. Today I am pleased to call many of these mentors my colleagues and friends.

I currently work in the film industry as a producer and development executive. With this book, I hope to share my knowledge and personal experiences in the business to help you make your own way in Hollywood simpler and more productive.

Most people will tell you that this is a particularly difficult and competitive business. That's the truth, but don't let it discourage you. Often, what is not said is that making it in Hollywood *is* possible. So no matter who you are, where you're from, or where you fit in, always remember that you *can* make your Hollywood dreams come true.

I had toyed with the notion of moving to Los Angeles to pursue my film business dreams for quite some time. However, I didn't know if I had what it took. Nothing in Tinseltown seemed tangible to me. I didn't want to be just another anonymous fish swimming in a huge celluloid sea. Many of you probably feel the same way.

If you have a burning desire to work in the movies, *Hollywood 101* is geared to help you realize your career goals. It's for the videographer who wants to be the next Steven Spielberg; the construction worker who would rather be building a movie set than a strip mall; the stylist at Supercuts who could be coiffing movie stars instead of the folks back home; and the perpetual diary keeper whose journals should be turned into lucrative screenplays.

When I came to Hollywood, I didn't have a book like this to help me. This guide points you to career opportunities that you might not have known existed. It will give you ideas and inspiration to make the leap; and it will answer many of your questions about how Hollywood really works. It is designed to put you steps closer to turning your reel dreams into *real* dreams.

DON'T PACK YET!

Don't rush out to buy your one-way ticket to Southern California just yet. After all, if you had never gone swimming before, you wouldn't jump right into the ocean. Prepare for your film career, to the best of your ability, *before* you leave home. There's a lot you can do productively from home in anticipation of your move to Los Angeles. The more educated and experienced you are about the world of entertainment, the better your chances are for success.

RESEARCH, RESEARCH, RESEARCH

Learn as much as you can about the film business. Reading this book is a great start, but others also are worth reading, such as William Goldman's authoritative *Adventures in the Screen Trade*. Visit your local library and search the Internet for other resources on Hollywood and the film industry. Surf film-related Web sites and subscribe to various news/user groups on the Internet so that you can electronically network with other people who share your career passions. See appendix A for a list of other movie industry books and Internet film resources.

EDUCATE THYSELF

Many high schools and most colleges and universities offer classes relating to film. These courses range from introductory surveys to more specific seminars on topics such as screenwriting and editing. Choose courses on the subjects that most interest you and, if you already know your specific goal, pertain to your future Hollywood career. Even if the craft you're interested in—hair and makeup or construction, for example is learned outside the realm of film school, you should endeavor to learn as much about film as you can if you want to work in the business.

Most local cable TV stations and many local TV affiliates offer on-site workshops on video production. Although video and film differ in form, these courses prove quite valuable to aspiring filmmakers, as many of the same principles apply to both mediums.

BUILD YOUR MOVIE REPERTOIRE

Watch as many movies as possible and develop a sense of judgment and perspective. You need to become fairly knowledgeable about the industry's end product. I've turned down many potential employees because they hadn't seen enough films or simply didn't have an opinion on what they had seen. Some couldn't even name their favorite film. Others told me the last movie they saw in a theater was something from a decade ago!

"You try never to push your opinion, because then you're pushy. If you're asked for your opinion, you'll always have one," says KristieAnne Groelinger, director of production at Jerry Bruckheimer Films. "There are a lot of assistants who don't even read the material. When I was an assistant, I read everything. That way, in the event your boss asks you about a script, you have an opinion ready."

See as many new releases as possible, good and bad, special-effects extravaganzas and art-house films, megahits and disappointments. You can learn just as much from watching a successful film as you can by watching failures. Also, rent older movies that you've never seen from the video store. Consult the lists below as a starting point.

The following is a complete list (ranked in order of importance) of the American Film Institute's (AFI) 100 greatest American movies as selected by a blue-ribbon panel of more than 1,500 leaders from across the American film community. Panelists chose from a list of 400 nominated movies compiled by the AFI. The nominated movies were all feature-length fiction films produced during the first 100 years of American cinema (1896–1996).

The American Film Institute's List of America's 100 Greatest Movies	
Film	Year
1 *Citizen Kane*	1941
2 *Casablanca*	1942
3 *The Godfather*	1972
4 *Gone with the Wind*	1939
5 *Lawrence of Arabia*	1962
6 *The Wizard of Oz*	1939
7 *The Graduate*	1967
8 *On the Waterfront*	1954
9 *Schindler's List*	1993
10 *Singin' in the Rain*	1952
11 *It's a Wonderful Life*	1946
12 *Sunset Boulevard*	1950
13 *The Bridge on the River Kwai*	1957

14	*Some Like It Hot*	1959
15	*Star Wars*	1977
16	*All About Eve*	1950
17	*The African Queen*	1951
18	*Psycho*	1960
19	*Chinatown*	1974
20	*One Flew over the Cuckoo's Nest*	1975
21	*The Grapes of Wrath*	1940
22	*2001: A Space Odyssey*	1968
23	*The Maltese Falcon*	1941
24	*Raging Bull*	1980
25	*E.T. The Extra-Terrestrial*	1982
26	*Dr. Strangelove*	1964
27	*Bonnie and Clyde*	1967
28	*Apocalypse Now*	1979
29	*Mr. Smith Goes to Washington*	1939
30	*The Treasure of the Sierra Madre*	1948
31	*Annie Hall*	1977
32	*The Godfather, Part II*	1974
33	*High Noon*	1952
34	*To Kill a Mockingbird*	1962
35	*It Happened One Night*	1934
36	*Midnight Cowboy*	1969
37	*The Best Years of Our Lives*	1946
38	*Double Indemnity*	1944
39	*Doctor Zhivago*	1965
40	*North by Northwest*	1959
41	*West Side Story*	1961
42	*Rear Window*	1954
43	*King Kong*	1933
44	*The Birth of a Nation*	1915
45	*A Streetcar Named Desire*	1951

46	A Clockwork Orange	1971
47	Taxi Driver	1976
48	Jaws	1975
49	Snow White and the Seven Dwarfs	1937
50	Butch Cassidy and the Sundance Kid	1969
51	The Philadelphia Story	1940
52	From Here to Eternity	1953
53	Amadeus	1984
54	All Quiet on the Western Front	1930
55	The Sound of Music	1965
56	M*A*S*H	1970
57	The Third Man	1949
58	Fantasia	1940
59	Rebel Without a Cause	1955
60	Raiders of the Lost Ark	1981
61	Vertigo	1958
62	Tootsie	1982
63	Stagecoach	1939
64	Close Encounters of the Third Kind	1977
65	The Silence of the Lambs	1991
66	Network	1976
67	The Manchurian Candidate	1962
68	An American in Paris	1951
69	Shane	1953
70	The French Connection	1971
71	Forrest Gump	1994
72	Ben-Hur	1959
73	Wuthering Heights	1939
74	The Gold Rush	1925
75	Dances with Wolves	1990
76	City Lights	1931
77	American Graffiti	1973

78	*Rocky*	1976
79	*The Deer Hunter*	1978
80	*The Wild Bunch*	1969
81	*Modern Times*	1936
82	*Giant*	1956
83	*Platoon*	1986
84	*Fargo*	1996
85	*Duck Soup*	1933
86	*Mutiny on the Bounty*	1935
87	*Frankenstein*	1931
88	*Easy Rider*	1969
89	*Patton*	1970
90	*The Jazz Singer*	1927
91	*My Fair Lady*	1964
92	*A Place in the Sun*	1951
93	*The Apartment*	1960
94	*GoodFellas*	1990
95	*Pulp Fiction*	1994
96	*The Searchers*	1956
97	*Bringing Up Baby*	1938
98	*Unforgiven*	1992
99	*Guess Who's Coming to Dinner*	1967
100	*Yankee Doodle Dandy*	1942

Every year since 1929, the Academy of Motion Picture Arts and Sciences presents the Academy Awards, or Oscars, in recognition of outstanding achievements in filmmaking. Below is a list of the films that received Best Picture to date. It makes a great checklist to start or improve upon your repertoire, but make sure you consider seeing films that won—and even those nominated—in other categories as well.

Several reference books on Oscar are available, including *70 Years of the Oscar* by Robert Osborne.

1998	Shakespeare in Love		1969	Midnight Cowboy
1997	Titanic		1968	Oliver!
1996	The English Patient		1967	In the Heat of the Night
1995	Braveheart		1966	A Man for All Seasons
1994	Forrest Gump		1965	The Sound of Music
1993	Schindler's List		1964	My Fair Lady
1992	Unforgiven		1963	Tom Jones
1991	The Silence of the Lambs		1962	Lawrence of Arabia
1990	Dances with Wolves		1961	West Side Story
1989	Driving Miss Daisy		1960	The Apartment
1988	Rain Man		1959	Ben-Hur
1987	The Last Emperor		1958	Gigi
1986	Platoon		1957	The Bridge on the River Kwai
1985	Out of Africa		1956	Around the World in 80 Days
1984	Amadeus		1955	Marty
1983	Terms of Endearment		1954	On the Waterfront
1982	Gandhi		1953	From Here to Eternity
1981	Chariots of Fire		1952	The Greatest Show on Earth
1980	Ordinary People		1951	An American in Paris
1979	Kramer vs. Kramer		1950	All About Eve
1978	The Deer Hunter		1949	All the King's Men
1977	Annie Hall		1948	Hamlet
1976	Rocky		1947	Gentleman's Agreement
1975	One Flew over the Cuckoo's Nest		1946	The Best Years of Our Lives
1974	The Godfather, Part II		1945	The Lost Weekend
1973	The Sting		1944	Going My Way
1972	The Godfather		1943	Casablanca
1971	The French Connection		1942	Mrs. Miniver
1970	Patton		1941	How Green Was My Valley

1940	*Rebecca*		1932/33	*Cavalcade*
1939	*Gone with the Wind*		1931/32	*Grand Hotel*
1938	*You Can't Take It with You*		1930/31	*Cimarron*
1937	*The Life of Emile Zola*		1929/30	*All Quiet on the Western Front*
1936	*The Great Ziegfeld*		1928/29	*Broadway Melody*
1935	*Mutiny on the Bounty*		1927/28	*Wings*
1934	*It Happened One Night*			

There's something to be said about a box-office smash vs. a box-office dud. If you haven't already, make a point to check out movies that raked in the receipts. Popularity aside, there must be something about these films that kept people coming back for more. Below are the 40 all-time box-office champs to date according to a compilation of industry reference sources such as annual editions of *Weekly Variety*.

Rank	Film	Distrib	Yr	Domestic Box Office Gross (in Millions)	Overseas Box Office Gross (in Millions)	Worldwide Box Office Gross (in Millions)
1	*Titanic*	Par	97	$600.8	$1234.3	$1835.1
2	*Star Wars*	Fox	77	461.0	337.0	798.0
3*	*Star Wars: Episode I— The Phantom Menace*	Fox	99	427.6	461.1	888.7
4	*E.T. The Extra-Terrestrial*	Uni	82	399.8	305.0	704.8
5	*Jurassic Park*	Uni	93	357.1	563.0	920.1
6	*Forrest Gump*	Par	94	329.7	350.0	679.7
7	*The Lion King*	BV	94	312.9	454.0	766.9
8	*Return of the Jedi*	Fox	83	309.1	263.7	572.9
9	*Independence Day*	Fox	96	306.2	503.0	809.2
10	*The Empire Strikes Back*	Fox	80	290.2	222.7	512.9
11	*Home Alone*	Fox	90	285.8	248.0	533.8
12*	*The Sixth Sense*	BV	99	260.4	52.2	312.6
13	*Jaws*	Uni	75	260.0	210.6	470.6
14	*Batman*	WB	89	251.2	162.0	413.2

15	Men in Black	Sony	97	250.1	336.0	586.1
16	Raiders of the Lost Ark	Par	81	242.4	141.5	383.9
17	Twister	WB	96	241.7	253.0	494.7
18	Ghostbusters	Col	84	238.6	53.0	291.6
19	Beverly Hills Cop	Par	84	234.8	81.6	316.4
20	The Lost World: Jurassic Park	Uni	97	229.1	385.3	614.4
21	Mrs. Doubtfire	Fox	93	219.2	204.0	423.2
22	Ghost	Par	90	217.6	300.0	517.6
23	Aladdin	BV	92	217.4	285.0	502.4
24	Saving Private Ryan	DW	98	215.9	263.2	479.1
25	Back to the Future	Uni	85	208.2	140.0	348.2
26*	Austin Powers: The Spy Who Shagged Me	NL	99	205.4	94.6	300.0
27	Terminator 2: Judgment Day	TriStar	91	204.8	312.0	516.8
28	Armageddon	BV	98	201.6	353.0	554.6
29	Gone with the Wind	MGM	39	198.5	191.9	390.4
30	Indiana Jones and the Last Crusade	Par	89	197.2	297.6	494.8
31	Toy Story	BV	95	191.8	167.0	358.8
32	Snow White and the Seven Dwarfs	BV	37	184.9	N/A	184.9
33	Dances with Wolves	Orion	90	184.2	240.0	424.2
34	Batman Forever	WB	95	184.0	151.0	335.0
35	The Fugitive	WB	93	183.9	185.0	368.9
36	Liar Liar	Uni	97	181.4	125.0	306.4
37	Grease	Par	78	181.3	198.5	379.8
38	Mission: Impossible	Par	96	181.0	271.6	452.6
39	Indiana Jones and the Temple of Doom	Par	84	179.9	153.2	333.1
40	Pretty Woman	BV	90	178.4	259.8	438.2

* Indicates film still in release at time of printing.

Finally, Hollywood's at its best when it's dissecting itself. Herewith a selective list of movies about movies: self-reflective films on the movie business.

... And God Spoke (1993)
The Bad and the Beautiful (1952)
Barton Fink (1991)
The Big Picture (1989)
Bowfinger (1999)
Boy Meets Girl (1938)
Burn Hollywood Burn: An Alan Smithee Film (1998)
Contempt (1963)
Ed Wood (1994)
Get Shorty (1995)
Hollywood Shuffle (1987)
I'll Do Anything (1994)
In a Lonely Place (1950)
Living in Oblivion (1995)
Mistress (1991)
My Life's in Turnaround (1994)
The Muse (1999)
The Player (1992)
Singin' in the Rain (1952)
The Star (1952)
A Star Is Born (1954)
Stand-In (1937)
Sullivan's Travels (1941)
Sunset Boulevard (1950)
Swimming with Sharks (1995)
Two Weeks in Another Town (1962)
Wes Craven's New Nightmare (1994)

Analyze the movies that you see. Why do certain films make more money than others? What makes a movie good or bad? What do you like and dislike about particular films? "Develop taste levels of what you like and what you don't like," recommends producer Marty Katz. "Try to read the scripts from the films you liked and didn't like, and try to figure out why somebody would or would not have made that movie." Are the characters in the movie well developed and multidimensional, or are they obtuse? Are the film's set pieces fresh and exciting, or have they been used time and time again?

Start to associate names of directors, producers, and studios with the films you screen. If you are particularly impressed with a production's costumes, watch the credits to see who designed them. Find out what other screen projects that person has worked on as a costume designer. Have you noticed that certain directors like to work with the same crew over and over? Why do you think that is? This thought process will help you gain a better understanding of the film business.

POP CULTURE JUNKIES

Become a pop culture junkie. Read as many magazines about pop culture as possible. Browse Web sites devoted to the movie business such as Film.com and E! Online (see appendix A for a listing of sites). Watch *Access Hollywood* or other news and entertainment magazines on television. Keep up with the latest buzz on upcoming films. Learn which actors and celebrities are hot. Find out what's new in the worlds of architecture and fashion. Know the latest trends and crazes. Keep an eye on the box-office charts and TV ratings.

GET IN TRAINING

Training is an important element of the traditional classroom approach to learning about the film industry. In fact, it's hard to imagine a class on camera techniques or editing without a component of hands-on experience with the necessary equipment.

Local cable stations generally offer classes to members of the community who want to learn how to operate video equipment. Many of these people go on to produce their own cable access shows. Inquire about the availability of internships at local TV broadcast stations. Getting an ancillary job as a secretary or runner at a broadcast station will put you in a creative environment where you can observe and learn the business.

If you do hair, get a job at a local salon. If you want to become a set dresser, score a position at the department store designing window displays. If you want to become an on-set still photographer, start snapping pictures for the local newspaper. It's all valuable work-related experience and it looks great on a résumé.

LOCAL PRODUCTION

Many films today are made outside of Hollywood. More production is done out of state, on location, than on a sound stage at one of the major studios.

To learn about employment opportunities on movies being filmed near you, contact your local film commission. Every state in the United States and practically every country in the world has its own film commission, which monitors all local film production activities. See chapter 2 for information about directories that list film commissions.

Working on a local production is the best way to gain hands-on experience. In fact, most on-set labor is hired locally. Although some key crew are brought in to work on a project, it's simply more cost effective to hire locals than to house an entire Los Angeles crew.

As you read this book, you'll discover that the majority of movie business jobs in Hollywood are union positions. Some states have a right-to-work policy, which means you do not have to be a union member to get work. California is not a right-to-work state. It's actually easier to get work on a film if there is no union requirement. Generally, in order to get into a union, it is necessary to work a predetermined number of days on non-union productions. Earning your days on a non-union film crew outside of Los Angeles makes it easier to get in to the local Hollywood craft unions.

PLANNING YOUR MOVE

Once you've exhausted all the opportunities where you live, it may be time to make your move. Like any big relocation, you need to do your homework. Plan out as much as you can in advance regarding costs, logistics, etc. Consider taking a short planning trip a few months before you relocate to map out the lay of the land. See appendix A for more information about Los Angeles.

When you think you're ready, go for it. Don't look back. And don't forget to pack this book!

WELCOME TO HOLLYWOOD

If you are really serious about film, ultimately you
will end up in Los Angeles, so why not start here?

ANGELA CHENG, literary agent

It doesn't matter whether you've lived your whole life in or near Los Angeles, or if you've just gotten off the plane at LAX. You can make it in Hollywood if you try.

This chapter is a crash course on the film industry. It's not intended to teach you *everything* there is to know about the business. Rather, it's meant as an organized starting place for information.

Pore over current issues of *Daily Variety*, the *Hollywood Reporter*, and other film industry publications. Familiarize yourself with names of agents, directors, executives, producers, and writers who are the leaders in today's Hollywood. Learn the names of major studios, production companies, and agencies, where deals are put together and movies are made. These data provide the basic foundation for the motion picture industry.

FILM SCHOOL 101

You don't necessarily have to go to film school to make it in Hollywood. Some knowledge of the filmmaking process, however, is helpful as you read through this book. Subsequent chapters discuss various industry careers. To gain a better understanding of how these professions relate to the making of a film, I have outlined the general steps below.

DEVELOPMENT

Before you can make a movie, you need a script. Thus begins the development process, affectionately termed *development hell*. Perfecting a script is a tremendously subjective process, and development can take months, if not years, to complete.

The first step is finding material. The traditional source is through submissions from literary agents. Other ways to find material are through established relationships with writers, unsolicited queries from new authors, ideas born in-house, or pre-existing material such as screenplays, short stories, books, plays, magazine and newspaper articles, old films, or TV shows.

Rarely is a script submitted in a sufficiently usable form that is fit to produce as is. Sometimes the idea is a good one, but the writing needs additional work. Sometimes the characters are terrific, but the story is too familiar. With certain material, a screenplay doesn't yet exist. Perhaps there is only a concept or a limited treatment. Whatever the case, the second step in the development process is working with a writer to improve or adapt the existing material into a workable screenplay.

Once a screenplay has been polished, it's ready to be set up for possible production. With a studio film, the producer submits the screenplay to a creative executive at one of the studios. If the studio responds to the material, it will agree to further develop, finance, and/or distribute the movie. With an independent film, the producer takes the screenplay to potential investors who then decide if the movie could be a financially profitable venture.

Often, a producer works with the agencies to package a project before bringing it to a financier or studio. Submitting a screenplay with attachments, such as a director or star, makes it more attractive, and less of a risk, for a studio or investor. See chapter 6 for more details about the development process.

How Films Originate: A Sampling

Film	Source
Batman & Robin (1997)	comic book
Beauty and the Beast (1991)	fairy tale
The Brady Bunch Movie (1995)	TV show (1969–1974)
The Empire Strikes Back (1980)	sequel to *Star Wars* (1977)
Flubber (1997)	*The Absent-Minded Professor* (1961), film starring Fred MacMurray
Grease (1978)	Broadway musical
Gross Anatomy (1989)	pitched as an idea
Jurassic Park (1993)	novel by Michael Crichton
Love! Valour! Compassion! (1997)	Broadway play
Mortal Kombat (1995)	video game
Outbreak (1995)	magazine article
Reindeer Games (2000)	spec script
South Park: Bigger, Longer, and Uncut (1999)	cartoon
Stand by Me (1986)	short story by Stephen King
Superstar (1999)	skit on *Saturday Night Live* (1975–present)
Three Men and a Baby (1987)	French film, *Three Men and a Cradle* (1985)

THE STAGES OF PRODUCTION

There are three phases in the actual process of making a motion picture. They are pre-production, production (also known as principal photography), and post-production. In their simplest definitions, *pre-production* is everything that occurs before the camera rolls. *Production* is the entire filming process. *Post-production* is everything that takes place after principal shooting is completed, until the film is actually released.

PRE-PRODUCTION When a project is greenlighted (i.e., the go-ahead is given) by the studio or financier, pre-production begins. The studio or financier likes the script (and package), and they want to move forward and make the movie. The first step is to hire the key crew, or department heads. These people are the director, cinematographer, editor, production designer, and line producer/unit production manager (UPM). All of these jobs are explained in greater detail in the following chapters. Ultimately, these people hire the rest of their crew members.

The producer must finalize a budget and shooting schedule, which are then approved by the studio or financier. A casting director is hired and immediately begins auditioning actors for roles. When the cast is in place, they rehearse with the director. Filming locations are found through location scouts, and permits to use these locations are secured. Any equipment (cameras, trucks, lights, etc.) that will be needed is also reserved. Costumes are designed or bought once the actors are hired. Sets are built if needed. Pre-production ends when the camera rolls.

PRINCIPAL PHOTOGRAPHY Also known as *production*, principal photography is the actual filming process. Actors and crew arrive on the set. Actors go to wardrobe and makeup, while the rest of the crew sets up the equipment. The director does a quick rehearsal or run-through with the actors of the scene to be filmed that day. Sometimes the director and cinematographer work with the actors' stand-ins to properly light the set.

When everything is ready, the actors perform the scene while the cameras roll and capture the action on film. Sometimes the director watches the action unfold on a video playback monitor to get a better idea of how it will look on screen. Each scene is shot several times from many different angles. Generally, no more than two and a half pages of script are shot per day. After filming is completed for the day, the producer, director, and several key crew screen that day's footage in dailies.

POST-PRODUCTION The final phase in the making of a film begins after the shoot is completed. All footage is put together by the film editor, who sifts through all the footage taken for each scene and selects the most workable shots. The soundtrack is then added. This includes mixing together the score, production sound, sound effects, and additional music. The film is then sent to the lab and prints are made. Finally, the film is test-screened and the marketing campaign commences before the picture is ultimately released.

MARKETING Completed films are screened by the marketing department so they can plan out a strategy to sell the film to the public. The marketing campaign can take the form of paid advertisements (TV, print, billboards, the Internet), one-sheets (movie posters), trailers (previews of a forthcoming film), promotions (contests, giveaways), or a combination of any of these methods.

Prior to opening for the general public, press screenings are held so that journalists and film critics can review the movie in print and on television. Usually, a star-studded premiere is held to provide photo opportunities for camera crews and to further promote the film. The movie's stars are booked as guests on popular TV and radio talk shows and Internet chat rooms to garner additional notice for the movie.

Marketing is an essential component of the film industry. With so much competition in the marketplace today, a movie has to open to great box-office success in its initial weekend in order to survive commercially. As a result, the marketing expenses for a film often are just as costly as the production of the movie itself.

DISTRIBUTION Distribution is the process by which prints of the film are physically sent to theater chains around the globe for exhibition. Distribution is divided into domestic (United States and Canada) and foreign (everywhere else) markets.

Movies can be financed by pre-selling the foreign distribution rights to certain territories before a project is even made. Say a company in Spain pre-buys the right to exclusively distribute a film in that country. This money is then used by the U.S. production entity to finance (or partially finance) the feature. When the movie is completed, money can still be made by selling off remaining territories, but distribution automatically goes to the pre-sale territory—in this case, Spain—that put up the initial production funds. By pre-buying a film, a territory may gain a lower price than if they waited until the film is completed. Like anything else in Hollywood, the greater the risk, the greater the potential reward.

All of the major motion picture studios have their own distribution arms. When a studio finances a project, it generally retains worldwide distribution rights. When the film is released, the studio needs to strategize the number of theaters in which to show it. See chapter 16 for information on distribution strategies.

Most of the revenue from box-office ticket sales is returned to the distributor. Believe it or not, multiplexes make the majority of their earnings through concession sales. The revenues earned by the distributor offset the cost of making and marketing the film. A percentage of any profit, after expenses (net profit), is contractually paid to certain above-the-line participants such as the actors, writer, director, and producer. Of course, the distributor, studio, and/or financier also gets a piece of the action.

KEYS TO THE (L.A.) KINGDOM

You wouldn't arrive for the first day of school without a notebook and pencil, so don't arrive in Hollywood empty-handed either. This section provides a list of materials to help in your initial pursuit of the Hollywood dream.

HOW TO GET HERE FROM THERE

Los Angeles is like no other city—anywhere. The freeways have ten lanes and the traffic doesn't move, it frequently takes a half hour *minimum* to get anywhere in town, and reliable public transportation simply doesn't exist, so you definitely need a car. To avoid road rage, you should at the very least, have a good idea where you are going before you get behind the wheel. For directions anywhere in Los Angeles, drop by an L.A. bookstore and purchase a *Thomas Guide*, the best detailed, portable street map of Los Angeles that's available.

For those who are Internet proficient, visit maps.yahoo.com/py/maps.py to get step-by-step driving directions between any two addresses. This Web site also provides a map that you can print out and take along with you in the car.

GET ME SCORSESE ON THE PHONE

The cellular (cell) phone craze has taken the nation by storm, but the fad started right here in Hollywood. That's because always being available is the primary key to success. I'm not advocating rushing out to purchase a cell phone; however, it might be a smart idea to invest at least in a pager.

Business in Hollywood happens quickly. If someone can't come in to work, someone else has to cover *immediately*. You could very well get a job because you were the first person reached. People have gotten jobs for stranger reasons. Just remember, accessibility is key to making things happen for you.

Get an answering machine or voice-mail service and check for messages frequently. In the fast pace of the film business, movers and shakers do not have the time or the patience to keep calling until you answer your phone. If there's no way to leave you a message, they'll just hang up and call the next name on their list.

POLISH THAT RÉSUMÉ

Always have your résumé complete, updated, and handy. If someone asks you to fax your résumé, don't wait until the next day to send it. The position may be gone by then. If your résumé is always current, you won't have to scramble to update it at the last minute and risk missing an opportunity.

Résumés are a reflection on you. If there are misspellings, or if you send a sloppy, disjointed résumé, you'll be thought of as a messy worker and probably lose the opportunity before you even have a chance to interview for the position.

"If an applicant presents a résumé that doesn't have typos, I'd be impressed," says Pauline Cymet, president of The Right Connections, a showbiz personnel recruitment firm. "If a potential employer does find errors in a résumé, an applicant would be wise to be nondefensive, offer a short apology, and send in a quick revision. A well-written résumé is the applicant's calling card. If he doesn't hit his mark the first time, he may expect intense competition from wannabes who 'get it' and get the job."

Résumés A (page 24) and B (page 25) are examples of a bad résumé and a good résumé, respectively, for a fictitious job-seeker named David Lawrence. David is determined to become a filmmaker.

There are many problems with résumé A. First, there are several spelling and format mistakes. There's no need for the poor graphics around his name; they're more distracting than helpful. No job objective is stated, so it's not clear what he's applying for. The content itself is padded and opinionated, and the paragraph style looks too dense. The type is too small and the italics make it that much more difficult to read.

Résumé B is David's revised résumé. If he sent this *good* version to me, I would certainly call him in for an interview.

Both résumés were created by Susan Ireland, author of *The Complete Idiot's Guide to the Perfect Résumé* and owner of Susan Ireland's Résumé Service (510-524-5238 or www.resumesthatwork.com).

Maintain several versions of your résumé to emphasize different strengths depending on the job you're applying for. For instance, if you are sending your résumé for an assistant's position, you'll want to stress your office and computer skills. If you are applying for a production job, you'll want to emphasize your on-set experience.

In addition to printed résumés, certain industry professions, such as directing and cinematography, rely on reels to showcase the artists' work. Other craftspeople such as production designers, art directors, costume designers, and makeup artists maintain portfolios of their work. Publicists and development executives keep samples of their writing on hand. Composers make audio tapes of their music.

LOGGING ON

With the ever-expanding information superhighway, it's advisable not only that you be computer literate, but also that you own a computer. Hollywood has always been on the forefront of the technological revolution, so you need to be equipped to work here.

Having a computer will allow you to access and amend your résumé conveniently, quickly key in a personalized cover letter, send and receive e-mail, do job background research, and maintain a database for your Rolodex. Probably the most important computer skill you can have is the ability to access the Internet. See the listing of film-related Web sites in appendix A if you have any doubts about Hollywood's obsession with the Internet.

If you can't afford your own computer just yet, you can rent time on one at most major chain copy-making stores, such as Kinko's, throughout Southern California. If you're not yet computer literate, make sure you add "Take computer course" to your to-do list *before* you move to Los Angeles.

MAKING CONTACT

Several directories are available that contain useful contact information. The *Hollywood Creative Directory* has accurate contact information for all the major studios and production companies in Hollywood. In the *Hollywood Agents & Managers Directory*, you'll find information for all the major agencies and management companies in Hollywood. Both books are published and updated triennially.

Other helpful directories include the *Hollywood Reporter Blu-Book* and *LA 411*. These guides have similar (but not as detailed) information about

★★ David Lawrence ★★

344 Lois Lane • Los Angeles, CA 90036 • (213) 555-2456

SUMMARY OF QUALFICATIONS

Writer/producer of four independent films; Winner of the Boston Film Festival. Career goal: to be a professional film director along the lines of Steven Spielberg, the greatest director of all time. Computer Skills: Windows and Macintosh; proficient in Microsoft Word, Scriptware, Script Wizard, and Final Draft. Able to work collaboratively and creatively on a production team.

INDEPENDENT FILM PROJECTS

STOUGHTON NIGHTS

Wrote and directed this 16mm, color romantic student film sponsored by the Boston Film Festival Junior Division as part of the Winter Workshop. Produced by Shaina Douty.

SEA MONSTER FROM BEYOND

Wrote and directed this low budget independent 16mm, color horror film. Winner of Boston Film Festival, Junior Division. Produced by Alex DesLauriers

FOOTBALL FRENZY

Served as production assistant on this horrifyingly amateur Stoughton High School film-course project written by and starring quarterback Stuart Paul and produced by Sam Schneiderman.

THE LAWRENCES

Produced this family documentary to be packed away along with my baby pictures.

WORK EXPERIENCE

1996 - pres., Clerk, TINSEL TOWN VIDEO, Los Angeles, CA
Expanded my knowledge of films by handling rentals and sales in this store with over 1,500 titles. Located videos, made recommendations, and generally tried to spare customers from the abominations that manage to pass as films.

1994-96, Ticket Taker, STOUGHTON CINEMA, Stoughton, MA
Stood at theatre entrance, checked, ripped, and collected tickets of admission. Also, cleaned the sticky floor of the theatre.

EDUCATION

Univeristy of Southern California, 2000
Stoughton High School, 1996
Various workshops at BFVF (insanely expensive, but worth all the early mornings)

— *Demo reel and writing samples available upon request.* —

Résumé A

David Lawrence
344 Lois Lane • Los Angeles, CA 90036 • (213) 555-2456

Job Objective
To obtain a position as a director's assistant

Summary of Qualifications
- Windows and Macintosh proficient in:

Microsoft Word	Script Wizard
Scriptware	Final Draft

- Experienced at working collaboratively on a support team.

Work Experience
(Concurrent with education)

1996–pres.   Clerk, TINSEL TOWN VIDEO, Los Angeles, CA

- Member of a seven-member team of sales clerks who perform the following:

Film research	Phone follow-up
Video filing	Customer service
Ordering	Data entry

- Organize and write *Weekly Flick Picks*, a newsletter that lists each clerk's video recommendations.

- Cataloged the store's inventory of over 1,500 titles using customized software.

1994–96   Ticket Taker, STOUGHTON CINEMA, Stoughton, MA

- Collected tickets and directed customers to theaters and concession stands.

- Coordinated maintenance duties with four co-workers to handle up to 24 shows a day in this eight-theater complex.

Education
M.F.A., Film Production, University of Southern California, 2000

Filmmaking projects:
- Wrote and directed several independent films
- Winner of Boston Film Festival, Junior Division

Résumé B

How Trying Too Hard Lost the Job

The following is a true story.

Sally Wannajob came to Hollywood to make it in the Biz. She did all the right things. First, she bought a copy of *Hollywood 101*. Then she began to collect the essential materials. She bought a *Thomas Guide* and a pager. She borrowed an old *Hollywood Creative Directory* from a friend. She even had four different versions of her résumé—each of them updated and ready to be sent out.

One day, Sally's pal, Andy Assistant, heard about a job as the assistant to a producer at a local film production company. Andy thought Sally would be perfect for the opening, so he called his friend, Gary Gottajob, who worked at the firm, to learn the scoop and recommend Sally. Gary was happy to do Andy a favor. He told him to have Sally fax over her résumé right away and he would personally hand it to the producer. Andy paged Sally and within minutes she returned his call. Andy repeated Gary's instructions.

Sally, eager to please, thought she'd go one step further. She lived down the street from the studio where the producer's office was. She decided to drop off the résumé in person.

When she arrived at the studio gates, Sally was not allowed on the lot. She did not know that she needed a drive-on pass. She asked the guard to call the producer's office. They would surely verify that it would be okay for her to come on the lot to deliver her résumé.

The guard phoned the office, but to Sally's surprise, he did not receive the necessary authorization. Sally insisted he call back and ask specifically for Gary.

Reluctantly, the guard called again. Gary was at lunch. No one else in the office knew anything about Sally or her résumé.

Continued on next page

---

production companies and agencies, and they also include contact information on services ranging from production equipment and facilities to location, transportation, and travel services. The *Pacific Coast Studio Directory* is a less expensive alternative filled with many great contact numbers, including those for film commissions, unions, and guilds. It is published quarterly.

MAINTAINING A ROLODEX

It doesn't have to be anything fancy, but devise a system to keep track of important names, addresses, phone numbers, and e-mail addresses of the people you meet in Tinseltown. The key is ease of use and accessibility. Because success in Hollywood stems from the people you know, an organized and updated Rolodex is an essential tool.

Remembering that persistence is the key, Sally walked over to a pay phone and called the producer's office. She would clear up the confusion. After carefully explaining the situation to the receptionist, Sally was convinced she'd be let on to the lot. The receptionist apologized for any confusion, but until Gary could verify Sally's story, there was nothing she could do.

A frustrated Sally went home in defeat. Not long afterward, Andy received a call from Gary.

"Andy. What is Sally's problem?" Gary asked.

Andy was baffled. What did he mean? Sally is smart, persistent, and hard-working. Did she send a poor résumé? What could she have done wrong?

"I just got back from lunch," Gary explained. "Apparently, your friend showed up in person to drop off her résumé, and, obviously, nobody knew anything about it. What's more, she wouldn't let it go. She insisted the guard call again and again, and then she called herself."

"I'm so sorry," Andy said.

"That's okay," Gary replied. "It's just that Sally can't follow directions. She should have just faxed the résumé like I said. The producer heard what happened and now she thinks Sally is nuts. Definitely doesn't want her working here. Sorry, bud."

"No, I'm sorry," apologized Andy once more before hanging up the phone.

The phone rang again. It was Sally.

Sally had all the right qualifications for the job: availability, updated résumé, speed, and persistence. Her fatal flaw, however, was in not following directions properly.

NEWS YOU CAN USE

The trade papers are *the* source for news about the entertainment industry. Read them religiously. The two major local trade publications are the *Hollywood Reporter* and *Daily Variety*. Both are daily papers and cover much of the same information. Both have weekly editions as well.

Reading the trades will keep you in the loop about what's going on in Hollywood. You'll start getting familiar with names, places, projects, and deals. The trades publish data on script sales, casting, studio changes, executive moves, industry trends, and other helpful information about the business. The news reported in the trades will seem a little more clear to you after you familiarize yourself with the names and companies, buzzwords, and lingo discussed in the remainder of this chapter.

THE PLAYERS

Every year, *Premiere* magazine rates the top 100 Hollywood Power Players in the film industry. These are names you should be familiar with, because they are the industry's current leaders. Check your local library for a copy of the most recent list.

THE STUDIOS

Movie studios are giant entities that have the financial backing and methods of distribution necessary to make and release films. Studios generally have multiple labels that oversee dozens of productions each year. Labels loosely define the type of product released. For example, the Walt Disney Studio has the Walt Disney Pictures label, which releases family-oriented films, and the Touchstone Pictures and Hollywood Pictures labels, which release movies for all audiences. The Miramax label, which is also owned by Disney, is used to release independent and art-house fare. Dimension Films, a division of Miramax, releases genre films, mainly horror, sci-fi, and urban.

Studios have production deals with many independent production companies (see below). Deals are structured in many different ways, but the most common one is known as a *first-look deal*. The terms of a first-look deal are such that a studio covers all overhead expenses (rent, employee salaries, entertainment, research, bills, etc.) in exchange for a first look at any material a production company wants to make into a film. The studio has the first opportunity to finance and distribute this project before any other studio in town. If they decide not to take the project on, the production company is free to shop the project elsewhere.

You should be familiar with all the major studios (DreamWorks, Metro-Goldwyn-Mayer [MGM], Paramount, Sony Pictures Entertainment, Twentieth Century-Fox, Universal, Walt Disney, and Warner Bros.), their film labels, what types of movies they produce, their talent and production deals, and the companies' principals. See chapter 16 for more information about studios.

THE PRODUCTION COMPANIES

A production company oversees the acquisition, development, and packaging of material for production. Production companies typically range in size from two people to twenty but are smaller than a studio. The *Hollywood Creative Directory* has a complete listing of all currently active studios and production companies in Hollywood.

THE AGENCIES

There are hundreds of agencies in Hollywood representing talent, writers, directors, and below-the-line artists. The four major agencies are Creative Artists Agency (CAA), International Creative Management (ICM), United Talent Agency (UTA), and the William Morris Agency (WMA). Contact information for these and other agencies can be found in the *Hollywood Agents & Managers Directory*.

The main focus for an agency is to get work for its clients. Many of the large agencies concentrate on packaging. For instance, an agency offers a package to studios consisting of a screenplay by a writer they represent, with another client attached to direct, and yet another attached to star. This process generates work for multiple clients and, in turn, multiple commissions for the agency.

INTERACTION

Here's an example of how all these different entities interact. A writer completes a screenplay and submits it to his agent. The agent reads it, thinks it's good, and sends it out as a spec script to production companies. Each production company is assigned a territory (i.e., a studio). If the company likes the script, they have permission from the agent to take it to the assigned studio. The studio reads the script. If they like it, they option or purchase it from the agency and make a deal with the production company that submitted the screenplay to produce the movie.

Studios and agencies interact again when clients (e.g., director, actor, cinematographer) are hired, fees and perks are negotiated, and contracts are drawn up. The production company continues to develop the screenplay, with guidance from the studio, until they have a shooting script to which the studio gives a greenlight.

SO WHERE DO YOU FIT IN?

If you're not on information overload by now, it's time to start thinking about where you fit in. Throughout the remainder of this book, various positions in Hollywood are explained in detail to give you an idea of what job you might want to undertake in the movie business.

You already may have a clear idea of where you see yourself working in Hollywood. This book provides you with an opportunity to examine the big picture and better understand how everyone in this community interacts to make movie magic.

If you're having second thoughts about a career in the film business, get rid of them. When I came to Hollywood, I knew I wanted to work in the movie industry, but I didn't have a specific idea of what I wanted to do. Sure enough, after experimenting with various jobs, I found my niche. Sometimes that's what you have to do.

If you want to make Hollywood happen for you, I truly believe you can. Read on to find out how.

STAYING ALIVE

The best advice anyone ever gave to me is, 'Take the job. Get in the door and you'll meet somebody who'll get you in the next door.'

KRISTIEANNE GROELINGER, director of production,
Jerry Bruckheimer Films

Now that you're in Hollywood, you'll have to find work. Chances are that your first job in the entertainment business won't be what you ultimately want to do. Don't get discouraged if offers to direct or do the production design on your first feature aren't pouring in just yet. Everybody almost always starts at the bottom. Even entry-level positions in Hollywood are hard to come by. Without knowing someone who can give you a break, your chances are slim for obtaining that first job in the biz. Don't get discouraged, however; you can make it happen.

THE LAY OF THE LAND

Los Angeles is a large, spread-out city. Although the term Hollywood is used to refer to the entertainment industry in general, geographically it is only a small section of greater Los Angeles, and not the hub of all entertainment activity. Contrary to what you might think, the major centers of activity are not all adjacent to one another. As a result, deciding where to live may prove to be a major headache.

On a map, Hollywood seems to be the city most centrally located, but it is not the cheapest place to be based. The San Fernando Valley (a.k.a. the Valley) is less expensive and close to some of the major studios (Disney, DreamWorks, Universal, Warner Bros.), but what if you get a job at Sony in Culver City? Palms and Culver City on L.A.'s Westside (which generally encompasses the area between Brentwood and LAX) are less expensive cities to live in and are close to a handful of industry centers (Twentieth Century-Fox, MGM, Sony, all the major agencies), but what if you get a job at Panavision in Woodland Hills (which is in the Valley)? For relocation assistance, key: digitalcity.com/losangeles/relocation.

As a commonsense rule, live in an affordable area where you feel most comfortable. If you know people who already live in L.A., ask them for pointers. Give yourself at least thirty minutes to get anywhere in Los Angeles at nonpeak hours. Allow an hour *minimum* to get from point A to point B during rush hour. Rush *hour* in Los Angeles generally is Monday through Friday, 7 A.M. until 10 A.M., and 4 P.M. until 7 P.M.

SUPPORTING YOUR HOLLYWOOD HABIT

Some people move to Los Angeles, give it a few months until they deplete their savings, and ultimately return home, head hung low. Don't let this be you. For the rest of your life, you will wonder what might have happened if you had stayed. If you come here with realistic goals and a practical understanding of how things work, you will survive and eventually make it. Trust in your ambitions and yourself.

Since earning that initial paycheck in the business can be difficult, think about getting an interim job when you first relocate here. It's better to have cash coming in instead of only flowing out. This will surely increase your opportunity to go the distance and give Hollywood your best shot. It also will eliminate a great deal of unwanted stress so that when you snag that industry interview, you will be more relaxed and aware.

The interim assignment probably should be a somewhat brainless job. Since your objective is to get a start in the entertainment industry, you don't want this temporary position to be a full-time career that interferes with your primary goal. Flip burgers, wait tables, work retail. It doesn't matter what you do as long as you save sufficient free time and energy to concentrate on obtaining your first entertainment job. Be cautious not to get sidetracked in a nonpro job. Many people make it all the way out here and are so turned off and/or frightened by the unpredictability of show business careers that they subconsciously settle for anything just to pay the rent.

ADVANCING YOUR CAREER

There are several other ways you can advance your career while searching for that first break. Many of these opportunities may even propel you into that first industry job and continue to help you build your career.

STUDENT FILMS

Student films are a great way to build experience working on a crew. Ads for crew positions usually appear in the pages of *Back Stage West*. Ads also can be found on bulletin boards at local films schools, such as those at UCLA and USC.

Most student films do not pay salaries, but you'll garner valuable experience. Better yet, you just may be working with future filmmakers who will take you along for the ride. Directors Bryan Singer (*The Usual Suspects*) and John Singleton (*Boyz N the Hood*) both made films while students at USC. Many of the people with whom they work on studio projects today are the same people who worked on the movies they made in film school. You do not always have to be a student at the university to work on the crew of a student film.

ORGANIZATIONS

Professional and social organizations, both formal and informal, may be a good way to meet people with allied entertainment aspirations. Writers groups and similar clubs allow you to perfect your craft and get feedback from others who share your passion. The *L.A. Weekly*, a free newspaper available at music stores and elsewhere throughout Los Angeles, has listings for various entertainment organizations. There are also social and fraternal groups that you can join such as Independent Feature Project/West (IFP), the Production Assistants Association (PAA), the Set Decorators Society of America (SDSA), or Women in Film (WIF). See appendix A for a list of film organizations.

SEMINARS

Throughout Southern California, seminars, lectures, and classes constantly are being offered that deal with all aspects of the entertainment industry. There is no such thing as learning too much as long as you continue to absorb new information. Audit seminars on topics that interest you. You may discover a niche you love and never knew existed.

Several extension schools, such as UCLA Extension and Santa Monica College (SMC), offer classes specifically geared toward the film business. The Learning Annex also offers a good selection of speakers on various film-related topics. Other seminars, like Robert McKee's Story Structure, are given periodically throughout the year.

NETWORKING

All of the career-advancing avenues above provide an excellent opportunity to network. Networking, the art of making contacts to further your career, is vital for success in Hollywood.

Most business in Hollywood is conducted within a social ambience. As a result, networking is an important tool. If you don't know how to schmooze, you'd better learn soon. It is how you make contacts, learn about opportunities, and advance through the ranks.

"Make friends with your peers," advocates Angela Cheng, literary agent at the Writers and Artists Agency. "If they stay in Hollywood, you will rise with them. All the people that I do business with are people that I was an assistant with when I was answering phones. Through aggressiveness, motivation, and a lot of hard work, they too have slowly risen through the ranks and are now creative executives and producers."

The best advice I can give you about networking is: Just be yourself. People can easily spot a phony. Don't focus on what someone can offer you; rather, focus on what you can offer them.

HOLLYWOOD—THE GAME

Think of Hollywood as one giant game. The object is to make it in Hollywood. One sign of making it is being someone everyone knows and can identify. For instance, Steven Spielberg, David Geffen, and Michael Eisner all are names easily recognized (not only in Hollywood, but throughout the world). They've won their game.

The challenge you are faced with is to meet as many industry people as possible until you change from someone trying to meet others into someone others are hoping to meet. It always amazes me when I meet someone for the first time and they say, "I've heard so much about you."

Networking happens round-the-clock, but most often occurs at nightly Hollywood gatherings. "Industry parties to me are not parties," states Joel Dean, a talent agent at the Agency for the Performing Arts (APA). "You're going there to be seen and to do business. You're there to grab fifteen seconds of somebody's time and put yourself in front of their face, but that's not my idea of a good time."

That kind of cynicism springs from having done it for so many years. Dean, an industry veteran, admits that he used to get enthusiastic about attending parties when he first started out and that networking is indeed a necessity, especially when you're new to the business. "I don't think you have to be at every single [party]," says Dean. "Then your face is too familiar. So you've got to pick and choose; otherwise you're just known as someone who goes to the opening of an envelope."

HOW TO FIND A JOB IN THE INDUSTRY

The simplest way to find out about a job opening in the industry is through someone you know. This is easier said than done, especially if you are new to Los Angeles and don't know anyone yet. See if people you know from home have any connections in Hollywood. "If your cousin's sister's ex-college roommate used to know a roofer who once worked on a producer's house, call him," advises Jeremy Garelick, an assistant to an agent at Creative Artists Agency (CAA). Well, it certainly can't hurt.

As you continue living in Los Angeles, you will meet increasingly more people. You will hone your networking skills and eventually have a support system of contacts and acquaintances in place. These people will hear about jobs and hopefully alert you to them. Once you are established, you will do the same for others.

JOB LISTS

Several job lists actually exist in Hollywood. The most famous is the United Talent Agency (UTA) job list. The list is maintained by UTA assistants and covers many industry job openings in Hollywood. Everything from entry-level positions to executive opportunities are tracked and updated. You can get this list only from someone at UTA. If you don't know anyone at UTA, find someone who does. Do not call UTA directly and ask for the list; they will not send a copy to you. Officially, it is only for in-house use.

YOUR ALMA MATER

Another way to meet people in the business is to find out which working-industry professionals share your alma mater. Don't limit this strictly to college. Look into your high school records to determine if anyone from your hometown made it in Hollywood. Drop them a letter, send them a fax, or even e-mail them. In your note, indicate the connection and suggest a brief meeting to get their advice. Most people are willing to meet with you, and it may be fun for both of you to reminisce about that seventy-year-old instructor who is *still* teaching freshman English.

PRODUCTION CHARTS

Every Tuesday the *Hollywood Reporter* publishes production charts. This includes a listing of all films in production, going into production, and in development. While this is not the only such list that exists, it is thorough and complete. If you want to get a job on one of these movies, look up when shooting starts, where the shoot is taking place, and who the unit production manager (UPM) is, and fax that person your résumé. Be forewarned: The UPM is likely to receive a hundred résumés from other job seekers and may respond only to one or two. If you get a job from one returned call, however, then it was well worth the concerted effort. Remember, availability is key. Your résumé may come through the fax machine at the same moment someone on the shoot quits.

READING THE TRADES

Collect information about potential job opportunities by continually reading the trades. If an executive negotiates a new position, chances are he'll need to hire an assistant. Get on it—immediately! If a company was recently formed, new staff will be needed. Seize the opportunity at once to send in a résumé.

FOLLOW-UP

Another vital ingredient to obtaining "that" job in Hollywood is intelligent follow-up. Don't sit around waiting for the phone to ring. You need to be aggressive and follow through with everyone to whom you sent your résumé. Keep detailed notes, including the name of the person with whom you spoke, her job title, and what she suggested you do as a next step. If the job in question has been filled, cross it off your list, but if they haven't hired yet, ask when would be a good time to check back. Ask if it would be possible to be interviewed. Be aggressive, but don't be a pain. If you can, make friends with the support staff so that they'll put your call through, give you intelligence, and be alert for you when an opportunity arises.

"I used to get lots of letters when I worked at Miramax. 'I'm moving to Los Angeles and I would love to talk to you about any opportunities at Miramax, etc.,'" says Jonathan King, now president of production at Laurence Mark Productions. "I would put them at the bottom of my in-box and save them for a week, and if the person called and sounded OK, I would generally give them some time on the phone. If they asked to come see me, and I had time, I generally would do it. It's amazing how many people expected me to call them. We're all too busy for that, but if someone called me, I generally would take the time to talk to them. So I would say, write the letters and follow up."

TEMP AGENCIES

Getting a job as a temp can help you get into otherwise impenetrable companies. In fact, many entertainment companies hire full-time employees from their temp pools.

Temping is a great way to learn about different areas of the film business. When I was a temp, for example, I worked in almost every department at Walt Disney Studios. During one month I worked in casting, music, home video, and creative affairs. Finally, I got an assignment temping for a producer on the lot, and this opportunity segued into a job as his assistant. Several years and many promotions later, I hold the title of vice president of that producer's company.

Going from job to job also allows for networking and an opportunity to increase your industry contacts. Not every job you temp at may offer you a full-time position, but do good work and they'll remember you and maybe even recommend you for an open position they hear about later.

The downside of temping is that, obviously, it is not permanent and does not include benefits. It also may not be steady. If you are temping, it is a good idea to sign up with several agencies simultaneously to ensure a regular paycheck.

There are several temp agencies in Los Angeles. Many provide employees solely for entertainment companies. Some provide full-time placement in addition to temporary assignments. "There's no better way to get a full-time job than by temping," says Pauline Cymet, co-owner of The Right Connections Personnel Service. "If they like you, you have had the chance to make the impression without going through the formality of the interview." See appendix A for a list of employment agencies that provide temps for the entertainment industry.

INTERNSHIPS

Internships are not a unique concept to Hollywood. No other industry, however, thrives so vibrantly on free labor. Because getting your foot in the door is the key to getting started, internships are a viable entrée into the biz.

Not everyone can get an internship. Technically, these positions are reserved for students as part of their educational training. Although

Temporary Employee, Permanent Success

One of the many success stories born at The Right Connections Personnel Service is that of a temp who was assigned to the late Dawn Steel, past president of Columbia Pictures. The temp was asked to take notes during a production meeting with Steel, creative executives, a director, and various writers. At one point, when creative contributions reached an impasse, Steel challenged the temp and asked for his input. Taking Steel's cue, he offered suggestions. "Rather than being pushy or obnoxious, the temp displayed respect, intelligence, and humility," explains Right Connections co-owner Pauline Cymet. After the meeting, one of the executives asked Steel who the person was with the good ideas. She told him it was her temp. "I am convinced that it was a pivotal point in his career... right time, right place, right connections."

Two weeks later the temp was hired as a creative executive in Steel's production company. Today he runs the film division of a multimedia entertainment company and has several impressive producer credits on various feature films. "[I] predict an Oscar in his future," says Cymet.

companies legally cannot hire nonstudents for unpaid internships, the reality is, they sometimes do. At the same time, most nonstudents cannot afford to work for free when they need to worry about rent and food. There are those who can, however, and they will have a head start on the others.

"I think this industry knows how to exploit the youth better than any other, but in what turns out to be a very good way," explains casting director Amy McIntyre Britt. "When you're twenty-one years old, you can afford to be working for very little money, existing on a very low level of income and still know you're working for something. You don't have life's responsibilities yet."

Internships can be very exciting, especially in Hollywood. Picture this scenario: You just moved to Hollywood from Wichita, Kansas. You score an internship with a famous producer who has an office on the Sony lot in Culver City. Your first assignment is to deliver a script to Sharon Stone, an actor whom you greatly admire. You arrive at her Beverly Hills home. She opens the door herself, thanks you kindly for delivering the script, and asks you in for a drink. Not a bad first day on the job.

Could happen, but probably won't. The more likely scenario is that you are asked to make twenty copies of a script on an old photocopier that jams every five pages. One of those copies is going to Sharon Stone, and you'd better count the pages in that one three times just to make sure they are all there when your boss personally hands her the script later that evening. Nonetheless, feel proud that you were an integral part of the process. The truth is, your boss may not even know where the copier is located, let alone how to make a copy. Without you, he'd be in big trouble. So congratulations—you've done a great job.

The key to a successful internship experience is to gain as much out of it as possible. This means turning rather mundane tasks like copying into something more important and fulfilling. Instead of just copying and filing the item, read it and ask questions. This enables you to acquaint yourself with common terms, and when you hear them again, they'll be familiar to you.

Adapt this strategy to all situations. If you're working on a set, hang around the crew and listen to what they say. Ask questions during downtime or at dinner. "They were talking about a rolling dolly shot. I'm not sure I know what that is." Listen, read, absorb, ask questions, and you will learn.

Lost and Found

At twenty years old, the most outrageous task KristieAnne Groelinger was ever asked to do was to find a lost shirt belonging to the producer for whom she was interning. She went to the cleaners where the item was misplaced, and they opened the door to a back room where they kept all of their unclaimed garments. "The room was piled eight feet high with clothing," recalls Groelinger. "So I took off my sandals and got in this pile and started rooting through to find the shirt. And I found that damn shirt and I brought it back. And the producer said, 'See, I told you it was there.'

"They don't care *how*, they just care that you've checked off the [task]," she points out. "I think that's why I made a good impression. He said to me, 'Did you find my shirt?' and I said, 'Yes, I found your shirt.' I didn't say, 'I opened up the door, there was an eight-foot-high pile of clothing…' because they don't care about the drama. Your job is to manage the drama so they can concentrate on making movies.

"The impression is what's important. That producer won't remember that you were the person that really had a knack for finding shirts, they'll just remember that you were resourceful and could get things done. It's important to remember that they *will* recommend you for bigger jobs if you've done a good job with all the little things."

Once you are in, the next step is to make a good impression. The key to doing this is subtlety. Otherwise, you run the risk of becoming a nuisance. But be assured, opportunity will present itself, and now that you've got the internship, you're in the right place to grab it.

WORKING ON THE OUTSIDE

Certain entertainment professions may dictate not getting an industry job, for instance, writing. If you become an assistant to a writer, you will be constantly busy doing tasks to make that person's life run smoother so that he can concentrate on his craft. When will you ever have time to write and perfect your own talent? It may make more sense to get a no-brainer position to pay the bills so that you still have energy to write at nights and on weekends.

ACHIEVING YOUR GOALS

Make a list of career goals. Long-term goals might include: direct a film, sell a screenplay, get an agent, become an agent, become a UPM, or style the hair of the lead actor on a film. Short-term goals might include: write ten pages of a screenplay by the end of the month, send out a hundred résumés this week, find out how to get into the costumers union, work on a student film, or sign up with a temp agency.

Whatever your ambitions, make them realistic and map a constructive, creative path to achieving them. If your goals are too large and unattainable right now, break each one down into steps until the path to achieving them becomes clear. If you go about meeting your goals in a methodical manner, you will attain them. Before long, you will be wheeling and dealing, cutting and styling, hammering and nailing, or doing exactly what it is you've always wanted to do in Hollywood.

PART TWO

ABOVE-THE-LINE

4

WRITERS

I as the screenwriter am dealing with the written word, not the filmed word. So I've got to learn how to put into writing what I see. To this day, I find myself sitting in a movie, seeing a scene being played, and I'll sort of cross my eyes, zone out on that, and imagine what it would look like type-written.

DEAN PITCHFORD, writer

Each person involved in a film, from executive producer to those who work in the production office, takes pride in his or her contributions, which merely underlines the fact that making a film come together is indeed a group effort. The initial vision for the film, though, springs from the minds of its key creative talent, referred to as *above-the-line*: actors, writers, directors, and producers.

FOOTLOOSE AND FANCY FREE

Dean Pitchford was enjoying a successful career as a song lyricist, which culminated in an Academy Award for the title song in the movie *Fame* (1980). This propelled him to make the career move from New York to Hollywood to pursue similar songwriting opportunities within the motion picture industry. Despite making a name for himself in the pop music scene, writing songs for the likes of Kim Carnes, Melissa Manchester, and Diana

45

Ross, when it came to the movies Pitchford was becoming frustrated. Even though he hailed from a background on Broadway, where the songwriter often creates the music for the entire show, Pitchford was getting only one song, at best, into each movie. Long before Matt Damon and Ben Affleck wrote *Good Will Hunting* (1997) as a vehicle for themselves to star in, Pitchford, who had never taken a screenwriting class, had the novel idea of writing a movie that required many songs, all of which he could supply.

"I wanted to find something that was so far removed from *Fame* that I wouldn't be accused of simply redoing that formula," says Pitchford. That's when he saw an article in the press about a small town in Oklahoma that had banned dancing since the late nineteenth century and was now repealing its own self-imposed ban. Pitchford researched this event as an idea for a script, and then wrote the first draft of what was to become the movie *Footloose* (1984). He created the character of a wisecracking, city-bred teenager who arrives in a small town and rattles the cages of its uptight citizens.

A Note on Notes

Much to the chagrin of the writer, it is standard procedure in Hollywood that everyone involved in the development of a film, from the producer to the studio executives—sometimes even the assistants—gives her or his input on the screenplay. This generally comes in the form of notes. Notes might include comments on any suggested changes in the script ranging from character and plot to story and dialogue. Rarely is a screenplay filmed exactly as it was originally written.

Pitchford took his draft screenplay and signed with an agent. She put him together with several different Hollywood producers, all of whom were kind and encouraging but did not quite see what he was attempting through the project. Ultimately, it was picked up by Twentieth Century-Fox for producer Dan Melnick, who, like Pitchford, had previously worked on Broadway. (Melnick was also the son-in-law of Richard Rodgers.) Unlike the other producers, who did not quite appreciate the material, Melnick understood it completely.

Pitchford was given development money to fly to Oklahoma to undertake additional research. He returned to Los Angeles to write the script, full of ideas that eventually made it into the picture. He also took notes and suggestions from Melnick and incorporated them into the screenplay.

Everything was going along perfectly for the novice screenwriter on his first feature. Then Melnick had a disagreement with Marvin Davis, who then controlled Twentieth Century-Fox. Shortly thereafter, when the producer submitted the rewritten script to the studio, Davis put the project into turnaround, reverting the rights back to Melnick.

Within twenty-four hours, however, the script was picked up by Paramount Pictures. *Footloose* had new fans in its then president, Don Simpson, and its vice president, Dawn Steel. For Pitchford, however, it meant a new set of notes to incorporate into the screenplay, and he went back to work.

Within weeks of Pitchford's rewrite, Simpson left the studio to produce *Flashdance* (1983). While Steel remained as vice president, in charge of the production, Jeffrey Katzenberg and Michael Eisner came in to run the studio. "So, now we're at our second studio, and at that studio we're on our second set of executives," recalls Pitchford. And of course, the new executives had their own sets of notes.

Once all of the new executives' notes had been incorporated into the screenplay to everyone's satisfaction, it was time to hire a director. Herbert Ross (*Funny Lady, Pennies from Heaven*) was everyone's first choice because of his musical background. "He came on board and we were very excited about his involvement," says Pitchford, who went right to work incorporating Ross's notes into the ever-evolving screenplay. Unfortunately, a deal could not be struck with Ross and he exited the project—for the time being.

The next director the studio hired was Michael Cimino. This was to be his first feature assignment since the expensive flop *Heaven's Gate* (1980). But as Pitchford recalls, Cimino's notes were all over the map. The demanding director butted heads with the studio on other issues, and soon he too was off the project. Suddenly it was back to square one, without a director.

Although Pitchford was hectically rewriting, he was paid for each new draft. "They wanted to keep this low-budget," he explains. "If they wanted to trade up in terms of screenwriters, they were going to have to pay a lot more." Because this was the first script Pitchford wrote, they were able to pay him union scale only for each polish. Besides, the studio was always happy with Pitchford's work, so they had no reason to replace him as the film's writer. Unfortunately, in today's Hollywood, this is far too rare.

Ultimately Herbert Ross came back on board, and the studio cemented his deal. Pitchford went back to Ross's draft, did further polishing, and finally production began. "My position on this film was unique in that I was there when the first piece of paper was rolled into the typewriter, and I was there at the very end when the last piece of music was dubbed into the movie," says Pitchford, who was hard at work in Los Angeles preparing the soundtrack while the movie was filming in Utah. "It gave me a chance to enjoy a perspective on the movie that most screenwriters don't have."

All in all, Pitchford wrote twenty-two drafts of the screenplay in three years. While this may sound discouraging for would-be writers, the movie did get made. In fact, it became enormously successful and spawned a hit soundtrack album as well. Pitchford's mission—to write a movie to service his music—has been fulfilled. In 1998 the live stage version of *Footloose* opened on Broadway, a sweet addendum for the man who started his career on the Great White Way.

THE WRITER'S LIFE

Pitchford could have written his initial screenplay anywhere. Once his agent started circulating the script to producers, however, it was necessary for him to be in Los Angeles to attend meetings with interested executives. This holds true for aspiring screenwriters. They can write anywhere, but when they are ready to work professionally, they need to be close to the business.

"It's very rare that somebody is on their own in some remote part of the world coming up with one slam-dunk idea after another and is able to sustain a career at the beginning," says Pitchford. "The business changes every six weeks—every six minutes. People move from studio to studio, and what the studios are looking for is constantly changing. Once they get a feel for the business and once they get to know the executives they are working with, and the executives know to call them about this rewrite and this book that they bought, or about this idea that the studio wants to work on, it's very important to be here. This is a business of relationships."

Screenwriter Daniel Yost (*Drugstore Cowboy*) agrees, "It's possible to do anything, but it's far more likely that you'll have a career if you live here. I think it's only beneficial to live somewhere else if you are in demand, because you've written a couple of things that have made a significant amount of money for somebody. Then you can live anywhere you want."

Anyone can be a writer. If you like to write, and you do it well, you're a writer. It's that simple. But, not everyone can make a livelihood as a writer. Before you decide that this is something you want to do for a living, you need to examine why you are writing in the first place.

"It's hard to make a living as a writer, but not at all impossible," says Yost. "You just have to keep working. You can't just have one screenplay that you keep taking around forever. You cannot insist that your first screenplay be made exactly as written. If you walk away from a deal because somebody's going to change it, you're not going to have a career here [in Hollywood]. You have to be flexible and you have to keep writing. If you care about it a lot, and you work hard, and you have some intelligence, you'll probably eventually succeed, but it's not easy. It took me several years before I actually started to make money at it."

TO WRITE OR NOT TO WRITE

I work out at the gym five days a week. I do it because it's fun, it feels good, it's a great way to relieve stress, it keeps me in physical shape, and it helps my creative juices flow. I don't want to be an athlete. I have no desire to be a personal trainer. I have never wanted to enter professional bodybuilding. However, I'm as committed to working out as someone with any of these specific goals is.

Writing can be very similar. Some people create for fun. Some do it to relieve stress. Some would claim writing keeps them mentally balanced. For many, it can be even more personal. Inner passion. Lifelong desire. Self reflection. Are these good reasons to choose screenwriting as a profession?

Certainly you want to enjoy your career. You want to do something that brings you satisfaction. Maybe your goals are even larger. Perhaps you want to use writing as a medium to educate through entertainment. Maybe you want to make an impact on culture and society. These are all valid reasons to write. None of them, however, will get you any closer to paying your rent every month. It doesn't mean that these are inappropriate reasons to write. In fact, these are all very sound reasons to write.

As with any creative profession, though, you must face the economics and reality of the situation.

In an ideal world, you could write a story about anything you're passionate about, sell it, and turn it into a film. In reality, if you want to sell your screenplay, you need to cater to the industry's current demands. Sometimes the business will call out for your passion piece. More often, it will call out for something else altogether. What do you do?

Establish yourself. Write something you can sell to make your mark and let Hollywood know you have arrived. You will begin to generate heat, and then you will have more leverage to write whatever you want. Regardless of *what* you're writing, make sure you *are* writing. Don't ever lose that focus. Yost worked as a sportswriter while he was in college, "That got me into the habit of writing. A lot of people have good ideas and say they want to be writers, but they are not in the habit of it."

Make writing your full-time job. Each morning after you have eaten breakfast and gotten dressed, work begins. In your case, this means unplugging the television, turning the phone ringer off, and booting up the computer. It may mean arriving at the Los Angeles Public Library with a list of topics to research, or showing up at the local coffeehouse with a laptop or notebook and pen. Whatever the scenario may be, for eight or more hours a day, Monday through Friday, you are at your writing job.

Dean Pitchford advises writers to treat their writing schedule as an appointment. "Rather than thinking of it as, I'll write when I get inspired or I'll write when I solve that problem, I just simply show up at my office every morning at ten o'clock, turn off the phones, and work for a set amount of hours. At the end of that time, whatever I got done, whether it's one page or ten pages, is the work that I've done for that day. It stops me from beating myself up for the rest of the day because I only got one page done."

Trying to write for a few minutes whenever you get a chance is mostly unproductive. Pitchford talks about the necessity to get back into his groove before he can resume writing. "I start reading what I wrote the day before. I have to remember all of the things I was thinking when I turned off the computer. It takes me about twenty minutes to a half hour to sink down to...cruising speed. Fifteen minutes of work, or twenty minutes of work doesn't get me to that level; I can cross some *t*'s and dot some *i*'s, but I can't really get inside it in any kind of appreciable way. When you have sessions that are fruitless, it discourages you from coming back to your next session. When you have sessions that are fruitful, I can't wait to go back and work again."

But how do you expect to pay your rent if you write full time?

When you're just starting out, get a second job to pay your bills. Work at a coffeehouse. Wait tables. Work retail on the weekends. Teach night school. It doesn't matter what you do, as long as it's *second* to writing.

It has to be secondary because *writing is your full-time job*. Remember, you want to *make a living as a writer*. If you take a job with responsibilities that overshadow your primary objective, then your main goal will not be achieved. If you have a job that requires long hours, involves taking work home, or makes you mentally or physically exhausted, you won't have the energy or desire to write when you're through.

Obviously there are night owls, and some people actually write better in the evening than during the day. This doesn't make a difference in terms of priorities. You still need to get a no-brainer job to pay the bills. Write when you do it best, but don't chance having your creative energy burn out from a stressful occupation.

Tim Garrick, who, with writing partner Scott Russell, wrote *Stranger Than Fiction* (1999) got very lucky. Garrick moved into an apartment just as the building's manager was fired. The owner asked if he wanted to manage the building. "I started off managing that building, and they gave me four more buildings," says Garrick. "I hired my writing partner as my assistant, and the two of us managed four buildings. We got our rent free, and we got a little salary. It wasn't easy. Mainly I lived on a credit card, but I was always able to write full time. When I got a legitimate agent later, I was always able to attend meetings whenever they took place."

EXQUISITE AGONY: THE PROCESS OF WRITING

Every writer has a particular process of writing that is personal and unique to each individual. It can be discovered only by trying different styles of working and determining which is best for you.

Anne Lamott's *Bird by Bird: Some Instructions on Writing and Life* is about the process of writing. The book has a chapter called "The First Shitty Draft," in which Lamott advises beginning writers to accept the fact that the initial draft you write is not going to be the best you can do.

"After I read that book, every time I would start a screenplay I would name the file in my computer *first shitty draft*," says Pitchford. "So every day, when I clicked on it, I would realize I was laying down the bare bones. This scene did not have to work like greased lightning at this point; this character did not have to be fully realized. It's very important that you get the big, bold strokes laid out."

After Pitchford writes his shitty draft, he tells the plot to a friend. "I think that at heart, all screenwriters are storytellers," says Pitchford. "I've always had a theory that unless you can tell a joke well, you can't write a screenplay because the same setup, delivery, payoff is used for both.

"If somebody stumbles by saying, 'These three nuns are walking down the street—no wait, it's a priest, a rabbi, and a minister, and they're walking down the street—no wait, they're in a bar. Let me start again...,' that person should not write a screenplay because it is not a picture in their head. And until it is a picture in their head, they can't make it a picture for you."

Several years ago Pitchford took a writing class called *Writer's Boot Camp* that taught him a structured approach to creating screenplays. "I start out with a premise line where I try to sum up the story in one line that incorporates the major character, his misbehavior [i.e., the thing that is holding him back], the journey that he will be on, and who will oppose him on that journey. You move from that into a general outline that basically breaks the 120-page screenplay into ten-page beats, so that every scene changes directions slightly, but every ten pages changes the course of the characters."

Next, Pitchford creates a character list that indexes all of the characters, their relationship to one another, and their function within the piece. He then plugs these characters into his outline. From there he breaks down the ten-page segments even further, giving each its own slug line:

`Int. Church -- Day`

What's going to happen in the church? Vinnie shows up and decides he is going to leave the priesthood and become a disc jockey.

`Int. Vinnie's Home -- Night`

In this scene, Vinnie fights with his mom about his decision to leave the priesthood.

"It's easier to make changes when you are in the outline stage," says Pitchford. "I have tried to fool myself, skip ahead, and say I'll solve that when I start writing it—and then you get to page eighty and you discover that you have done stuff that is going to have a ripple effect and is going to alter things that happened back on page eleven. I could have answered those questions had I been more arduous about asking myself all the necessary questions in the development."

Daniel Yost follows quite a different approach in his scriptwriting. "I'm more interested in the texture, characters, and ideas in the story as opposed to having a complete plot outlined beat by beat. To me, that destroys the spontaneity of writing a screenplay. I love to discover a lot of those beats as I'm writing, and I hate figuring them out ahead of time."

Find the style that works best for you. Once you make the commitment to write as a profession, you need to work toward the goal of selling a screenplay. After all, the first sale is vital to your screenwriting career because it puts you in a stronger position, and with strength come options.

WRITING FOR HOLLYWOOD

That said, what should you write?

Write what sells.

Look at the most current box-office grosses to see what is selling. They're usually printed in the calendar or arts section of your local newspaper at the beginning of the week, or you can always find them on the Internet (e.g., www.k2nesoft.com/movies/boxoffice.html). If a film does well, Hollywood wants to duplicate its success.

When *Titanic* (1997) was released, it became the highest grossing movie of the year. (In fact, it became the highest grossing movie to date!) Hollywood's response to this was: find another *Titanic*. Just weeks after *Titanic* was deemed a success, Twentieth Century-Fox announced plans for *Hindenburg*, a movie set on the ill-fated dirigible that will center on an American naval intelligence officer and a female German documentary filmmaker in 1937.

Another way to exploit the success of a currently popular film is to bring the idea to the next level, or give it a creative twist. From the success of *Titanic*, two screen spoofs have been put into development. New Line Cinema is making *Gigantic*—the story of a ship that rivaled the great *Titanic* but, because it is two and a half inches shorter, receives no publicity on its equally tragic maiden voyage. The Motion Picture Corporation of

America (MPCA) is preparing *Titanic Too—It Missed the Iceberg*, in which the *Titanic* misses the iceberg but then encounters other hazards ranging from sea monsters to asteroids.

It's not enough, however, to write what sells. Unless you can turn out a polished screenplay virtually overnight, you need to be able to predict industry trends and have the property that everyone wants waiting in the wings. Take the case of *Scream* (1996). This satiric, youth-oriented slasher was so hot it took Hollywood by storm. When it came out, everybody wanted to find the next *Scream*. The results: *I Know What You Did Last Summer* (1997), *Disturbing Behavior* (1998), *The Faculty* (1998), *The Rage: Carrie II* (1999), *Idle Hands* (1999), and others.

When *Scream* was deemed successful, the even smarter writer didn't begin another *Scream*. Instead, this person predicted the trend. If *Scream* was teen horror, the next step may be teen comedy. A year after *Scream* was released, Hollywood had more than thirty teen comedy film projects in the pipeline, including *Can't Hardly Wait* (1998), *She's All That* (1999), and *Ten Things I Hate About You* (1999).

FRANK DARABONT WRITES SMALL, CHARACTER-DRIVEN FILMS AND MAKES A LIVING AT IT ... WHY CAN'T I?

Frank Darabont is one of the most sought-after writers in Hollywood today. His film *The Shawshank Redemption* (1994), based on a short story by Stephen King, was essentially a small, character-driven drama—the pinnacle of anticommerciality.

And yes, it's true, Mr. Darabont can write his own ticket today. He can pen virtually anything he wants and be paid for it. This is because he has proven himself.

But it wasn't always like that. Darabont's first three movies were anything but small, character-oriented passion pieces. In 1987 he co-wrote *A Nightmare on Elm Street 3: Dream Warriors* for New Line Cinema. In 1988 he co-scripted *The Blob* for TriStar. In 1989 he co-wrote *The Fly II* for Twentieth Century-Fox. It wasn't until 1994 that he not only wrote but also directed *The Shawshank Redemption* for Columbia.

Darabont's dreams of writing anything he wanted *and* getting paid to do so came only once he was established. His passion never waned. His desires did not change. He simply knew what he needed to do to establish himself as a *working writer* and escalated from there.

WHAT IS COMMERCIAL?

Something is commercial if it has widespread appeal. Take another look at the most recent box-office grosses. The top five movies probably are all quite different in style and subject matter. Yet, they are all commercial because they appeal to a wide range of audiences.

Part of your job is to monitor trends and predict what will be commercially viable, then infuse your creativity and passion into a saleable vehicle. The end results will be something you can sell and be proud of. "Frequently writers will do something, or do a series of things that are very, very commercial, in an effort to have the luxury of doing something more independent next," notes literary agent Angela Cheng.

SCREENPLAY FORMAT

The art of writing may be an inherent trait, but there's no excuse for incorrect screenplay format. "I didn't even know what screenplay format was," Daniel Yost remembers about first starting out. "I put the dialogue at the extreme far left of the page, all the way across like I'd seen in plays that were printed up. Finally I took a screenwriting class and learned the format."

It's a good thing too. Had Yost's script come to my office with the wrong format, I'd have sent it back. I receive too many screenplays written without attention to detail. Here are some rules to write by:

When formatting your script, avoid:

- using difficult-to-read print
- sending dirty pages
- using both sides of the page
- using graphics
- leaving out important information, such as your address and phone number
- binding your script in any way other than three-hole punched and held together by three brads (brass fasteners)
- using weak or sharp brads

In general, do not:

- editorialize
- make spelling or grammatical mistakes
- overuse parentheticals

- overwrite description
- submit a script that is too short or too long; 120 pages is the standard length
- submit a script with missing pages
- use camera directions
- use *Cut to*, *Continued*, or scene numbers. You're not writing a shooting script.
- use inconsistent character names
- use incorrect formatting
- use irregular margins or typeface. Margins should be one and a half inches on all sides. Standard typeface is `Courier 12-point, 10-pitch, nonproportional.`
- use passive verb tenses

Remember always to:

- capitalize slug lines, a character's name the first time it appears, sound effects, and emphasis on an important prop
- number pages in the upper right-hand corner

THE SPEC SCRIPT

A spec script is one that is written *on speculation*. In other words, the writer has not been commissioned to create the screenplay but has simply decided to write a script in hopes of selling it once it is completed.

Obviously, in order to get an agent, writers need to have available examples of their work. The best samples for future screenwriters are spec scripts that they've created. From this, an agent can judge your writing, and if she likes the script, she can try and sell it for you.

Established writers write specs all the time. It's not that they can't be paid to adapt other people's ideas; they can. However, sometimes they just want to tell their own stories. They may first try pitching the story to producers, but if no one options it (pays a generally non-refundable deposit up front for possible purchase later; see glossary) or buys it right away, they will probably just write it on spec and see if their agent can sell it for them.

See chapter 17 for more information on the spec script market and how a spec script is sold.

UNSOLICITED MATERIAL

For legal reasons, most production companies and studios will not look at material unless it is submitted by an agent or attorney. Thus, if you ever send a screenplay directly to a production company, they will probably send it right back to you, unread.

What often is not known, however, is that by signing a release form, a writer can have his material read by a producer or studio executive, even if he is without representation. How do you get a producer to send you a release form? You first need to send a query letter that gets them excited enough to want to contact you and request your script. Similar letters also are used to solicit agents.

QUERY LETTERS

Many executives in Hollywood, including myself, read and respond to query letters. Although I do read them all, my time allows me only to respond to those that intrigue me.

"A lot of people try to do gimmicky things," says literary agent Debbie Deuble. "They'll enclose something cute, or they'll try to write a really outrageous letter. That will usually get my attention. But if the story is not interesting to me, forget it. However, you can't just completely dismiss query letters because you never know who the next great talent is."

"I get five to ten query letters a day," says Angela Cheng. "I find that a lot of people don't do their homework. When it's 'Dear Sirs' or 'Dear Madame' or 'Dear Literary Agent,' or they get my name wrong, I'm not really going to give them the time of day."

Following are two examples of query letters.

Get to the point quickly in your query letter. In one paragraph tell me what your story is about and why I should read it. Choose your words carefully and sparingly. This is also my opportunity to evaluate your writing. If you cannot express your idea clearly in the letter, I don't want to struggle through 120 pages of poor writing.

Avoid movie references. I dislike when people write "It's a cross between *Psycho* and *Bambi*." If you have to rely on other movies to describe your own original idea, how interesting could it be? Referencing screenplays by movie titles is a tool development executives use to describe a script's tone to studio executives.

Tammy Jasons

February 14, 2000

Fredrick Levy
Levy Entertainment
5555 Gower Avenue
Hollywood, CA 90000-0000

Dear Fred:

I wrote a movie called *When Harry Was Sleepless with His Mail*. It's the best script you'll ever reed. It's a scross between *When Harry Met Sally* and *Sleepless in Seattle*.

It starts off with this guy Harry. He's so damn funny, you'll pee your parnts. Anyway, Harry got no money, so he decides to rob a post office.

So Harry comes up with a plan, along with his neigbor Lyndsay and the local paperboy, Sam. They like to hang out at the local pizza joint where this plan was hatched. One time, in this really funny scene I wrote, they have a pizza eating contest and Sam gets so sick, they have to pump her stomach.

Everything turns out OK. They pull off their plan. Just when they think they got away with it, they chased by the mail police. (I actually researched this and found out that there really are actual mail police!!!)

At the last minute, Sam throws a paper at the police, temporarily blinding them, and the trio escapes. As I'm sure you'll agree, this is a great set up for a sequel. You'll have no problem getting top actors on board because of the original concept and the funny dialouge.

I've included a twenty page treatment of my project for you to read more. I'll be waiting for your call.

Best regards,
Tam

Letter A

Jill Karen Jeffreys
Screenwriter
1313 South Main Street
Stoughton, MA 02072
(781) 555-5555

September 18, 2000

Mr. Frederick Levy
Levy Entertainment
5555 Gower Avenue
Hollywood, CA 90000-0000

Dear Mr. Levy:

I have recently completed a screenplay for a teen horror film
called *A Screaming Nightmare from Dusk Till Halloween Dawn*.
Per your company's listing in the *Hollywood Creative Directory*, I
believe this is the type of film you're looking for.

Four teens go camping for the weekend. Only one comes back.
Years later, still haunted by the deadly events of his past, he
goes on a killing spree in the small town where his friends mys-
teriously disappeared.

Please let me know if you would like to see a copy of my
screenplay. I would be happy to sign your standard release
form and get you the script as soon as possible.

Best regards,
Jill Karen Jeffreys

Letter B

> ### Fear of Plagiarism
>
> Don't let your fear of being plagiarized prevent you from sending out query letters. If you're explaining the story's concept generally and succinctly, there won't be enough detail for anyone to steal it from you.

Finally, query only one project per letter. If you bombard an agent or executive with several screenplay pitches all at once, at best he'll request to see only one. They'll also probably wonder why this writer hasn't sold a single screenplay yet.

The first thing I notice when I look at letter A is that the writer misspelled my name. Big no-no. She also addresses it "Dear Fred," like she's known me for years. That's mistake number two. Like a résumé, this letter is your opportunity to make a good first impression, and because our relationship is strictly professional at this point, you must pay extra attention to these kinds of details.

Next, I read the first paragraph and notice more spelling mistakes and typos. If the writer cannot proof a one-page letter before sending it, I don't know that I want to stumble through a script probably filled with errors. Also, can't the writer come up with anything more creative than two movie titles to describe her screenplay?

Then I must wade through four paragraphs of a poorly constructed story. They're filled with unnecessary plot points and commentary. All I want is a simply constructed paragraph to learn the basic premise and idea. At this point, I absolutely do not want to read the attached twenty-page treatment. If I'm at least intrigued, I may want to contact the writer to ask her to forward a treatment or screenplay. Of course, it will be virtually impossible for me to do so in this case. She forgot to include any contact information. Good thing I'm *not* interested!

Letter B is one that would grab my attention and that I would consider seriously. It's professional in format and appearance. It also gets to the point. The writer tells me her story in three lines. Also, this person has done her research and knows that this is the type of movie I'm generally looking for. She has included an address and phone number so I can contact her if I'm interested in the project.

GETTING A LITERARY AGENT

Query letters are fine while you're still looking for representation, but having an agent gives you a certain degree of credibility and also makes your job as a writer easier. The agent can worry about selling your material while you expend your energy writing the best screenplays you can. Most important, it's usually the only way to get in many industry doors.

"If they are looking to get an agent, they should use the resources that they have at college, their friends, the uncle of your next-door neighbor from childhood who has an ex-girlfriend that is in the business—use their names because that's the way to get in the door," recommends literary agent Debbie Deuble.

Yet finding representation is not that easy. If you have no one to refer you to an agent, it might be necessary once again to rely on the query letter. A good query letter or a referral will only open a door; it still may not be good enough to get you in.

The only ticket over the threshold is a great script. You have only one chance at each door, so make every one count. Do not send a query on a script until the screenplay is as good as it can possibly be. If it still needs improvement, work on making it better. Don't send out letters until the screenplay is finished. I'll read each screenplay only once.

Be careful which doors you enter. Unfortunately, not all people claiming to be agents are certified. First, check with the Writers Guild of America (WGA) that the firm is a signatory of the guild. Also, the standard agency fee in Hollywood is 10 percent. They shouldn't take a dime more from you, and never pay them anything up front for taking you on as a client. Also, make sure that an interested agent has good taste and that you're both on the same page with regard to your career. Sure, it's important to have an agent—but it will do you no good to have the wrong one.

Writing team Tim Garrick and Scott Russell started looking for their first agent after they had done four scripts. "Since neither one of us had gone to film school or had taken any writing courses, we really considered each script that we wrote like a semester of film school," explains Garrick. "We felt that we had gotten better and had learned a little bit more each time, so we were more self-assured that maybe what we had could be shown around."

The struggling writers did what everyone else was doing. They sent out query letters providing synopses of their projects. "We tried to be as interesting as possible," says Garrick. "We sent out about forty letters. Just one [agent] responded. In retrospect, the agent we got was a joke."

At this point in their career, the writing team didn't have much of a choice. Was it better to go with a small agent or no agent at all?

"Having no agent is impossible. No one will read your stuff," insists Garrick. "But after we realized what a joke we had as an agent, we left her." Eventually they did acquire a legitimate agent. "By script number eight, we had written a script that was commercial, so it was easier for people to really grasp the concept of what we had written. I would say by this script, I was proud of what we were doing. It was entertaining. We had learned a lot along the way. We were on par with what was out there."

Once again, they sent out query letters, but this time they went only to appropriate places—not the biggest firms, but legitimate boutique (smaller) agencies. This time around, they actually had a choice of agencies that were interested in signing them.

THE HIRED PEN

Writers usually cannot get hired to write a screenplay, until they already have sold something. Once they are in the category of *writer for hire*, however, assignments are a great way to earn a living in between creating your own material. Daniel Yost advises, "Whatever I want to write, that's what I write, unless I take a job for pay. But I always try to find a way, in whatever I'm writing, to enjoy it, because if I'm not enjoying it, I can't write well anyway, so I might as well stop. You've got to write because you care about it. Of course, it doesn't hurt to say, 'Well I care about it and I want to make money.'"

THE BLAIR PITCH PROJECT

Established writers can go to a studio with their own ideas and verbally pitch the executives. If the creative execs like the story, they will hire the scribe to write the screenplay. This is a privilege reserved for established screenwriters only.

"Once *Drugstore Cowboy* [1989] came out, that was something that everybody had seen. It got a lot of critical acclaim and won a lot of awards for screenwriting," says Yost. "Suddenly I was the same person walking in with the same screenplays to meetings, but now people gave me credibility. They trusted me, and they were willing to take a chance and pay money for me to write projects. I had ideas, and some of those ideas I got deals on. There were other things, over the course of the next few years, that I got to write based on producers' ideas, or books, or things like that."

Pitching ideas is an art unto itself. I've seen excellent writers fail miserably at verbally selling their ideas to a room full of executives. However, I've also seen mediocre writers dazzle the room and walk away with deal after deal after deal.

All of the same principles of writing apply to pitching—they just need to be transmitted verbally. If you're selling a comedy, make them laugh. If you're describing a thriller, keep them on the edge of their seats. If they can see the movie poster in their mind as you leave the meeting, you've done a good job.

WRAPPING IT UP

When a writer's first screenplay is finally put into production, it is a time for celebration. It's amazing to think that a movie is actually being made because of an idea you created. "One thing that is so shocking is that you're there on the set and all these people [costume, special effects, etc.] have a job because of something you sat down and wrote," says Tim Garrick.

While Garrick's script *Stranger Than Fiction* (1999) was filming, the writer spent a lot of time on the set. He was amazed to see people running around trying to find specific props that he had placed in the script on a whim. "We needed some bar mitzvah wrapping paper," he remembers. "The whole reason I put that in there was I thought that was just odd because [the characters really] needed wedding wrapping paper [and couldn't find any]. These people were calling New York and Hallmark and all over the country trying to find bar mitzvah wrapping paper, which just did not exist. And they were freaking out, and it was so funny watching all this chaos around me that I had created."

Not all proved to be harmless fun and games, however. It's difficult watching your script change and grow. "You write something, you have it in your mind, then you see an actor or a director change it," says Garrick. "Sometimes they would do something that you hadn't thought of, and it was interesting or funny, and you'd be pleased. Other times it was so opposite of what you'd expect, and you have to keep your mouth shut. But I learned so much, and that's what's important. During the whole ordeal, no matter how upset I got, whether or not I was crying or storming off the set or whatever I was doing, which I did all of the above, I never forgot how fortunate I was to be where I was."

No one can teach you how or what to write. There are books and seminars to teach format and structure, but writing is a talent that gets better only with disciplined practice. Like acting, writing is one of the most difficult and competitive professions in show business. Successful screenwriters in Hollywood can map their own future, and many writers today get the opportunity to direct their own screenplay. Spec scripts have sold for as high as $4 million. An average script sale is generally a six-figure deal. Obviously, writing can be an extremely lucrative and rewarding profession. See appendix B: Guild/Union Minimum Payments to find out how much writers can earn.

5

DIRECTORS

*What's important for a director is a voice that is
distinct to that director, and a sense of practicality
that understands that you are working in both a
collaborative medium that has strict economic
demands, and an artistic medium that has some
tried and true rules that need to be followed, and
other rules that need to be broken.*

JON TURTELTAUB, director

WHILE YOU WERE BLINKING

There's a little scene in the romantic comedy *While You Were Sleeping* (1995) starring Sandra Bullock and Bill Pullman, in which a paperboy, riding his bike on an icy sidewalk, tosses a newspaper and wipes out. When director Jon Turteltaub was filming that scene, everyone from the production manager to the producer said to him, "We don't have the money. It's an unimportant scene. Don't shoot it." However, something inside of Turteltaub said, "I know this is good," and the production team spent a third of a day and a lot of money putting fake snow up and down a Chicago street for this one establishing shot that everyone but the director thought was unnecessary.

Turteltaub was sitting with one of the producers at the initial test screening of the film. When the scene with the paperboy unfolded, "the whole audience roared," says Turteltaub. "It got the biggest laugh in the entire movie. My producer turned to me and said, 'Dammit, you're a

65

genius.'" That is one of Turteltaub's most satisfying moments to date as a film director.

"[Filmmaking is] such a hugely collaborative job that sometimes it's hard to know what you did right and what you did wrong," concedes Turteltaub. "You don't want to take the blame because there are so many other people involved. But you also have trouble taking credit because there are so many other people involved. And every now and then there's a little moment that you know is just you. And you hang on to those."

But What I Really Want to Do Is . . .

There are as many ways to make it as a film director as there are directors. "No two of us have taken the same route," says Turteltaub, director of *Cool Runnings* (1993), *Phenomenon* (1996), and *Instinct* (1999). When contemplating a career as a director, you should consider two questions. First, how do you get to be a director? Second, how do you get to be a good director? "One is about having a job; the other is about having a career," Turteltaub explains. "The fact of the matter is, it's a lot about luck and timing, and timing's a lot about luck.

"Every job you take before directing helps you once you become a director. "I would say to any student, if you want to be a film director, study something besides film, otherwise you're not offering anybody anything. If you have a great sense of human behavior, an amazing sense of music, or an incredible understanding of history, then you've got something to offer. The film industry is looking for new voices who can do the old stuff in a new way because the old stuff has become old stuff because it works. The question is, how can you present it in a way that is fresh and unique?"

The three biggest talent pools for feature directors are writers, television directors, and commercial/music video directors. But directors can come from anywhere. Actors such as Penny Marshall (*Laverne & Shirley*), Ron Howard (*Happy Days*), and Rob Reiner (*All in the Family*) are now directors. Jan De Bont (*Speed*) was formerly a cinematographer. Robert Wise (*West Side Story*) began his career as a film editor. Risa Bramon Garcia (*200 Cigarettes*) was a casting director before she directed her first feature. Even Bob and Harvey Weinstein, chairpersons of Miramax Films, directed a movie (*Playing for Keeps*).

FILM SCHOOL: WORTH THE BUCKS?

"When you come out of medical school, you're a doctor. When you come out of law school, you're a lawyer. When you come out of film school, you're a waiter," jokes Turteltaub, who graduated from USC's School of Cinema-Television graduate production program. "Would I suggest you go to film school? If you want to learn, yes. But nobody hands you a job when you get out."

So why pay thousands of dollars for an education that in no way guarantees you a job? "Film school taught me an enormous amount about all the technical things that I knew nothing about," says Turteltaub. "It was extremely helpful to me to have gone to film school to learn what everybody else's job is. I didn't learn a hell of a lot about directing, but I learned a lot about lighting, and shooting, and sound, and gripping, and all of that stuff, which then helped me later on as a director because I could speak in the vocabulary of all these other people. I rely more on my theater major than my film major in terms of directing—understanding story structure, drama, acting, and communicating with actors, which is more important to me when I make movies than the technical things. Other directors rely much more on the technical aspects to tell their stories."

Marshall Herskovitz, director of *Jack the Bear* (1993) and *Dangerous Beauty* (1998), attended the American Film Institute (AFI), which is where he met his longtime business partner, Edward Zwick, director of *Glory* (1989), *Legends of the Fall* (1994), and *Courage Under Fire* (1996). "That was really how I got into the business," says Herskovitz. "I got my first job writing for television while I was still at the school, through a contact I had made at the school. That's exactly how you want film school to operate."

As far as which film school one should attend, there may be differences in the curricula, but there's not much difference in the outcome. The three major film schools are AFI, New York University (NYU), and USC. "You're going to succeed on your own anyway," says Herskovitz. "Those schools aren't going to make you succeed. But you have an equal chance to succeed at any one of them."

When Herskovitz was at AFI, actor Anne Bancroft was enrolled in the Directing Workshop for Women. His classmate Stuart Cornfeld was helping Bancroft with her project. "Anne would go home and talk to [her husband, writer-director] Mel [Brooks] about 'Stuart this' and 'Stuart that,' and how great Stuart was. So we get out of AFI and Mel hires Stuart to be his assistant. A year later he's producing a movie [*History of the World, Part I*] for Mel. That's the best case of how it works."

<h2 align="center">LANDING IN THE DIRECTOR'S CHAIR</h2>

Today, if you want to be a director, all you need to do is go out and make a film. I'm not saying that you should attempt to make the next $100 million special-effects vehicle for a $20 million star like Jim Carrey. Maybe your first project should be less ambitious. The fact remains, you need to have a film to show if you are to be a director. This is an even more vital tool in this field than a résumé.

THE REEL FACTS

The most important calling card you can have is a sample of works you've directed. A reel is a video that consists of shorts, scenes, and other footage you've shot. It is a showcase of your talent. Make it look as professional as the best résumé. Not only should the contents be impressive, indicate a reflection of your taste, and show a range of what you can do, but it also should be cut together neatly and packaged well. Type the labels and put the reel in a nice case. The reel itself will be your first impression to those who matter. Make it count.

In addition to getting you jobs, a great reel is the way for you to obtain an agent. Writers send out their scripts to be read and evaluated. Directors send out their short film, or reel, to be viewed and evaluated. "I got my first agent right out of film school, screening my short film," says Jon Turteltaub.

"While I was [at Brandeis University] I decided that I wanted to go into filmmaking," Herskovitz details. "So after I graduated, I took all the money I had in the world, which was about $6,000, and I made my own dramatic, sync-sound, 16mm epic film—thirty-nine minutes long. I took it to California and couldn't get anyone to look at it. It was just a nightmare. I remember looking through the Yellow Pages under 'Film Production Companies.' I was just completely lost."

Debra Hill, producer of *Halloween* (1978), *The Fisher King* (1991), and *Crazy in Alabama* (1999), explains, "Today you have so many things available to you, such as a video camera. The idea is to get something that's tangible, that says I can tell a story that's unique and unusual in ten minutes. Essentially, if you can do that and do it well, you're going to get noticed."

A perfect example is director Jamie Blanks. "He was in film school in Australia, and he got a hold of the script for *I Know What You Did Last Summer* [1997]," Hill says. "He went out with his own money and the resources that he had from school, and directed a trailer. That trailer got seen by an agent, who showed it to some studio executives, and he went on to direct *Urban Legend* [1998]. Now he's developing a big-budget feature, *Blood Relative*, for Phoenix Pictures. He didn't even decide to tell his own story. He obviously knew what would succeed in the marketplace and sort of hooked his success on that. He told a story that made people who were willing to put up money understand that he understood the genre, and he is now launched."

Although directing a short film may be more feasible than financing an entire feature, making your own full-length movie is not entirely impossible. Director Robert Rodriguez began making home movies at the age of thirteen. When he graduated from the University of Texas at Austin, he raised $7,000 from family and friends, to shoot his first feature, *El Mariachi* (1992). Hollywood was amazed with the finished product and Columbia Pictures signed Rodriguez to a directing deal. Since his feature debut, Rodriguez has made *Desperado* (1995), the sequel to *El Mariachi*, one segment of the anthology film *Four Rooms* (1995), *From Dusk Till Dawn* (1996), and *The Faculty* (1998).

One common way to raise a large amount of money to make a movie is by maxing out your credit cards. It may not be the best way to finance a project, but it is a tried and true method. Other ways might include fundraisers, begging your parents or rich relatives for cash, asking friends for favors and to work on the film for free, getting sponsors who believe in your filmmaking ability, and keeping your vision to a manageable budget. You also might try bartering for services and asking for favors. Be creative. Better yet, partner with a would-be producer who will raise the money so you can focus on your directing chores.

COMMERCIALS AND MUSIC VIDEOS

Another viable source of entrée into the world of directing features is through directing TV commercials and music videos. Many of today's top directors started this way, including Michael Bay (*The Rock*,

Armageddon), who directed commercials for Bugle Boy, Nike, and Levi's, Tony Scott (*Top Gun, Crimson Tide*), and Antoine Fuqua (*The Replacement Killers*), who directed a Coolio music video. After all, when directing a commercial or music video, many of the same principles of filmmaking apply, especially the elements of storytelling.

Mary Lambert got her start directing music videos before she went on to helm such features as *Pet Sematary* (1989), *Pet Sematary II* (1992), and *Clubland* (1999). "I was very naive about the business," Lambert admits. "I didn't really want to be a director so much as a filmmaker."

Lambert had gone to college at the Rhode Island School of Design (RISD) where she studied painting. While there, she realized that she was not a very good painter in the traditional sense, and that the canvas she wanted to paint on was film. So she began making experimental short films. It was the late 1970s, the music video scene was just emerging, and MTV was on the horizon. That's when Lambert saw a music video for Rickie Lee Jones, and she thought that's exactly what she had been already doing with her shorts.

A lot of Lambert's friends were musicians. In fact, she was classmates at RISD with the rock band the Tom Tom Club, for whom she directed her first video, "As Above, So Below." The video received a lot of attention on MTV and earned Lambert her next directing assignment, Madonna's "Borderline." Lambert directed a total of five videos with Madonna and continued to make a name for herself in the music video scene, working with a diverse range of artists from Sting to Mötley Crüe.

In the late 1980s, Lambert found a feature she wanted to direct. "It was just one of those very difficult independent films that gets put together and falls apart, and finally it came together." The project was *Siesta* (1987), which starred Ellen Barkin and Jodie Foster. While it was neither a critical nor financial success, Lambert is extremely proud of the movie.

Lambert's jump from music videos to feature films was not a planned move. "It was not so much a deductive reasoning, like, this will advance my career in such and such a way," admits Lambert, who just wanted to start telling her own stories. "I wanted to put the music with the pictures instead of the pictures with the music. I wanted to be able to explore that more on my terms than on the terms of the musicians that I was working with.

"You should do something that you have an affinity for, if writing and telling stories is something you're good at, then that's where you should try to get your start. Music videos is a good entrée, but not if you're not interested in it."

If you want to direct music videos, you have to sell yourself to the bands, record companies, and video production companies. "I would suggest that you become as much a part of the music scene as you care to. If you want to be a commentator on the scene, which is what a music video director is, then you have to be part of that scene," Lambert suggests. "Working as a PA [production assistant] is a perfectly acceptable way to do that. You have to do whatever it is that you have to do. It depends on how important it is to you."

Music Video Production Association (MVPA)

The MVPA is the trade organization of the music video industry. Members include the majority of music video production and post-production companies, and artists working in the music video industry. Its purpose is to promote and uphold professional production standards, to provide a forum for members to exchange ideas, and to educate members about the latest developments in the music video industry.

HYPHENATES: THE WRITER-DIRECTOR

One of the biggest challenges facing directors in Hollywood today is finding a great script. As such, if you've written an incredible screenplay, it will be in great demand. If you've written a great script and you've got your eye on directing, the script may be your ticket to the director's chair. Of course, a great script is a screenplay that others, besides yourself, consider great. Many of today's top directors started out as writers. They include Quentin Tarantino (*Reservoir Dogs, Pulp Fiction, Jackie Brown*), Luc Besson (*La Femme Nikita, The Fifth Element, The Messenger: The Story of Joan of Arc*), and Kevin Smith (*Clerks, Chasing Amy, Dogma*).

"I couldn't get hired as a director, so I was a writer for many years," Marshall Herskovitz acknowledges. "I basically had to create a television series and hire myself to direct. That's how I became a director."

Herskovitz got his start writing for the TV show *Family* (1976–80). "I languished as a writer for several years, doing freelance episodic work and hating it," he says. "Then I just threw it all over in 1981 and just said I'm not doing it anymore. I wrote a script on spec that Ed [Zwick] and I developed together and everything sort of came from that. That was a turning point for me. It was really putting everything on the line."

The script he penned but never made led directly to Herskovitz writing a movie-of-the-week for NBC called *Special Bulletin* (1983). "That put us both on the map. [Ed] as director, me as writer, and we produced it together," says Herskovitz. The telepicture won Herskovitz the Writers Guild Award, earned Zwick the Directors Guild Award, and for the two of them, the Humanitas Award and four Emmys, all for their first time out. "We were a little bit spoiled," says Herskovitz. "All of a sudden I had a feature career as a writer, and not long after that I made a blind directing deal at TriStar with [then president of production] Jeff Sagansky to write and direct a movie. Ed got his first feature off of that. It was a very significant moment in our lives."

When writers are experienced enough, they essentially are already equipped to direct because they're just following their own vision. They don't have to be technically versed. They don't have to have experience working with actors. They just have to know what they want and be able to articulate it, so that the actors and the crew can act accordingly. "They know exactly how to direct because they see the movie in their head," says Herskovitz.

"My training is as a filmmaker, and that's a generalized term," he adds. "In order to be a filmmaker, you generally have to be a hyphenate. You have to be a writer-director, or a producer-director, or all three. That's what a filmmaker is. A filmmaker is the author of the film, in some way, and the person responsible for the film. In that way, I prefer to produce and direct, but I need to have somebody there who's holding up the producing end for me so I'm not literally doing both. I'm certainly not line producing while I direct. But in terms of the battles with the studio and all that, that's why Ed and I have each other. I just think it's necessary in the business today, in order to protect yourself, to be a hyphenate."

THE SMALL SCREEN

"When I directed the pilot of [the TV show] *thirtysomething*, I won the Directors Guild Award," recounts Herskovitz. "The next year I won the Directors Guild Award again. I won it two years in a row. All of a sudden I was on the map as a feature director."

The most successful television directors cross over into theatrical movies. In fact, Mimi Leder (*The Peacemaker, Deep Impact*), John Pasquin (*The Santa Clause, Jungle 2 Jungle*), and Sam Weisman (*Bye Bye, Love; George of the Jungle, The Out-of-Towners*) all started out directing for television. "It's a good way," Herskovitz points out, "but you have to become successful and established in television. In some ways that's begging the question, because that, in and of itself, is a major struggle."

ASSISTANT TO THE DIRECTOR AND ASSISTANT DIRECTOR

Ironically, neither the route as an assistant to a director nor as an assistant director is a straight path to becoming a director. In both positions, you work closely with the director and learn through observation. However, unlike being an assistant to an established agent or a producer, where you could logically grow into the higher capacity because you're training along the way, assistants to directors do not have an opportunity to prove their creative ability in that position. The only way to do that is by directing something themselves.

The assistant director route is a means to becoming a production manager (see chapter 8).

THE FILM FESTIVAL CIRCUIT

Film festivals create an opportunity for new moviemakers to screen their independent projects. These competitions allow movies that ordinarily would not be seen to be screened by top industry distributors who regularly attend festivals seeking new product. Emerging filmmakers look to such festivals as a chance to screen their work in front of an audience. Entertainment executives come to festivals hoping to discover fresh talent. For anyone with an entry to screen, this is the big league.

There are hundreds of annual film festivals all over the world. Three of the more prominent ones that encourage entries from new filmmakers are the AFI Los Angeles International Film Festival, the Slamdance Film Festival, and the Sundance Film Festival. See appendix A for information on these festivals.

SHAKESPEARE IN TURNAROUND

Just because directors are established does not mean that it's easy for them to get a film made. OK, so maybe it's a little easier since they already have one or more features under their belt, but making each movie is still an uphill battle. They face the same challenges we all do in getting their new projects greenlighted.

Shakespeare in Love (1998), for instance, was a film that director Edward Zwick developed with writer Mark Norman as part of Bedford Falls (the company Zwick and Marshall Herskovitz co-own). They brought in writer Tom Stoppard to do additional work on the script, and in 1991 Zwick went to England to direct it with Julia Roberts set to star, but he did not yet have a leading man cast. At the time Universal was producing the picture and insisted on a major star for the title role or the studio would not make the movie. Zwick couldn't find a personality who fit that bill, so Universal put the project into turnaround just four weeks before shooting was scheduled to start.

As we all know, several years later the project was resurrected in 1998 with Gwyneth Paltrow in the lead. Zwick did not direct the film, however, and served solely as a producer. Nonetheless, much of Zwick's vision remains in the movie, since he helped create, shape, and develop it. *Shakespeare in Love* went on to win the Best Picture Oscar.

A similar thing happened to Marshall Herskovitz one year prior to Zwick's attempt at making *Shakespeare in Love*. Herskovitz was in pre-production on a film about Robin Hood. However, there were two other films on the bandit being made at the same time. A month into pre-production, an industry rumor circulated that Kevin Costner was thinking about playing Robin Hood in one of the other Sherwood Forest entries. "I think he [Cost-ner] called [his agent] Mike Ovitz and said, 'I don't want to be the second Robin Hood,' " says Herskovitz who still did not have a leading man for his own production. "Mike Medavoy, who was head of TriStar at the time, wanted us to back off. We were supposed to start [set] construction the next week and it was going to cost $60,000. He said, 'I don't want to start con-struction if we don't have a leading man.' And I begged him over the phone and said, 'The other Robin Hood is at Shepperton [Studios in Middlesex, in England]. We're at Pinewood [Studios in Buckinghamshire, also in England], these guys all talk. If we don't start construction, they will know in one hour, and it will be known [soon after] in Los Angeles that we have slowed down, and that will be the message to Costner that it's safe to do it. If we keep going, Costner will not sign to do that movie, and we'll be OK.' "

Medavoy still would not allow construction to begin. Not a week later, as Herskovitz had predicted, Costner signed on to do the competing version. "We continued for another month trying to find an actor, but this was my first lesson in Hollywood politics," says Herskovitz. "My agency was CAA [Creative Artists Agency], and Costner's agency was CAA, and I don't fault anybody, it's just the way the business works, Costner was a lot more important to them than I was. And his *Robin Hood* suddenly became a lot more important than mine. There was no way that I was going to get a CAA client to star in that movie. We were dead."

A Team Effort

While certain directors such as George Lucas and Steven Spielberg have carte blanche to pick and choose the movies they wish to make, many directors are just hired hands, like everyone else on the production crew. This sometimes poses a question of artistic integrity when offered an assignment.

"Even when you're just a director for hire, when you're just out there trying to get a job, you don't take just anything you're offered," advises Jon Turteltaub. "You still have to choose the material that you know, in your gut, you can turn into a great movie. If you don't think you can make a great movie out of it, don't do it, because you won't."

"Part of the myth at AFI is the director as auteur," says Herskovitz. "AFI is very steeped in the tradition of great American filmmaking—John Ford, William Wyler, Frank Capra—and I didn't understand that those days were gone." He learned it quickly on his first feature, *Jack the Bear*, because he was not the producer, he was not the writer, he was only the director. "I had no idea the extent to which I had to please all of these other people. It was a real eye-opening experience. The politics on that movie were very difficult."

Working with Writers

Good writers are so important to directors because without a solid script, there is no movie to direct. Of course, by the time a movie is finished, nobody feels a greater sense of ownership on that film than the director. "Even writers have to concede that by the time it's all done, the director has put at least as much as the writer has into that project, assuming they did their job well," says director Jon Turteltaub.

"I think a director who is working with a writer has to do as much of the work of writing as they can without getting in the way of the writer," says director Mary Lambert. "I feel that it's my responsibility working with a writer to do all the things that the writer does except put them on the page. You don't tell them what to write because you want them to come up with something that you wouldn't come up with. You want them to go through their own thought process and come up with the dialogue, or the location, or the set piece, or whatever it is they're coming up with. At the same time, I expect to talk to the writer enough and spend enough time with [the writer] in the process of it so that we're totally in agreement on who the people are, and what the world is they're living in, and what the story is we're trying to tell so that when [the writer] does come up with something that doesn't seem right to me, then we can discuss it in terms of the world that we're both living in at the time. I think working with a writer is almost as exhausting as writing it yourself."

WORKING WITH ACTORS

"All of us care about casting as much as we care about any other process in the film," Turteltaub offers. "Most directors care more about casting than lighting. It's a rare film that's lit well and acted poorly that people like. Yet there are many films lit poorly and acted well that people love. Your actors are your primary tool for telling your story. Aside from having a good script, there's nothing more important than having a great cast. Nothing even comes close."

Sandra Bullock auditioned just like every other actress for the leading role in *While You Were Sleeping*, the 1995 movie that made her a Hollywood star. She actually read for the director twice. "When she left the room, Joe Roth and Roger Birnbaum, the producers, said, 'That's our girl.' I said, 'I'm not so sure yet. I hear Nicole Kidman's still available,'" jokes Turteltaub.

"What I saw Sandra Bullock do in that room were two things that made me say, this is who I want for this movie," he explains. "She made me laugh, and I believed that she believed the words coming out of her own mouth. It felt real. The most important thing an actor can do is make you believe that they mean what they're saying. It's not dialogue. It's coming from inside. That's how it was with her. It's a gut thing. It doesn't matter if you're casting a man or a woman. Some part of you as a director wants to fall in love with these people. There's something about their charisma and their charm that makes you want to be with them. It's not a sexual thing. It's a deeper kind of instinctive, romantic, somehow twisted thing."

Mary Lambert's film *Clubland* (1999) is about a teenager from Riverside, California, who comes to Los Angeles with his band, hoping for a record deal. He discovers what a twisted business it is, and in the process his relationship changes with his brother and his bandmates. For the lead role, Lambert and producers Glenn Ballard and Mimi Gitland cast a complete newcomer named Jimmy Tucket. "My agreement with Glenn was we would find a kid that truly had the potential to become a rock star because that's what we're saying in the movie," says Lambert. "This kid has it. It's just a question of whether he's going to make it or not."

From the time Lambert joined the project, six months were spent looking for this pivotal performer. Lambert and her associates talked to a lot of interesting actors, but they couldn't find "the one." They finally ended with an open call one day, and Jimmy walked in. "He had been sleeping on the streets for three days," says Lambert. "He had been in Italy for eighteen months, and he heard that Glenn was doing these auditions, and he wanted to work with Glenn. He didn't even care about the movie. He wanted to cut a record with Glenn."

Lambert actually gave the actor a hard time in the audition process because everybody thought his story was so cute. She really didn't care about his story; she cared about her story, the film. "He just kept convincing me, though. Every obstacle that I would put in his way, he would just slide around it or under it in this very charming way." After he was cast, Tucker conceded, "OK, I'll be in the movie, but do I still get to cut the record?"

WORKING WITH CREW

Some directors use the same crew on every film they make. Other directors like to meet new creative talent and work with an entirely different crew on each production. "There's a lot to be said for using the same [crew] people every time," says Turteltaub. "You feel comfortable with them. You have a shorthand with them. You know their strengths and limitations, and they know yours. The advantage of working with new people is new ideas come from new people."

Once the crew is assembled, the director has a support group. "You can start to use their talents to help you imagine things very, very specifically," Lambert details. "Anything is possible, and you haven't put down anything—there's no hard copy yet. There's no evidence to the contrary that this is going to be the best thing you ever did. It's a really great time."

Lambert tries to choose people to work with who both understand her vision of the project and will bring an extra something to that vision. "I don't want someone who is going to do exactly what I tell them to do, because that would just be like working with a robot," she advises. "I like to work with all of them in pre-production so that we're all pretty clear about what's going to come down, and the way scenes are going to lay out emotionally and visually.

"Sometimes I'll have a very specific idea about how I want something to look, or how I want a shot to be composed, and then the cinematographer will say, 'OK, but we could do it this way, or we could move the camera way up here and look at it from down here, and then do the coverage,' in a completely different way than I had thought of. Sometimes I'm blown away. 'Wow. That's great. Let's do it that way.' But I always try to think before I change my mind. Is this still going to tell the story in the way that I wanted to tell the story, or is this just eye candy that's going to distract from the story that I'm trying to tell?"

THE SUITS

One of the nicest benefits to working in film production is that you can wear anything you want to work. Virtually every day is a casual day. Of course, if you are employed as an executive, attire is more formal. As such, studio execs and agents have earned the title *suits*. And everyone knows when an agent or executive visits a set because over the production assistant's walkie-talkie you'll hear, "The suits have arrived."

On studio features there's long been an unspoken animosity toward the power of the studio exec in the production of a film. Some moviemakers are quite apprehensive about the presence of studio executives on the set because it usually means something is wrong. In reality, however, that's not always the case. They're mainly there to support the filmmaker.

"I think the studio should have a say in the movie," says Turteltaub. "They bought their say in the movie. The studio hires me to make a movie for them. If I wanted to make a movie that only I liked, then I should go pay for it myself. My job is to make a movie that will make money back for the studio. I owe them my best effort to do that. However, I can never let that be at the expense of what I think is the most artistically correct, dramatically correct, creatively correct film. And they are counting on me to know that. They're counting on my taste. They're counting on my ability to be able to put on screen the things we discussed in the conference room.

"The other thing that's assumed, which isn't quite fair, is that if it's the studio's idea, it's a bad idea. That's a wrong assumption. There are a lot of very intelligent people who work in production companies and studios. You might be shocked to find out that a lot of them actually have something to contribute to the process, as might anyone. Good ideas can come from anywhere. It's just about finding the balance of how often to listen and which ideas to take. The next step comes in giving credit for those ideas, and that gets tricky too.

"As a director, it is a collaborative process from day one," Turteltaub continues. "The producers and the studio are turning to the director to say, guide us. Have an opinion. Have a voice. Have a vision. Give this film a uniqueness that makes it a very specific film. They may have suggestions as to how to do that, but they do want you to do that. That is your job. To know what you want and how to get it. For me, once you've worked out the kinks and all of your issues, trust that the script is right, and basically let your actors and crew help you to take pictures of what it says in the script. If it says, 'Man walks up to a house,' take a picture of a man walking up to a house. It's that easy. Sometimes there are better pictures of men walking up to a house than others. But just take pictures of what it says, and that's what you're doing really. Infusing that with a voice and a tone and a mood is the catch.

THE REVIEWS ARE IN

"Audiences will often read a review before going to a movie," says Turteltaub. "They'll buy a $190 pair of shoes just because they want to, but for an eight-dollar movie, they sit down and read a review first. And bad reviews hurt. You try not to read them. It's not that they matter. I don't know that any filmmaker changes his style or does different work because some reviewer didn't like his film, but your feelings still get hurt because you want people to like the work you do. If the person didn't get what you were saying, you feel that you either missed or that person wasn't paying attention. Look, here's all this filmmaker did: They spent a year and a half of their life working really hard so that you will have a nice night out. That's all we did. If we failed to do that, we failed at trying to give you a nice night out. That's it. And for that, people are called stupid, and failures, and dumb, and weak, and simpleminded, as if we just invaded a sweet little country for no reason.

"There's never been a person who has seen a movie who isn't a film critic," continues Turteltaub. "You walk out and your husband says to you, 'Did you like that?' Now you're a critic. What makes some people authorized to write it down in the newspaper versus other people who just talk about it in the car as they're paying the baby-sitter, I have no idea. But it's an unfortunate reality. One good argument I can make for critics is that were it not for critics, a studio's marketing department is the sole voice that the consumer hears. That would mean that every single movie, according to every single studio, was the greatest movie ever made."

6

PRODUCERS

Producers put together sports teams. They put together the best people that they know to do a job and then they guide the team from beginning to end.

JERRY BRUCKHEIMER, producer

LOVE AT FIRST OINK

A producer's role is that of problem solver and troubleshooter, no matter how strange the situation. For example, in the comedy *Big Top Pee-wee* (1988), Pee-wee Herman (Paul Reubens) experiments with hydroponic gardening at his farm. One night, a hurricane hits and the circus literally flies into town. All of the big top animals are mixed up with the barnyard ones. Pee-wee's best friend, Vance the pig, is drinking at a water hole when a hippo approaches—it's love at first sight.

"I'm trying to figure out how to do this scene without the hippo eating the pig," recalls the film's producer, Debra Hill, with a laugh. "So I searched all over the country looking at performing hippos. I found these two hippos in Sarasota, Florida, [who] were in love with each other for real. You couldn't separate them, but if you did, one would run to the other. We were going to have the hippo way up on the hillside," says Hill. "You see Vance come into the scene, and he sees the hippo, and suddenly the hippo starts to chase Vance. So to get the hippo to run towards the camera, we put the other hippo next to the camera. Not only did the hippo hit his mark, but he also hit the camera, and he almost ran over the pig! Everybody had to get out of his way."

WHAT A PRODUCER DOES

There are all types of producers in the motion picture industry. In the truest sense, a producer acquires material, arranges for financing, and then works with the financing source, typically a studio, to put together the rest of the elements (i.e., a director and the cast). Once all the pieces are together, the producer continues to supervise the preparation and the making of the movie, working with everyone as the glue, keeping the project together and moving forward. The producer stays involved throughout post-production and the release of the picture.

There are those who are producers by virtue of the fact that they havea key relationship with talent that is attached to the project. They could be the manager of an actor, the partner of a director, or possibly the owner of a piece of literary material. Based on the strength of their relationships, they are able to leverage a producer title, even get a fee, and sometimes have a voice in the actual production of the movie.

Then there are those who are dealmakers. They are good at bringing all the right elements together: cast, script, money. Having accomplished these steps, they take a title and hire someone who actually goes through the process of making the film, which they're usually not adept at.

Marty Katz, producer of *Lost in America* (1985), *Man of the House* (1995), and *Reindeer Games* (2000), falls into the first category. "So much about producing is talking and communicating with other people and sharing your vision with them. You have to be able to tell a story well and have others recognize its creative and financial merit. You must have a good sense of story as well as good business acumen, because the motion picture business is still a business, and yet it's the art of making motion pictures."

"Some of the qualities that make a good producer are never giving up, not taking no for an answer, persevering, and having a vision," adds Bonnie Bruckheimer, producer of *Beaches* (1988), *For the Boys* (1991), and *That Old Feeling* (1997). "I think that a lot of my feminine qualities make me a good producer because I'm very fair, I'm nurturing, and I consider everyone who works for me on a movie important."

THE ESSENTIAL INGREDIENTS

There are three essential elements to being a film producer. They are talent, material, and money. Bringing any one of them to the table will secure you a producer's title. What makes them essential is that individually each has the power to get a film made.

ACCESS TO TALENT

The term *talent* refers to writers, actors, and directors, all of whom are essential in the making of a film. A person other than a handler (i.e., agent or manager), who brings a piece of talent to a project before it is set up, will become a producer on the film if she has savvy.

Logically, if you have access to talent whom you can bring to a screen project, you too can be a producer. Not all talent is meaningful, however. Tom Cruise, Julia Roberts, Steven Spielberg, Michael Crichton—these names certainly mean *something* to a studio or financier. And if one of them happens to be your neighbor, cousin, best friend, or significant other, then you may be in luck.

If your connection is an actor on a midlevel television sitcom, chances are this performer won't matter enough to get a project made. Usually such people just don't carry sufficient weight with the financing entity. Of course, the more pieces you bring to the puzzle, and the stronger the package you build, the greater the chances are that you will form a combination that is meaningful and attractive enough to get your movie set up.

Each year the *Hollywood Reporter* ranks actors' star power (i.e., bankability). This is done by tallying an actor's standing before a film is made by gauging the ability of his or her name alone to raise financing for a project. To calculate this figure, such factors as the box-office receipts of each actor's most recent films are taken into consideration. Only a handful of directors are bankable when attached to a project. Even fewer writers are significantly meaningful to a package. Therefore, the remainder of this section focuses on actors and directors. Writers are covered later in this chapter under "Access to Material."

What if you don't know any pertinent talent? This is where the access part comes in. Sure, it helps if you have a personal relationship to fall back on, but as long as you can get a script into the hands of a bankable star, you can still attach that actor to a project.

LOCATING TALENT

You've got a script that is perfect for Brad Pitt. The only problem is, you don't know him personally. Not only that, you don't even know how to go about finding him, or if finding him at all is even possible.

The first step in locating Brad or any actor is to contact the Screen Actors Guild (SAG), the union that represents film and television actors. By calling Actors to Locate, SAG's referral department, at 323-549-6737, you can find out what agency and/or management firm represents an actor. For more information about SAG, log on to their Internet Web page at www.sag.com. An agent's job is to find work for her clients and negotiate contracts and salaries; a manager is involved in helping to guide his client's career and work choices. An actor often is represented by both an agent and a manager. More information on agents, managers, personal assistants, and other handlers is in chapter 17.

The Directors Guild of America (DGA) also has a department to locate its members. The number for Agency Listings is 323-851-3671. To learn more about the DGA, visit their Internet Web page at www.dga.org.

If contacting the unions yields no usable data, the next step would be to call the larger agencies and management firms to ask if the actor or director is a client. If this still doesn't provide the needed information, refer to the *Hollywood Creative Directory* to see if any of the actors and directors you seek have their own production companies. Contact information for all of these companies can be found in the *Hollywood Creative Directory* and the *Hollywood Agents & Managers Directory*. See chapter 2 for more details.

If all of these steps prove futile, it's time to be even more resourceful. What other handlers might these actors and directors have? Attorneys? Publicists? What projects are they currently working on? Where are these productions based? Who do you know who might have some connection with the person you are trying to reach? Who do you know who might know someone with that connection? Do your research, and do not give up. After all, *finding* them is only half the battle. Now you have to *contact* them.

CONTACT Once you learn the talent's representative, call the agency or management firm and find out the name of the point person for the actor or director in question. Most receptionists can give you this information. Sometimes they will transfer you to a department known as Client Information. Either way, you can get this data fairly hassle free.

The next step is to ask to speak with the talent's agent or manager. This person's assistant generally will answer the handler's phone. Be nice to the assistant, as he may turn out to be your biggest ally . . . or your worst nightmare. Assistants are well trained to screen calls. The following scenarios will give you a fairly good idea of what to do and what not to do when contacting an agent or manager.

Scenario 1: Someone Who Doesn't Know Better (SWDKB)

Assistant: Joe Agent's Office.

SWDKB: Hi. I have a script I'd like to send to your client, Jack Actor.

Assistant: Where are you calling from?

SWDKB: Um . . . I'm a producer.

Assistant: Your name?

SWDKB: Jim Producer.

Assistant: OK, where can Joe Agent return your call?

SWDKB: 323-555-1234

The phone goes dead, and most likely your call will never be returned. The reason for this is you do not sound confident, professional, or legitimate. Let's give you the benefit of the doubt, however, and say that Joe Agent does call you back.

Scenario 2: Someone Who Doesn't Know Better: Part Deux

SWDKB: Hello?

Assistant: I've got Joe Agent calling for Jim Producer.

SWDKB: This is he.

Assistant: One moment.

Joe Agent: This is Joe.

SWDKB: Hi, um . . . I've got a script I'd like to get to Jack Actor. . .

Joe Agent: Is it set up?

SWDKB: Not yet.

Joe Agent: Unfortunately, my client is booked through the rest of the year and he's not really reading any new projects at this time. Why don't you call back after the project is set up, and maybe things will have calmed down for him.

You stare longingly at the dead receiver, wondering where you went wrong. Could you have handled this situation differently? Would an agent, under any circumstances, take you seriously or actually consider reading your script? The answer is yes! Don't get discouraged; you didn't know any better. Besides, it wasn't such a bad call. This agent actually was being *nice*.

Scenario 3: Someone Who Knows Better (SWKB)

Assistant: Joe Agent's Office.

SWKB: Hi. Jane Producer calling for Joe Agent.

Assistant: One moment. (Pause) Could I ask what this is regarding?

SWKB: I'd like to speak with him about a project for Jack Actor.

Assistant: One moment.

Joe Agent: This is Joe.

SWKB: Hi, Joe. Jane Producer here. I've got a project you need to look at right away for Jack Actor. It's the best script I've read in the last year. Actor plays this ordinary guy who saves the planet when he discovers a cure for cancer. I want to give Jack first shot before it goes to Nicolas Cage.

Joe Agent: Great! Send it over.

SWKB: You'll have it this afternoon.

The reason this approach worked was because you sounded like you knew what you were talking about. You were not intimidated or hesitant; in fact, you jumped right in and got to the point. You described the script, made it sound attractive, and also gave him a reason he should look at it right away (possible competition from Nicolas Cage).

Dealing with managers and other handlers often will be similar to doing business with agents. Sometimes, however, these other handlers are a little easier to work with because they're not just looking for the monetary offer. They're generally more concerned with finding that career-making role for their client.

Production companies run by actors and directors operate a bit differently. These firms are formed so that these individuals can produce their own projects. A studio will make a producing deal with this company in the hope that the actor or director also will star in or direct some of the product they produce. Each company has a development executive whose job it is to find material to produce. This is the person you'll want to speak with.

PERSISTENCE IS THE KEY If nothing works right away, do not get discouraged. You gave it your best shot. Do not give up. If you couldn't find or contact a particular actor, there are others who might be just as good in your film. Some simply will be more accessible than others. Industry professionals face these same challenges every day.

I once had to get a script to the late Chris Farley. I called his agent several times, leaving messages each time. My calls were never returned. Discouraged but not ready to give up, I put a call in to the comedian's manager. He took my call but quickly told me that he's interested in reading scripts for Chris only if there is an actual offer on the table. Since this particular project was not yet set up, he would not even consider looking at it. After browsing through the *Hollywood Reporter*'s Production Charts, I discovered that Chris was shooting the movie *Almost Heroes* (1998). A friend of mine was working on the film's production staff. He told me where they were working and left a pass for my assistant to visit the set. I gave my assistant explicit instructions to march right up to Chris's trailer, knock on the door, and hand him (and nobody else) a copy of the script. I had enclosed a letter explaining this unorthodox approach to Chris.

The next morning, at one minute past nine o'clock, my phone rang. It was Chris's agent—the one who never returned my calls. He was ranting because I dared to go around him. "This was not proper operating procedure," he roared. When I told him that I couldn't use standard procedures if he didn't return my calls, he quickly became defensive and claimed he never received any of my messages. "Must have been that temp," was his best excuse.

Needless to say, the agent read the script. Promptly. He got back to me right away too. The downside is, he passed on the material. The upside is, now he *always* returns my calls.

ACCESS TO MATERIAL

Every once in a while a script comes along that everyone thinks is the best thing they've ever read. *The Shawshank Redemption* (1994), written by Frank Darabont, was one. *The Truman Show* (1998), written by Andrew Niccol, was another. Both screenplays were way above average, got bought right away, and were made into films. Niccol was attached to *Truman* as a producer. Darabont directed *Shawshank*. If you find that next great script, you too can become attached to the project, most likely in some sort of producer capacity.

The first time producer Bonnie Bruckheimer read the treatment for *Beaches*, she knew it was a movie she would produce for Bette Midler.

. . . But Bette Midler's Attached

"It always makes it easier if Bette's attached to a project," says producer Bonnie Bruckheimer, Midler's producing partner. "First of all, the material comes to us because people will say this is a great Bette Midler vehicle. Unfortunately, everybody who thinks that they have a great Bette Midler vehicle isn't always right. I would say we've had two thousand scripts submitted about a woman who always wanted to be a lounge singer but never quite made it because she was a housewife. But one day she steps on the stage and lo and behold, she can sing.

"Yes, we get the material," she continues. "We also get in the door [to major Hollywood players] a lot easier. Years ago we tried to do a TV series, and we went to see Brandon Tartikoff, then head of NBC. That was the easy part. Getting the show done was just as hard for us as it is for anybody else. So I think it does make it easier to have talent attached. But the actuality of the job is still just as difficult."

"A friend had called me up and said her girlfriend was writing a book called *Beaches*, which she envisioned as a movie, and she had Bette in mind. She gave me a twelve-page treatment of the book, and I read it, and I just cried and laughed while I was reading it. I gave it to Bette and I said, 'Wouldn't this just be a wonderful film?'"

Bruckheimer and Midler didn't have a production company at the time, so they didn't move forward with the project. In the interim, Disney bought the film rights. When they later got their deal at Disney, they asked to produce *Beaches* and the studio gave it to them. "It was the only time that something was ever just given to us," Bruckheimer admits.

FINDING MATERIAL If you're just starting out, you have to be both creative and resourceful in finding material. This is because most of the major agencies will not submit their screenplays to you if they don't know who you are.

"The most important thing is relationships," says Debra Hill, producer of *Escape from New York* (1981), *Clue* (1985), and *Adventures in Babysitting* (1987). "You build them throughout the years by being loyal, honest, [and] sincere. And you've got to be careful because you may pass a lot of people on your way down that are on their way up."

Start to establish relationships with agents and writers. Go out of your way to help new and undiscovered writers develop their material, and attach yourself to their work so you can produce their project. Go to the film schools and other colleges and universities. Find out whether the movie rights to an old book that you love are available. Ask your friends and family if they have a script. Put an ad in the paper. One thing's for sure, most everyone has written, or knows someone who has written, a screenplay.

ACCESS TO MONEY

The third key element is money. If you have the money to produce a film, what are you waiting for? The biggest stumbling block people face is in getting financing. The traditional method is to set up a project at the studios. But maybe you can pull together money from private investors.

Subsidiary Rights

To find out if the film rights to a published book are available, first call the book's publisher and ask for the subsidiary rights department. They will alert you to which agent represents the film rights to the book. Call that agent's office—you just need to talk to the assistant—and ask if the film rights to the book are available. If they are, either talk to the agent or fax them an offer.

In the mid-1970s, when producer Debra Hill first got into the film business, a tax credit was to be earned for high-risk tax investments, so there were many consortiums of doctors, dentists, and businesspeople who would risk $100,000 to $150,000 to make a film. "There were a lot of low-budget, independent pictures being produced, and it was a real education because if you couldn't afford to go to film school, you learned while you earned," she recalls.

Assault on Precinct 13 (1976) was financed by one such consortium. Hill was working as the movie's script supervisor. After the project wrapped, the film's director called and asked her on a date. Their date eventually led to a relationship, which ultimately spawned a professional collaboration. The director was John Carpenter.

"We took *Assault on Precinct 13* to England, where it was shown at the London Film Festival," remembers Hill. "While we were there, [producer] Moustapha Akkad saw the picture, and he responded to John's style, particularly the sound of the silencer in the movie. He came to us and said he wanted to do [a movie about] baby-sitter murderers. He wanted John to write and direct it, and John wanted me to collaborate with him, and having been a baby-sitter, we all came up with the concept of doing *Halloween*."

They wrote the screenplay in under four weeks and were funded $300,000 through Akkad. Hill and Carpenter worked on the film for no money upfront, and it went on to gross $55 million.

THE CAREER PATH

"The strange thing about being a producer is there are no rules. There are no steps that you follow," notes producer Marty Katz, who got his start in the business as a production assistant on various television shows. "If there was one path that you could take, then everybody would take it. Unfortunately—or fortunately—there is no one path."

ASSISTANT TO A PRODUCER

Being an assistant to a producer is a tried and true way to learn how to produce films while working your way up the industry ladder. That's how I started. I was temping at Walt Disney Studios, working as an assistant in various studio departments, doing mundane tasks like answering phones and typing letters. One of my assignments was to fill in for Marty Katz's assistant, who was on vacation. Katz was pleased with my performance and repeatedly requested me back. When his assistant finally left to attend graduate school, Katz offered me the job. That was in 1994. I've since been promoted several times and am now the vice president of the company, producing films with Marty as an associate and co-producer.

Over the years I have had the pleasure of seeing my own assistants and interns succeed in the business. My very first intern, KristieAnne Groelinger, is currently director of production at Jerry Bruckheimer Films. "I'm one of those idiots who always says yes," laughs Groelinger. "I think that's why I've gone as far as I have." Perfect example: At 7 P.M. a line producer asks Groelinger if she thinks it's possible to get an actor on a flight to New York—now.

Groelinger immediately responds in the affirmative. "Every day there are those little impossibilities that you make possible," she explains. "It's all about common sense. That I can't teach you."

Groelinger tells the line producer she can get the actor on a plane. "But you have to know the next nine questions that he's going to ask you. 'Do they have good seats available? Can you get him a ticket or does he have to fly ticketless? Is there a meal? What's the next plane? What's the plane before that?' You have to know all of those things before you say, 'I can get him on the nine o'clock.'

"The most valuable lesson that I've learned is do a good job no matter what you're doing," says Groelinger. "It's just so much better for you to hand them the tickets because then you're the hero. Don't hand them the tickets and say, 'Oh my God, you wouldn't believe what I've been through in order to get these tickets.' Never tell them the magic."

THE DEVELOPMENT TRACK

Even as a producer's assistant, I was reading scripts and writing coverage. Many companies also hire outside readers who work from home. Coverage is like a film industry book report. You start with a log line, a one-sentence description of the screenplay. Then you write a one- to three-page summary of the script. Finally, you provide a page of your own comments on the material.

When analyzing a script, I first want to know if it is a good story. Is it an original idea, a twist on an old concept, or just something stale and rehashed? If it's a comedy, is it funny and did it make me laugh out loud? If it's a thriller, is it exciting or entirely predictable? How is the writing? Maybe it was great, but the idea was not. What is the tone of the piece? Is this a project for Tom Cruise and Nicole Kidman, or is it better suited for Adam Sandler and Drew Barrymore? This information gives the development executive a "snapshot" of the material. Based on the company's needs, the development executive will be able to determine quickly if the script is worth considering.

Before development executives can read a script, they must first find scripts to read. The most obvious source for material is through agency submissions. Scripts also are submitted by managers, attorneys, and other producers. Sometimes scripts find their way to my office because the writer and I share a mutual friend. At other times they are submitted in response to an answered query letter.

Development executives work closely with writers to develop ideas in-house. A producer may pitch an idea to writers she knows. One of the writers may respond with his original take on the idea. If the producer likes the take, she will bring the writer to meet with creative executives at the different studios to pitch the story to them, hoping the creative exec will commission the writer to draft the screenplay. In such cases, the producer would be attached to produce that movie.

Development executives oversee a slate of projects that the production company has in development. They prepare notes when a writer turns in a new draft of a screenplay. They also put together lists of scribes who may be suitable for an open writing assignment.

Some development executives help package material. This involves attaching an actor or director to a screen project. With interested talent, it is much easier to get a project set up. Setting up projects is the development executive's final duty. This is where the financing source comes into play. Most likely he will try to set up a project at one of the major studios. If these attempts fail, the more ambitious executive will try to find independent funding.

ESTABLISHING CREDIBILITY

The hardest part about establishing yourself as a producer is credibility. "It's very hard to hit all the marks it takes for you to gain credibility with studios, with actors, and with other filmmakers," notes Marty Katz. It's something that can only be achieved by sustaining a career over the years, proving time and again that you are an expert at your craft.

If a producer like Katz places a call to an agent or studio executive, it will be returned promptly. If Joe Schmoe, wannabe producer, places the same call, it may be weeks before he hears back, if ever. That's because Joe Schmoe does not have the credibility that Katz's tenure and success in the business have earned him.

A MATTER OF PERCEPTION

Marty Katz spent six years (1969–75) as director of production for ABC/Circle Films, the television network's in-house movie-of-the-week production division. From 1976 to 1978, he was executive vice president of production for Quinn Martin Productions, where he supervised such TV shows as *Cannon* (1971–76), *The Streets of San Francisco* (1972–77), and *Barnaby Jones* (1973–80). Getting his first theatrical feature to produce wasn't easy, because his perception in the business at that point in his career was as a television producer.

Jonathan Kaplan was set to direct the feature *Heart Like a Wheel* (1983). The only producer on the film was Chuck Roven, who was lead actor Bonnie Bedelia's manager. At that time, Roven wasn't experienced at physically producing a film. Kaplan, who had previously directed a TV movie that Katz had produced, asked Katz to team with Roven to produce the feature. That was the break Katz needed to become a bona fide theatrical film producer.

This industry has a tendency to typecast you no matter who you are. If you work in TV, you don't work in features. If you are an editor, you're not a director. It is difficult to make any transition in Hollywood, but it is not impossible. It just takes hard work, persistence, and seizing the opportunity when it arrives.

"The skills I needed to be a theatrical producer were actually enhanced by working previously in television," says Katz. "There's always been an underlying perception that television production experience doesn't necessarily translate into theatrical production skills. Personally, I've found that my television experience, which was about knowing how to do things for less, how to make the most of an opportunity, and how to push the envelope creatively on the small screen, has helped me in being a better theatrical film producer where I'm able to work on a larger canvas. Television efficiency, ingenuity, and creativity transfer quite well to the big screen."

THE PRODUCER'S ROLE

A movie really is produced three times: in pre-production, when it is filmed, and in post-production. Because producers are on the film from the very beginning and oversee the project until the very end, they have a strong hand in moving the film along each step of the way.

DEVELOPMENT

Producers rely heavily on their development executives to find material and set up projects, but they are in no way absent from this process. If a producer is physically present during the making of a movie and is on the set every day, she's not going to be able to spend too much energy developing other projects. In between films, however, she may be extremely involved in the process, calling agents, soliciting material, and meeting with writers and creative executives.

Producer Bonnie Bruckheimer appreciates that development can be a tedious process. "It's never easy to get material," she says. "Even if you have material, you have to get a writer, and the odds of that are slim to none. Once you get a writer and you actually have a script, the process of getting a director—forget it. Every step of the way is difficult."

Yet eventually, the right project comes along. "You have to be passionate about what you want to do and you can never give up," says Bruckheimer. "Every time you take a step forward, unfortunately, you're knocked two steps back and you have to tell yourself that this part of the process is not personal, I'm just going to forge ahead."

PRE-PRODUCTION

"On *That Old Feeling*, we had a cast that came in and out a lot. Gail O'Grady, who played one of the major roles, had another movie that she wanted to do, but we had her on hold," recalls Bruckheimer. "She really wanted that part, and I knew that if we did some juggling around, we would be able to accommodate her. Some people would say, 'Well, I'm sorry. We have you for this period of time and there's nothing we can do about it. You're getting paid.' But I don't feel that way. I thought that if we moved some scheduling around and let her go do what she needed to do, she would come back a happier camper. Then if we got in a bind, she would be more likely to help us out." O'Grady was able to do both projects.

In addition to scheduling the actors, the producer also is busy working on the budget and cash flow, supervising the casting process, and hiring the crew. For Debra Hill, the most important aspect of pre-production is being there with the director and trying to understand his vision. "Hopefully it doesn't fall too far from my vision, even if it means I have to compromise," she says. "You have to be flexible and you need to roll with the punches. There's a lot of compromises to be made, not only in the differences in the director's vision, but in the studio's vision. Sometimes you've got a foot in each camp. And it's [about] merging those camps."

One of Hill's fondest memories is of scouting locations with director Terry Gilliam on *The Fisher King* [1991]. "We went to scout Grand Central Station [for] a scene where Robin [Williams] is following Lydia [Amanda Plummer]. It was about five-fifteen [P.M.], and we're standing above on this balcony near the bar, and we're looking at all these people, and they're coming from all these corners, and they sort of met in the middle. They kind of did a sidestep around each other to keep on going across. Terry observed this, looked at us and said, 'Wouldn't it be wonderful if they just broke out and waltzed?' [Producer] Lynda Obst and I looked at each other and high-fived. That's what you get Terry Gilliam for—to bring that incredibly visual moment to that written script."

Of course, Hill now had to budget for a thousand dancers. An even greater challenge lay in convincing the studio financing *The Fisher King* that the expense would be worth it.

PRODUCTION

"I am on the set all the time because I think that as soon as you leave the set to go do something, there's a disaster," says Bonnie Bruckheimer. "I like to think of myself as a disaster-control person, trying to stop a problem before it happens, or if there is a problem, solving the problem."

Marty Katz is no stranger to disaster. He worked as Twentieth Century-Fox's supervising producer on *Titanic* (1997). "At the time, the stakes were so high, the budget was in trouble, and there was no indication as to when the movie was going to finish, or when it could be released. So many people's reputations, careers, and futures were at risk. Every decision was crucial."

No one could jeopardize the ongoing production, however, because the investment was so high. While the epic was still moving forward, everyone had to remain supportive and figure out how to help it become more streamlined and efficient. They also needed to assist director James Cameron achieve what he wanted, while still retaining some degree of budget integrity.

One potential major problem that Katz foresaw on *Titanic* involved the jacking up of the ship. The vessel was intended to be hydraulically repositioned twice during the production so that it could be shot at both a three-degree elevation and a six-degree elevation. Had they adjusted the ship to both angles, the movie would have had to shut down for a long time to engineer the changes. Each time, while the production was halted, nothing could be shot and money would be wasted as the cast and most of the crew stood around.

To complicate matters, Christmas and the holiday hiatus was approaching, which would provide a limited window in which the ship could be readjusted. However, if the production was not able to finish shooting the necessary scenes before that window of opportunity, they would need to be completed after the hiatus. Then the production would literally have to shut down while the ship was repositioned to the three-degree elevation. Even if they did finish shooting before the hiatus, there would be another period of time where nothing would be shot while the ship was re-engineered to the six-degree angle, costing the production many millions of dollars.

"I talked to the engineers about this not being possible, and they agreed. They didn't know how they were going to get it done. They were just trying to get it done," recalls Katz. "So I pointed out to [James] Cameron that there was a way he could have his cake and eat it too, which is fake the shots that were supposed to be at three degrees, when the ship was at level, or the ship was at six degrees. And then just go right to the six-degree angle and use some visual-effects shots to fill in. Who better than Jim Cameron to figure out a way to do that? Basically, I posed a creative solution to a potential physical production problem and Cameron agreed." The company proceeded to reconstruct the ship at the six-degree elevation and the work was done without any shutdowns.

POST-PRODUCTION

Halloween II (1981) was a difficult and trying experience for producer Debra Hill. "I think that [director] Rick Rosenthal had a completely different and much more violent vision than we [the producers and the studio] wanted it to be," reveals Hill. "What was nice about John Carpenter's [first] *Halloween* is that it left a lot up to the imagination. I think that Rick was a little too heavy handed. He didn't quite know how to choreograph such a subtle thing and we had to come into the editing room and work on that picture a lot, and that was very hard."

These days it's a lot easier to deal with a problem like this because test screenings, which provide numbers that tell a producer whether a film is working or not, have become an industry standard. "You look at cards and you see, out of four hundred people, everyone hated the ending," says Hill. "It's very clear that you need to do something about the editing. Back then, it wasn't so clear, because there was no audience preview [for *Halloween II*]. In fact, John and I [brought] people in [to] do our own little focus groups, and that's how we arrived at the fact that the picture wasn't working.

"I like to be objective when everyone else has lost their objectivity. That means not hanging out in the editing, not seeing every cut, [but] being able to come in and do highlights. You want the director to have faith in your ability to be objective. So you have to gain a director's respect. When you make a movie, it's like going to war. You've got to be on the same side. Sometimes I think that the producer and director come back from war and they've been on opposite sides. If you've lost your director's respect, they're probably not going to listen to you."

MARKETING

"We had a bit of a disaster on *That Old Feeling*, and I learned a very good lesson about it," recalls Bonnie Bruckheimer. "*That Old Feeling* was supposed to be released on Valentine's Day, and we had a big promotional campaign for that release date because it was basically a love story."

One week before the opening date, Bruckheimer and her associates learned that Universal was going to release another film, its $100 million volcano actioner *Dante's Peak* (1997), the same day. "We started to panic," remembers Bruckheimer. "If they are releasing *Dante's Peak*, they're not going to pay any attention to our little *That Old Feeling*." They insisted Universal open their comedy on another weekend.

"That was crazy, because *Dante's Peak* bombed, and we lost our Valentine's Day weekend and went up on a weekend that wasn't successful for us," says Bruckheimer. "It's not a science, but you have to trust your instincts. All of our instincts were Valentine's Day, and we should have stuck with them."

PRODUCER SOUP

So many different producer titles roll by in movie credits these days: executive producer, producer, associate producer, line producer, and so forth. What do they all mean? There is no uniform definition for each title. However, the *possible* meaning of each can be explained. As a point of reference, the (sole) producer is the primary producing force on a film.

"Take my progression for a moment," says Ira Shuman, a unit production manager (UPM) who has received credit as an associate producer (*Newsies*), as well as a co-producer (*Airheads*, *The Wedding Singer*, *The Waterboy*). (See chapter 7 for more details on a UPM's responsibilities.) "I am a production manager on a movie. I do a couple movies for either a producer or a studio, and the next progression is another credit, a better credit, say associate producer, or co-producer."

ASSOCIATE PRODUCER

The title of associate producer generally goes to a development executive or someone else who has a hand in developing the original material. It also can be given to a junior-level producer who might assume some of the producer's duties on the set. Some actors give their assistants credit on their films as associate producer. Also, when someone comes already attached to a project (having probably brought in one of the essential elements) but really is not involved with the physical production of the film, this is a credit he might receive.

CO-PRODUCER

The title of co-producer usually is given to production managers who split their time between typical production manager work and line-producing issues. It also can be given as a next-level credit to junior level producers who have paid their dues and are ascending the credit ladder.

LINE PRODUCER

The line producer deals with the bigger issues that come up on the set and makes decisions on how to get the movie made. "He's watching the film being made," says Mark Indig, who has worn many different producer hats over the years. "He can make suggestions to the director that might not be appropriate coming from the production manager, which bridge the creative areas."

"You start to work either on bigger films, or with producers who have no production understanding," adds Ira Shuman. "Total deal-makers who need somebody to really run the movie in more areas than just hiring the crew and making deals on equipment, which is primarily the UPM's job.

"For instance, *The Waterboy* (1998). Mark [Indig] was the UPM, hired by me, the line producer," Shuman explains. "When I went into Disney, with the producer, Bob Simonds, and they looked us in the eye and said, 'Can you do this movie for $20 million?' and I said, 'No, we can do it for $22 million.' And they said, 'Can you do it for $22 million?' And I said yes. I was on the hook after that; Mark wasn't. They wouldn't have had that conversation with the UPM. I am somehow partnered with the producer in a different way than a UPM. Even though I'm employed by the producer, I'm kind of partnering with him as a team to make the movie. Then I have much more leverage with a director when I say, 'We're not going to do this.' UPMs don't walk into the room with that kind of clout."

EXECUTIVE PRODUCER

The executive producer title often is given to a financier or to a studio executive when the studio (such as New Line Cinema or Miramax) allows their executives to take a credit on the films they oversee.

Joel Dean was executive producer on *Summer Lovers* (1982) because he was director Randal Kleiser's former agent. "I knew how to put the deal together because I was good at making deals," he admits. "When it came time to produce the movie, I still can't do it, and I've produced four movies. I can't read a board to save my life. I look at it, but it's all Greek to me."

As executive producer, Dean was on the set every day. "The actor has his job, the production designer has his job, the makeup person has their job. The producer hasn't got a job. People get suspicious. Every time I would show up somewhere, they thought something was wrong," he says.

LEGGO MY EGO

"Ultimately, you have to know when [trying to make it as a producer] is not working, and move on," says producer Debra Hill. "The myth of the film business has grown. What other industry, besides the film industry, do we report our Monday morning grosses on? And everybody's wishing to get that spec script sold for seven figures. They read the propaganda in the *Reporter* and *Variety*, but it just doesn't happen to anybody.

"It takes people who are very thick skinned, who have the ability to notice talent, have the ability to know a good story, are willing to make the sacrifices it takes to work long, long, long hours for many, many years without getting the recognition, and even when you do get the recognition, know that the director, or the writer, or the star will probably get more recognition. You've got to either have the most tremendous ego that doesn't need to be filled, or none, so that you'll accept success gracefully and failure gracefully.

"I think one of the reasons I became successful is I knew that I had to make sacrifices in my daily life," says Hill. "I did not, like other people around me, grab that credit card and buy things I couldn't afford—a TV I can't afford, an apartment I can't afford, a car I can't afford. [Because] you need insurance, and you need gas, and all that kind of stuff." At that time, Hill put $10,000 in the bank, which is what she needed to live for one year. Her plan was, "What I'm going to do for the next year is I'm going to have tunnel vision. I'm not going to be distracted by dating; I'm not going to be distracted by going to the mall or going out to dinner. I'm going to write, and I'm going to find a piece of material that I know is going to launch me. So I think a producer has to be willing to do that too."

PART THREE

BELOW-THE-LINE

THE PRODUCTION OFFICE

Anybody can just sign a time card, but a good pro-duction manager is someone who can deal with emergencies, because when you're out there shoot-ing in the street, literally anything can happen.

MARK INDIG, unit production manager

Below-the-line refers to all workers on a film crew other than above-the-line creative talent. From assistant directors, directors of pho-tography, and set decorators, to editors, gaffers, and script supervisors, chapters 7 through 15 focus on these behind-the-scenes professionals.

BASE CAMP

It may not be as glamorous as an actor's life, but the production office is where a lot of the action takes place. It's the film's administrative base, where paperwork is generated, records are kept, and daily production details are arranged. It's where the production staff and accounting department are housed, and where the key crew keep offices, which they all but abandon once principal photography begins. The production office may be located on a studio lot near a sound stage where interiors will be shot, or in a non-descript building that is central to most of the project's shooting locations.

THE PRODUCTION STAFF

Depending on the scope of a movie, the size of the production staff may vary. On a typical feature film, the production staff consists of the unit production manager (UPM), or simply production manager; production office coordinator (POC); assistant production office coordinator (APOC); production secretary; and an office production assistant (PA). These jobs are outlined below.

UNIT PRODUCTION MANAGER

The last third of the high-tech movie *Strange Days* (1995) features the 1999 New Year's Eve celebration of the millennium in Los Angeles. Co-screenwriter James Cameron starts the sequence with a one-line description: Downtown L.A., the mother of all parties. "The director [Kathryn Bigelow] had a vision of it being like Times Square, packed with people, and confetti falling through the whole sequence," recalls UPM Ira Shuman. "I'm trying to figure out how the hell we're going to do this."

A large crowd of partiers was needed for the climactic scene, but there wasn't money left in the budget to hire sufficient extras. Shuman decided that the only chance they had to create a sizable crowd was to publicly advertise a giant promotion in the local media. "I'd been down this road before, and it's really scary," Shuman notes. "You're sitting there the day of the sequence and you're wondering if anyone is going to show."

Shuman hired a rock promoter and told him he wanted to have a crowd that was dressed wild and ready to party. But he knew that even if you're paying extras, at two in the morning everyone gets tired. "I didn't want them to go home," says Shuman, who paid the promoter $10,000. He then hired the band Deee-Lite for about $25,000 to attract the rave crowd. Once this was set, he began selling tickets. "I sold tickets because I wanted to know how many people were going to come. I wanted them to make some kind of a commitment themselves and put out some money so that they would show up that day."

The city of Los Angeles didn't want to give Shuman a permit to shoot the sequence downtown because they were afraid that with a big open casting call, the crowd would get out of control. "I convinced them that if I sold tickets, we would limit the crowd to the number I wanted," recounts Shuman.

The day of shooting, 7,700 people showed up to the party that had taken five weeks to prep. "At four in the morning, when the fire department wanted us to get rid of the crowd and send them home, the people didn't want to go," remembers Shuman, describing the fun everyone had that memorable night.

The production manager deals with any and all of the details of the production. This person is responsible for the budget, hiring the crew, making the deals with the crew, reviewing all the contracts, authorizing the payroll, making deals for the equipment, supervising the production staff, arranging travel and hotels, approving purchase orders and rentals, approving petty cash reimbursements, and making sure that safety and other issues are being enforced. "It's really all the minutia that has to happen on a movie that involves how that entity does business," explains Mark Indig, UPM on such films as *The Waterboy* (1998) and *Fear and Loathing in Las Vegas* (1998). Production managers divide their time between the set and the production office. An average film has one production manager, and the production staff falls under the auspices of that person.

The most common way to become a UPM is to join the Directors Guild of America (DGA) training program. See chapter 8 for additional data. "It's a structured program with huge competition. Maybe a thousand people apply a year, and fifteen get accepted," Indig notes. "You work as a trainee for a couple of years, then you become a second AD [assistant director], then a first AD, then you become a production manager."

Another path to becoming a production manager is to work on nonunion films. You also can work on union movies outside of Los Angeles in New York or Chicago, or in what is called *a third area*. A third area is a state where union requirements are less strict, if applicable at all. "You have to work a certain amount of days in that third area and then you can apply it to the Southern California area," advises Indig.

Production managers have to be prepared for anything. "You're shooting somewhere at three in the morning, and some piece of equipment fails," Indig says. "You've got to know how to get people out of bed and get something replaced. You've got to know how to react at a minute's notice if an actor gets sick and rearrange the whole shooting schedule and all the equipment and crew that goes with it. You've got to know how to deal with weather cover [an alternate indoor scene] if it starts to rain.

"The production manager is like the foreman," says Indig. "He's on the same plane [level] as the crew. He's in charge of the crew, but he's among the crew." More experienced production managers also act as co-producers. If there's a co-producer/UPM, this person spends half his time in the producer role, dealing with producer issues, and the other half of his time in a production manager role. This means that half of the production manager work has to be carried by somebody else. That is where the production supervisor, or the assistant UPM, comes into play.

THE PRODUCTION SUPERVISOR

A production supervisor is someone who usually is working toward becoming a UPM. Production supervisors are not in the DGA (which oversees production managers), so they cannot step up. They don't want to be a POC or location manager anymore. Working as a production supervisor essentially is an apprenticeship, and while they're doing this job, they're trying to figure a way into the guild to become a production manager, or they're going to skip this step altogether and aim straight toward becoming a producer.

As to the exact role of a production supervisor, Indig explains, "It depends how much rope the production manager wants to give the production supervisor. The odd thing is that they can all be doing the same thing on different movies." Different production managers will give more or less responsibility to their production supervisors depending on that production manager's style. The presence of a production supervisor on a film generally allows the production manager to spend more of her time on the set. This is because the production supervisor takes on many of the production manager's office responsibilities.

THE PRODUCTION OFFICE COORDINATOR

The production office coordinator runs the production office and is the production manager's (and/or production supervisor's) right-hand person. This person is one of the first hired and one of the last off the project. The POC handles all of the film's paperwork (crew lists, call sheets, wrap reports, etc.), communications (phones, pagers, etc.), travel (airlines, hotels, car rentals, etc.), deliveries, film shipments, equipment rentals, and coordination of dailies.

Think of a production office as a military unit. The POC is the captain. All requests must go through this person. Then the work is filtered down to one of the production staff. For instance, the lighting department tells the production office what equipment they need, and the POC assigns the task of ordering it. "The idea of the production office is to service all the needs and coordinate the entire functioning of the film," says manager Michael Valeo, who began his Hollywood career working in a production office.

THE ASSISTANT PRODUCTION OFFICE COORDINATOR

If the POC is the captain, then the assistant production office coordinator (APOC) is the lieutenant. While the APOC assists the POC in many of his joint duties, this person is not actually the POC's assistant. Usually, APOCs are given certain responsibilities of their own, such as ordering equipment, coordinating all travel for the crew and the actors, or making sure that the crew has all the information they need, such as maps and memos. The precise division of labor among the production office staff varies on different movies.

KristieAnne Groelinger started as a production secretary on *Bulletproof* (1996), starring Adam Sandler. "I was there for about two weeks, and they hadn't hired an APOC yet. The POC liked me so much she said, 'Let's just have her be the APOC.' So I made this light-year jump, which should have taken me two or three movies to work up to APOC, but because I went in, kept my head down, and did everything they said, they promoted me within the film. If you do a good job and you're in the right place at the right time, that's what happens."

THE PRODUCTION SECRETARY

In keeping with our military analogy, the production secretary would be viewed as the corporal of the outfit: think Maxwell Klinger on the old TV show *M*A*S*H*. This person is in charge of printed material and its distribution. The production secretary puts together crew lists, schedules, and the like. Of course, *M*A*S*H* took place before computers were commonly used. Today the computer is a production secretary's main tool.

THE OFFICE PRODUCTION ASSISTANT (PA)

The office production assistant (PA) is definitely the lowest person on the totem pole in the production office, the private in our ongoing military analogy. Office PAs do whatever they are told and whatever is needed. Essentially, this person is a gofer. A lot of grunt work (running errands, making deliveries, etc.) is involved. It's by no means a glamorous position, but it is a great place to start.

"An office PA is basically like an assistant to executives," says Valeo. "The executives you are working with in this case are the line producer, the production manager, and the POC. It may not be brain surgery, but you've got to know where you can get a 12K light if you need a 12K light. You've got to know who to call at Panavision to get the camera package to shoot that next day's scene. That's not something you can learn in school."

WILL WORK FOR PRODUCTION JOB

"The scariest thing, coming from a very blue-collar family, [was] explaining to my parents that I worked job to job, which sort of makes you sound like one of those people who stands on the side of the road," KristieAnne Groelinger admits. "I was very lucky in the years I worked production. In almost four years total, I never had a week off. If you hook yourself up with good people, those good people always work and they will always take a good team with them."

THE ACCOUNTING STAFF

The accounting department also is housed in the production office. The production accountant is integral to the financial success of a film. "If we don't approve certain stuff, you can actually affect the ability to make a day. And a day is too expensive," says Craig Cannold, a veteran film and television auditor.

Cannold has worked as a production accountant on many feature films, from *The Ice Storm* (1997) to *Titanic* (1997). A weird dichotomy exists because the accountant is representing the studio's interest on a project, but from a union perspective he is part of the crew. Even the union line is blurred because a production office can hire a non-union accountant. California Local 717, which represents production accountants, is not part of the collective bargaining agreement involving craft unions. While the union issue may or may not be abated in this scenario, like most jobs in Hollywood, the way in is still to start at the bottom and work your way up through the ranks.

CLERKS

A clerk is the entry-level position in the accounting department. If you're good with numbers and have a reasonable amount of computer skills, this could be a good place to start. The biggest part of this job is basic bookkeeping.

"The trick is to read every piece of paper you file," advises Cannold, "so you'll learn about what's going on." Look over the budgets and the cost reports, and if you don't understand something, ask. You're in a position where learning leads to advancement.

PAYROLL

Once you're a successful clerk, the next job up the departmental ladder is payroll. In this position, you'll learn everybody's salary and you'll become familiar with all of the union rules. This person's main job is to pay the crew every week and to make sure that the crew's time cards match what is listed on the production report.

"Nothing ever matches," reveals Cannold. "Everybody asks for more." Depending on the department, this could add up to a lot of money.

Take the camera department, for instance. "If they work one minute past fourteen hours, they get paid for the whole next hour. If they actually work 13.9 hours, they [may] put in for 14.1 hours because that means they have to be paid for fifteen hours. Then you have a fight and the payroll person has to get in the middle of it. Ultimately, the production manager will take care of it and unless it's really flagrant, you pay."

There are many union rules a payroll clerk needs to know and keep up with. Every local union has its own personal regulations. In addition, every production usually petitions the unions for variations on some of the rules. For instance, a production may request a thirty-minute grace period. That way, if lunch is delayed by a half hour, the production won't go into meal penalty. Sometimes a union will allow such a request, sometimes not. In either case, it affects the rate that union's members are being paid.

THE FIRST ASSISTANT PRODUCTION ACCOUNTANT

The first assistant accountant matches all of the bills to the purchase orders. If anything does not equate, he must research the variance. Once all of the bills are approved, the first assistant enters them into the computer and prints the checks for the UPM to sign. The first assistant also handles the disbursement and audit of petty cash.

THE ACCOUNTANT

Once the first assistant production accountant matches the bills with the original purchase orders, the accountant receives the paperwork and codes it. Each department of the crew has its own code for tracking purposes. After coding everything, the accountant checks the expenditures against what was budgeted. Assuming everything matches, the accountant signs off and the paperwork is given to the production manager for approval.

The accountant does not spend her entire life in the office. It's important for her to visit the set and communicate with the various crew departments. "There's a real value to speaking to them every day because they're spending money every day, since they're either building more, or buying more, or dressing more," says Cannold.

"Are they on top of their game? Do they know what's happening? Or are they barely making it through every day? If a department is super-organized and they are really good and are hitting their numbers, you never think about them again. Conversely, when they're disorganized, you're on their tail every day. You're always looking over their work and trying to figure out what's going on."

COST REPORTS

At the end of every production week, a cost report is generated. This charts how much is being spent by each department. Cannold explains, "Based on experience, you have a pretty good sense of which departments are in trouble and are only going to get worse, and which ones are OK. [For] the ones that are in trouble, my job is to alert the producer."

A daily hot-cost report is also printed. Hot costs track all of the major elements (such as crew hours, fringes, cast overtime, and film developing and printing costs) day to day.

BUDGETING

When preparing a budget, the accountant can use published rates, but alternately she can negotiate even lower to find the real going rate. Once the budget is approved, the department heads are given a dollar amount with which to draw up a budget for their own departments. It is the accountant's job to help the crew achieve their budgeted goals.

Two books are currently available that list the published rates and rules for most crew positions: *The Industry Labor Guide* and *Paymaster*. The same information can be collected from each individual union, but the benefit of these annual books is that everything is collected together in one volume.

"The budget is watched by the second," says Cannold. "The big fallacy is that the entertainment industry is crazy and irresponsible. But we know pretty accurately how much we've missed our mark on any given day."

As production on a film proceeds, budgets change. If you're doing a studio picture, studio executives are going to have input every day. Cannold gives an example. "You show your dailies, and a production exec calls and says we need this, this, and this. You have to sit down and do a new budget and say, 'You've asked for these things, and it's going to cost this much more.'" If the studio approves this budget increase, the amount of the increase is called an overage.

Budgets also can change on independent films. Since there's no monetary source to cover an overage, however, these productions have to be much more careful about any overspending. If they do spend more money than was allotted, the production will have to make up for that money by deducting it from another department's funds.

KEEP IT INTERESTING

To keep the job interesting, Cannold aligns with the producer or production manager. "You start to help them make their decisions, and you spend as much time as you can with them, so that you're learning more about what they do."

This may be one of the reasons that many production accountants go on to become production managers. "A lot of what a UPM does is around budgeting, tracking costs, and making deals," says Ira Shuman. "You can almost tell the difference between a UPM that was a first AD and a UPM that was an accountant. Certainly, one wears sneakers, and one doesn't."

Unfortunately, unlike the AD, the production accountant is not in the DGA, so he must find a way to get into the union. Shuman advises the accountant who may have trouble getting into the union to get hired on a non-union picture as production manager and work on out-of-area pictures for two or three years. Eventually, they'll earn enough days to meet union requirements and be able to work as a UPM in Los Angeles. But Shuman does not hide the fact that it's a tough business. "For years I've discouraged people when they've come to me to get into the business," says Shuman. "I had this conversation with my thirteen-year-old son, who had to write an essay to get into private school. He said that he wanted to get into entertainment. He likes what I do and would like to 'follow in my father's footsteps.' So I said to him, there's a hundred of me. There's a couple hundred thousand lawyers, and a couple hundred thousand doctors, and a couple hundred thousand engineers. Why don't you pick a profession that's not so luck based. It's not that I'm better than, or smarter than, or better at socializing than other guys. It's a huge luck factor."

ASSISTANT DIRECTORS

The assistant directors need to collaborate the vision of the director to all of the departments; it's not just standing there and calling the shots.

DAVID KATZ, assistant director

In its day, *Superman* (1978) had one of the longest shooting schedules in the history of motion pictures. In fact, much of *Superman II* (1980) was shot at the same time as the original, since both features shared many of the same sets, locations, and casts. As a result of shooting two pictures at once, the schedule was more than a year long. To complicate matters further, the movie was filmed in locations all over the world. "It was crazy," recalls Michael Green, an assistant director (AD) on the project. "One day, around the world, there were twelve cameras, all working on the same movie."

Green was directing one of the additional units. They had the camera mounted on a helicopter that was shooting high up on the Athabasca Glacier in Canada, on a large, flat snow plane. They were shooting the sequence where Lex Luthor (Gene Hackman) takes Eve Teschmacher (Valerie Perrine) to Superman's Fortress of Solitude at the North Pole. Luther's on a snowmobile and Perrine's wearing a big, fluffy orange coat. To conserve space on the helicopter, which could seat only eight people, they shot the sequence with stand-ins, or doubles. In fact, Green acted not only as the unit's AD, but also as its director and as Perrine's double—fluffy orange coat and all!

The nearest phone to where the crew was staying was forty-five miles away in Bath, New Brunswick. Green regularly phoned the producers to update them on their progress. One day during lunch, he flew by helicopter to Bath to make the call. He instructed the pilot to bring the rest of the crew back to the location after lunch, and then to return to pick him up.

Later, the helicopter arrived to take Green back to the location. He changed back into his Valerie Perrine costume and climbed on board. When he arrived on the set, he realized there was one extra person in attendance. "In my seat, where I should have been had I gotten back from the phone call in time, was the wife of the DP [director of photography]," recounts Green. If an emergency were to arise and people needed to evacuate, this could spell trouble, as every seat in the helicopter counts. But at this point there was nothing Green could do.

One of the eight crew members was a mountain expert named Bruno. They'd been shooting for about an hour, when Bruno approached Green and warned him of an approaching storm. "There were a few black clouds, but they looked a long way away," remembers Green. "In ten minutes they were right on top of us, and unfortunately, because this DP had brought his wife, there wasn't room in the helicopter for everyone to go back down in one trip. So I sent everyone off, and I stayed with Bruno."

Regrettably, the helicopter couldn't get back to them before the storm broke. Bruno had a survival pack and Green was able to keep warm because he was dressed in Valerie Perrine's insulated outfit. "We were up there for two and a half hours waiting for the helicopter to come back, but I had visions of us being snowed in overnight, some rescue operation helping out, and me being taken out in drag, with this orange furry coat! It was very bizarre."

As soon as the storm passed, they were rescued and all ended well. For Green, part of whose job it is to be a safety officer, it was valuable training for the future. "It's interesting how one learns how important that one seat is," he notes.

THE FIRST ASSISTANT DIRECTOR

The first assistant director, or 1st AD, is the eyes and ears of the director. This person's primary function is to relieve the director of many routine responsibilities so that the director can concentrate on the creative aspects of the job. Some of these tasks include helping to pictorialize the director's vision to the crew, keeping up the work pace, enforcing safety requirements on the set, keeping the production on schedule, and inspiring high morale. If the director is not very articulate, the 1st AD may call the shots under his mutual guidance. Every director works differently with the AD.

The 1st AD shows up at crew call and stands in the spot where the camera is supposed to be positioned for the first shot of the day. As the rest of the crew arrives on the set, the 1st AD is there to greet them and work with every department. He may say to the special-effects crew, "For safety reasons, I think you guys should be over here on the right-hand side," or to the stunt coordinators, "Why don't you guys set up over here and tell me when you need time to rehearse." The 1st AD thinks through the scheme of things and organizes the workday in advance, then informs the 2nd AD, who makes sure the procedure is inscribed on the call sheet. The camera is rolled in on a dolly, and shortly thereafter the director arrives.

On a typical day, the 1st AD greets the director, briefs him on the schedule, and tells him how much longer it's going to be until they're prepared to begin. The 1st AD actually has been giving time warnings (ten minutes, five minutes, etc.) up until the moment when the camera is finally ready. When it is set, it is the 1st AD who calls in the first team, and, on cue, the 2nd AD walks the actors in.

The 1st AD also sets up the background or extras with the 2nd AD. For example, the 1st AD might say, "Bring in ten people and let's put everybody on the left-hand side. Lets have them cross from left to right." The 2nd AD then rehearses the extras, and a rehearsal is done with the camera operator and the DP. The 1st AD works with them as they do the dry rehearsals to make sure that the lighting, the grip equipment, and everything else that is needed is set up and ready to go when they start filming. Once the 1st AD is sure the timing is right for the rehearsal, the principal actors are placed on their marks and a run-through of the rehearsed scene commences.

When the director is satisfied with the run-through, it is time to capture it on film. The 1st AD literally asks, "Is everybody ready? If anybody is not ready, let me know right now." If no one responds, the 1st AD will look around to make sure it's safe, and only then will say "Roll sound." The sound mixer will respond with, "Sound speed" to confirm that the sound is running at speed, or in sync with the camera. Then the camera operator will call out "Roll camera." The camera will be turned on by the first assistant cameraman. When the camera is working in tune with the sound, the camera operator will say "Speed." The second assistant cameraman will clap the slate to visually note the start of the take and to have a defined image on film that the editor can later use in syncing the sound with the picture.

At this point the 1st AD will motion to the director that the set is ready. Sometimes the director doesn't want to say anything, and thus will let the AD call "Action." During a stunt sequence, it's usually the 1st AD who is responsible for calling the shots so that the director can concentrate on collaborating with the actors. Sometimes the 1st AD will turn everything over to the stunt coordinator, who has more experience with explosions, stunts, and other dangerous sequences.

The 1st AD shares the duty of safety officer with the production manager. Together they must ensure that when the camera rolls and "action" is called, everything is safe and in compliance with union rules. It is important that everything be thoroughly thought out, because if something goes wrong, the industry and the unions hold both the AD and the production manager legally liable. In fact, if there is ever an issue of safety at stake, the 1st AD can override the director. "A lot of an AD's job is being able to think on his feet when something happens that isn't planned," says Green, 1st AD on *Burglar* (1987), *Child's Play* (1988), and *Thinner* (1996).

At the end of the day, the 1st AD will do a walk-through for the next day. All the key department heads will be present. The director, with the 1st AD, will read through the scenes and walk through the camera positions and setups for the following day's filming.

THE SECOND ASSISTANT DIRECTOR

The second assistant director (2nd AD), also called a key second assistant director, takes as much of the workload away from the 1st AD as possible, as outlined above. If the 1st AD is the eyes and ears of the director, the 2nd AD is the eyes and ears of the production manager.

PRODUCTION REPORT

The main responsibility of the 2nd AD is to handle all paperwork on the set, including the production report. Whereas the call sheet shows what the production intended to accomplish for a given day, the production report is the actuality, like a time card, that shows what the production actually did and did not accomplish.

."If we didn't complete a scene, we would note, say, one-eighth of a page not completed," explains David Katz, a 2nd AD on *Mr. Destiny* (1990), *In the Line of Fire* (1993), and *The Relic* (1997). "Or, still owe one pick-up shot—a close-up on Linda Hamilton's eye as she winks."

The 2nd AD also must collaborate with the personnel who have their own paperwork to do, including the script supervisor and the camera assistants. She also will integrate information from the Screen Actors Guild (SAG) sheet into another report that lists work, rest, and travel times for the actors. Since all time, on and off the set, is work time to an actor, it's the 2nd AD's responsibility to keep track of *all* of these things for *every* actor.

MEAL PENALTIES

Keeping track of everyone can be a difficult job, but it is extremely important. If time is not monitored correctly, it could cost the production a good deal of extra money. For example, meal penalties are incurred if actors do not break for lunch or dinner on time. These start at $1,250 for the first offense and swiftly rise in cost. Penalty periods start after six working hours. Every half-hour increment after that is another meal penalty.

"With sixty actors on a big motion picture, and extras that are also protected by the Screen Actors Guild, it's my responsibility to make sure that they're all [released] on time and don't incur meal penalties," explains AD David Katz. "If they do, I'd better have an explanation for the production manager as to why." Meal penalties apply to crew positions too. Meal penalties are for everybody's protection because when you don't eat and you're working for six hours straight, the potential for an accident is higher.

THE REMAINS OF THE DAY

The 2nd AD needs to make sure that everyone, cast and crew, receives a call sheet before he or she leaves the set at the end of the workday. This document tells them their call time for the following production day, which is the time either that they are to get into the van at the hotel in the morning, or that they are to arrive at the location for makeup, hair, and wardrobe (if they are cast), or to set up (if they're crew).

After the principal cast has left the set on any given workday, the 2nd AD's next responsibility is the crew. This person must literally stand at the edge of the set, between the parking lot where the crew will retrieve their vehicles, and the edge of the trucks where the base camp is located. As the crew walks past, the 2nd AD records each person's out time.

Call times can be anytime, day or night, but they are always protected by the turnaround time, which is the rest time required between the end of one shooting day and the beginning of the next. It's the 2nd AD's responsibility to make sure no one incurs a penalty for turnaround because these are even more costly than meal penalties. For a member of the SAG, it's close to $900 a day.

Before going home at the end of a workday, the 2nd AD must finish all the paperwork. This includes checking that the reports from the other departments were done correctly, and also totaling all of the background (extras) vouchers. If it's a location, a driver usually waits for the paperwork and takes it to the studio at the end of the day. From there it gets delivered to the production executive on the movie and is ultimately used to create a hot sheet for the day. The hot sheet is the hot-cost report, which is the actual cost for production, with the most up-to-date information for that given day. See chapter 7 for information on hot costs.

When the 2nd AD gets home, there is still a final check to be made. Everybody in the cast who didn't work that day but is working the following day must be contacted to confirm his or her call time. "The standard procedure is to physically speak with that person or the agent and confirm a call time for the next day, or else you haven't done your job," says Katz. Since an actor may have been working on another film and may not get the message until midnight, the calls can come in at any hour. If an actor is new to the set altogether, or if the actor is coming in from out of town, the 2nd AD usually will call that actor three days in advance to prepare the newcomer.

THE SECOND SECOND ASSISTANT DIRECTOR

A second second assistant director, or 2nd 2nd AD, is hired on bigger productions when more help is required. This person takes care of whatever the key 2nd AD can't handle. If more ADs are needed, additional 2nd 2nd ADs may be brought in.

In North American productions, the 2nd 2nd AD is responsible for the production reports and for communications with the base camp, where all the trailers are located. That allows the 2nd AD to be on the set and always within eye or ear distance of the 1st AD, leaving the 2nd 2nd AD to shuttle back and forth between the base camp and the set. In productions in Europe and other parts of the world, the 2nd AD and 2nd 2nd AD often switch duties.

The 2nd 2nd AD and any additional 2nd ADs generally start a film with very little or no preparation. The reason additional seconds are hired instead of production assistants (PAs) is because the additional seconds bring with them a great deal more experience. On more complicated shoots, this experience is vital.

BEING PREPARED

During pre-production, the 1st AD creates a schedule based on all information pertaining to actor and location availabilities as well as weather conditions. Ultimately, this person is responsible for making sure that everything is planned out and is going to work.

"In making a schedule, it's very important for an AD to know the director he's working with, or to find out how he goes about doing things," notes AD Michael Green. "I've worked with some really wonderful directors who've just amazed me, and I've worked with some directors who have amazed me by being so terrible. If an AD knows how a director works with actors, he is able to better prepare a schedule, allowing the right amount of time for the right kinds of scenes."

The 1st AD must think through every detail of the production to make sure the director has the best opportunity to get his vision across. Meanwhile, the 2nd AD is working with the production office to prepare cast and crew lists. The ADs work with the location manager to schedule the locations; they collaborate with the stunt coordinator on the stunt sequences, and with the heads of the other departments. "Any element that goes in front of the camera in production or post-production has to be considered and dealt with by the ADs so that it is actually feasible that it can be created on the day of shooting or in post-production," says Katz.

EXTRAS CASTING

ADs work together with the extras casting office to determine the need for and selection of the background actors. A script is sent to the extras casting director. The ADs then prepare an extras breakdown, which is approved by the director.

The production manager will tell the ADs how much money is in the budget for extras, which is measured in people days. For example, ten people days could mean ten extras on one day, five extras on each of two days, or one extra on each of ten days. So if there are only 300 people days for extras and there are a total of sixty days of shooting, the ADs can easily break it down to see how many extras they'll be allotted on any given day.

The ADs ask the director what's most important for the film. Would it be better to have twenty extras on one day and only ten extras on another day? Of these ten extras, how many ride bicycles, how many play catch, how many drink soda, how many are surfing, how many are babies? All these things have to be thought through ahead of time so that when the director arrives on the set that day, all the extra talent that was envisioned originally, or that the AD had created for the day's run, is actually there.

The extras casting director pulls pictures of extras from their files. The ADs can request to see the pictures that the extras casting director picks; interviews with the extras themselves, however, will cost money. From these pictures the ADs and extras casting director select the extras.

Michael Green was an AD on *Reds* (1981). "[Director] Warren Beatty was very interested in how every single extra looked, even if there were five hundred of them." So for eight weeks prior to shooting in Helsinki, Finland, Green flew to that city every weekend. He had an office where he photographed the locals. "I'd put them in a bracket of whatever scene I thought they'd function best. I'd fly back with the film on Monday morning. It'd be processed. And Monday lunchtime, Warren Beatty would look at every single extra."

DIRECTORS GUILD OF AMERICA TRAINEES

The Assistant Directors Training Program is sponsored by the Directors Guild of America (DGA) and the Alliance of Motion Picture and Television Producers (AMPTP). The purpose of this program is to train 2nd ADs for careers in the film industry. It is a highly competitive program, and those accepted are required to complete 400 days of on-the-job training as well as attend regular seminars. The training is spent working on actual film projects.

The program is designed to provide a basic knowledge of the organization and logistics of film production, set operations, paperwork, and the working conditions and collective bargaining agreements of most of the industry guilds and unions. Trainees learn to deal with all types of cast and crew members while solving problems in various situations. Upon completion of the program, trainees are eligible for employment as a 2nd AD.

SET PRODUCTION ASSISTANTS

Other than entering through the DGA trainee program, the best route to becoming an AD is to wrangle a job as a PA. "Good PAs are remarkable," says AD Michael Green. "A lot of people just want a job in the film business and they kind of slop around. They get sent off on jobs and they take two hours doing them. The PAs [who are] on the ball have done very well [because] the interest is there."

Even obtaining an entry-level PA job is extremely difficult and competitive. "All these things usually stem from a situation or a relationship," Green notes. "You've got to know someone who will let you in the door to give you a day's work."

Before he became a seasoned talent manager, Michael Valeo began his Hollywood career as a production assistant on the set of the movie *Holy Matrimony* (1994). Even back then, Valeo used his connections to get the entry-level position by contacting a production manager he knew. "You are basically a gofer," reveals Valeo when describing the job. "You keep people out of the way when you're shooting. You run around the sets getting things and telling people where to be. Or you do what's called a lock-up, which is when you're rolling camera and you station PAs all around the set so that they can yell, 'Quiet please, we're rolling.' You're basically just helping the ADs help the director get the shots made."

The best thing about being a set PA is that you will learn a great deal about how a movie is made, because there's nothing that can match that on-set experience of watching them set up the shots and light a scene. "It is amazing how long it takes to shoot just a few seconds of film," Valeo points out. "It takes hours and hours to set up the shot, relight it, change the angles and move the cameras around, and then relight the whole thing again. The only way to learn that is to be on-set."

That said, after working as a set PA on just one film, Valeo knew production work was not his calling. "I was working eighteen-to-twenty-hour days and not making anywhere near the kind of money one should be making if one is working twenty hours a day, six to seven days a week."

Being a PA, however, was the launching pad Valeo needed to start building relationships that would eventually lead him in the direction of management. No matter what your career goal, being a PA gives you a broad introduction to the entire production process. For those who specifically want to go the route of becoming an AD, it's a direct form of entry to an AD career.

Once a PA has accumulated 600 workdays (of which 300 must be shooting days), she can get a note from the production manager, take her organized call sheets, production reports, and paycheck stubs from all of those days, and turn them into the DGA to be "grandfathered in" (unionized) as a 2nd AD. Most PAs work on only a few projects before finding their niche elsewhere in the film industry. But for a wannabe AD, this is an excellent way to get into the union.

A 2nd 2nd AD becomes a 2nd AD by having 400 days. A 2nd AD becomes a 1st AD by having an additional 120 days. "No one wants to hire you as a 1st," explains David Katz. "You have to get a break. You have to get the producer that you worked the best with to help you make that move."

While the DGA allows its members to work back and forth in any of the guild-specified positions, it's not a good idea to bounce around like that. People generally do not want to hire a 1st AD that 2nd 2nded a movie the week before. They want a 1st that was the 1st on the last few projects they worked on. They want a consistent track record.

Despite the fact that ADs are guided by the DGA, the film industry is not set up for ADs to become directors. The stepping stone from AD is to production manager. This is done by being a 1st AD who has worked a combined 600 days in any of the AD positions. The industry does not hire production managers to direct. They are two different entities. One is below-the-line; the other is above-the-line. See chapter 5 for information about becoming a director.

9

Lights, Camera, Action

Look at all the variables that one little frame of film has to go through. Getting loaded and unloaded, going through the camera, being put back in the magazine, going to the lab; the lab unloads it, they clean it, it has to go through their baths, then the negative has to be mounted. It's lucky there's anything that comes out. Within four hours you have the dailies. I'm always amazed.

STEPHEN M. KATZ, director of photography

Cinematographer Stephen M. Katz was working as a waiter at the Factory, a swank Hollywood nightclub, to put himself through art school, where he was studying painting. Katz had recently acquired his first still camera and started photographing a model who would frequent the club. When he had the film processed, the lab was so amazed by what they saw, they blew up the prints and hung the photos all over their offices. They said to Katz, "You've got an eye." Shortly thereafter, Katz switched his major to photography.

Virtually everyone who worked at the Factory was an aspiring actor or filmmaker. One of the bartenders was going to direct a low-budget exploitation film and, having seen Katz's great photos, asked him to be an assistant cameraman. "There was a young English camera-man who got stuck with me," recalls Katz. "I never pulled focus—I didn't know what that was—but I was learning." (*Pulling focus* is when the assistant cameraman adjusts the lens while shooting is in progress to compensate for movement between the camera and subject without losing the sharp image.)

"I didn't think of it as a career at all," he admits. "It was fun. Just a month of my life." Well, one month turned into three, and soon Katz was heavily entwined in production when the director of photography announced that he was leaving for another gig. The producer was ready to bring in another cameraman, but Katz wanted to get a shot at it first. "So I did this little *All About Eve* number and said, 'I'm shooting the movie or I'm off to New York,'" he recounts. "They sort of looked at me strangely. I didn't know that you had to climb the ladder. But they said, 'OK. You shoot tomorrow. We'll see how it looks. If it works, you'll finish. If not, you'll go to New York.'" Clearly by now, Katz had learned how to pull focus!

He studied the schedule to see what was to be shot the next day. "They had this Hell's Angels rape scene," remembers Katz. "So I just went nuts. And it was violent, and it was stark, and at dailies women had to walk out. [The producers] loved it so much, I finished shooting the movie." The film was called *The Peace Killers* (1971). Katz's more recent DP credits include *The Blues Brothers* (1980), *Gods and Monsters* (1998), and *Baby Geniuses* (1999).

THE DIRECTOR OF PHOTOGRAPHY AND THE CAMERA CREW

The director of photography (DP), also called a cinematographer, is in charge of photographing a motion picture. This person not only plans the filming, but also lights and shoots it as well. The DP is both an artist and a technician. "It's all about your eye," says Katz. "The technical stuff comes later. But all the technique in the world doesn't mean anything if you can't see." That is why it's important to be able to look at the world through a camera and know how to catch that view on screen.

Cinematographers must be able to execute and oversee the lighting of both studio and location settings, the positioning and movement of the camera, the composition of the picture, and the use of any special optics or film material. They must have the ability to create convincing, believable, artistic shots under any conditions, in all climates, at all altitudes. This could mean shooting a scene underwater, in the snow, or even while hanging out of a helicopter.

A DP should be able to take light-meter readings, select lenses, and determine the necessity for filters. He should be able to identify and solve any photographic problems relating to the film. He also should have a working knowledge of the camera, composition, editing, lighting, optics, special effects, and staging.

The job does not end on the set. A DP must work closely with the labs that process and print the film, ensuring that the moods or color values of the scenes are preserved or accentuated in the way the DP and the director have chosen.

During pre-production, the DP carefully selects the camera, its accessories, and associated equipment. The film stock also must be chosen. Some DPs shoot with multiple stocks for the same film to help create specific looks for different scenes. The DP and the director spend a great deal of time preparing the shot list, a master list of all the different takes for every scene of the entire film. "Billy [Condon, director of *Gods and Monsters*] and I will spend months before the picture not only discussing it, but trying to get the feel of what we want," says Katz. "We sit at the locations and we act it out. It's the most fun of making the movie. We do this every which way until we find how he really wants to block it and what will work for lighting." Blocking a scene is when the director establishes the on-camera movements of the actors. "We get it into my computer, and we have this funny shot list—of which 90 percent works. It gives us a place to start off."

The first take is generally a master shot that captures everything on set in frame. *Coverage* consists of close-ups and different angles of the same scene that will be used to provide choices later on in the editing room. "Once I've done the master—and we've set it all up, if they really need coverage, I know right where to go," Katz explains.

"Some directors, all they care about is coverage," he adds. "They feel they have to have twenty-six shots a day. They're trying to create a performance. They don't even have a style. It's flat and it's boring, and it makes me f***ing crazy. Billy [Condon] and Bob [Clark] are brave because they'll go for a one-shot, with maybe a little piece of coverage."

On *Gods and Monsters*, Katz and Condon had only a few days to plan their shot list. "We sat in that art studio," recalls Katz. "I was worried about [too much static] plop and talk. But [Condon's] script was so beautiful that it worked. I didn't want the camera to overpower it. We talked about where we wanted the moves and where it felt good. "Like the scene around the table with Jack [Plotnick], the interviewer. It was eight minutes long. But we really thought it out. It's all extremely wide lenses and under-the-table shots of the shoes. Everything was planned with that scene. And it's really just about two people at a table. It works."

Other duties of the DP before principal photography commences include prepping the lighting and grip departments. The DP also runs film tests on various elements such as hair and makeup.

When production begins, the cinematographer supervises all of the various camera crews (first and second unit) working on the film. The DP works closely with the director in matching the action and screen direction of the shots and setting the camera positions, angles, and moves. "I don't move the camera just to move the camera," says Katz. "I always believe in the script first. I'm a little different than most cameramen. I don't care if the actors don't hit their marks. I've gotten over that. If they miss it, let them miss it. I'm not going to lose them. My poor assistant, who's pulling focus, is going crazy. If they walk out of light, let them walk out of light. It's OK. It's real."

The DP supervises all lighting. The cinematographer's directions are implemented by the gaffer and the key grip (descriptions of these jobs are provided later in this chapter). Some DPs are more involved than others with the technical side of lighting a set. Sometimes they merely discuss with the gaffer what it is they want to achieve and leave it to the gaffer's discretion as to how to achieve that special look.

Prior to each take, the DP must set the composition for the camera operator, determine exposures, and select the lens. At the end of the day, the DP walks through the next day's shots with the director. After leaving the set, the DP views dailies to make sure everything that was shot came out the way it was planned.

The DP's job during post-production is not lengthy, but it is very important. He supervises the timing of the work print (with which the editor works) and answer prints (the approval print from which subsequent release prints are prepared) of the film. He also supervises the transfer of the image from film to tape. This, too, is for quality control.

THE CAMERA OPERATOR

The camera operator is directly responsible for maintaining the composition, focus, and camera movement desired by the DP. This includes lining up and ensuring the proper functioning of the camera and related equipment, adjusting the ocular to the operator's proper visual focus, and determining that the lens and filters are properly flagged.

The operator refines the shot by actually working out the choreography of the move while the DP is lighting the shot with the gaffer. This is typically done with stand-ins. Then the actors come on set to rehearse the scene. The DP can ride the shot (literally sit on the moving camera dolly) if necessary, or leave it to the operator. The DP usually doesn't ride the shot nowadays, because he can watch it on video playback. *Video playback* consists of a video camera trailing the shot of the film camera so that the director, DP, and other key crew can watch the filmed action unfold on a TV monitor as it would on screen. Since only one person—the operator—can look through the camera at any time, playback has become an effective tool.

During rehearsals, the camera operator composes and frames the shot as instructed by the DP, perfects focus with the first assistant, refines dolly, crane, or boom moves with the corresponding grips, gives the sound team safe limits on boom positioning, and checks the shot for reflections. When the camera has reached the proper sound speed, the operator gives the camera assistant the cue to slate the sound.

As the title implies, the camera operator is the person who is physically operating the camera during filming. "I was raised out of low-budget, independent films where I did everything, and that's how I learned," says Katz. "I'm one of the few cameramen that operates a camera. I have to be in the lens. That's the only way I can see a movie. I can't see it on a video monitor, I can't stand beside it, it's just me. I'm naked without that camera.

"Seeing it in the lens is what turns me on. In fact, when we were shooting *Gods and Monsters*, I would watch Ian [McKellen's] performance. When the camera didn't move, I'd [sit] Billy [Condon] behind the lens and say, 'Look at it through the lens. Just stay there, because it's fabulous.' And he did. I was seeing things that Billy couldn't see. I feel like I'm in the audience watching the movie."

THE CAMERA ASSISTANTS

The first and second camera assistants work together as a team, but the first assistant oversees the second in all of his duties. The first assistant discusses with the DP what the basic requirements will be for the project, and then coordinates with the rental house to have the needed equipment prepped, inventoried, and shipped.

The first assistant services and cleans the camera. A great first assistant also should know how to build this essential piece of equipment from the ground up. He's like a teenager who gets his very first car. During shooting, he is responsible for focusing the camera. This includes taking care of any filters that go on the camera, setting the f-stop, shutter speed, and shutter angles for each and every shot, and changing the lenses. When the camera is not on a dolly, the first assistant must carry the camera and equipment to whatever position is needed for the shot.

"The first assistant cameraman is probably one of the most important positions," emphasizes Katz. "He's pulling the focus, and if he's off, we're dead in the water, or we're back there reshooting it."

Pulling focus is an art. "We design the scene and put marks for the camera and marks for the actors," explains Katz. "He physically goes out with a tape and measures each point. Then he figures on the lens and the light values, what the lens will hold depth-of-fieldwise [how much will be in focus], and calculates the position of the camera, where the focus should land, how much depth of field he has if the actors are moving, and what will hold them. He has to be watching the scene and watching the lens at the same time. He's like a chameleon, with his eyes going two ways. Now they have a little TV monitor on the camera for him, so he can just look at that if he has to."

The second assistant cameraman ensures that all the right equipment is on set, and that the camera batteries are charged. The actors' positions during rehearsals must be marked, and the beginning of every take has to be slated. All the paperwork for the camera department must be filled out on a daily basis. This includes the camera reports, time card records, camera equipment inventory lists, and daily film inventory sheets.

American Society of Cinematographers

Have you ever seen the initials A.S.C. after a cinematographer's name in the credits of a film? These initials stand for the American Society of Cinematographers, an organization founded in 1919 whose purpose is to advance the art form through artistry and technological progress. The initials are a recognized symbol of excellence in the field, and membership to this group is by invitation only. In addition to directors of photography, the organization also has some of the industry's leading visual-effects practitioners in its membership.

THE FILM LOADER

The film loader is the entry-level position on the camera crew. This person's main responsibility is to load and unload the film. The film loader must coordinate with the script supervisor to make sure that the correct takes of the film to be processed are marked on the camera reports. Other duties include completing purchase orders for the lab, and maintaining an accurate inventory of film stock. Film loaders must stay in this job for one year before moving up to second camera assistant.

THE GAFFER AND THE LIGHTING CREW

In the early days of Hollywood, the gaffer was known as the chief electrician. Today gaffers are sometimes called chief lighting technicians, which is more reflective of the job, since they really do not deal with electricity. The main responsibility of the gaffer is to implement the DP's vision of the lighting. "Some cameramen just want to be able to tell the gaffer where to put every light. That's all they want," explains Katz. "I hire people because they're talented, and I let them do their job. I want them to create, [to] show me something better.

"My gaffer is an artist. He's been with me long enough that he has a good sense of what I like and don't like. Once we talk about it—I don't set lights—I explain where it's coming from and how I want it to be. Nine times out of ten, it's perfect. Very rarely do I have to relight the set."

During pre-production, the gaffer scouts locations for potential lighting problems and assesses the availability of power and cable runs (how far the cable will have to extend). He must order the necessary lighting and electrical equipment.

When setting up a shot, the gaffer and grip (see the next section for a full description of this position) will coordinate the rigging of any lights, whether on the ceiling or attached to a moving vehicle, and accommodate needed diffusion. The gaffer gives orders to the electricians regarding placement, diffusion, and color correction. He will meter the scene, direct the electricians in focusing and balancing the light, spot and flooding, and adding or removing scrims and dimmers, as well as direct the grips in the placement of flags, nets, cutters, and diffusion frames.

During location filming, the gaffer will monitor the scene for changing conditions, shifting sunlight, or clouds. "It's problem solving on the spot," says Katz. "You're set up with challenges. Some people just throw their hands up. I usually take what's given to me and try and make it work. I have to."

In one of the final scenes of *Gods and Monsters*, Clayton Boone (Brendan Fraser) and James Whale (Ian McKellen) head off into the night, imitating the walk of director Whale's famous screen creature, Frankenstein's monster. "I had the black-and white-clouds. I saw the rehearsal and we had it lit fully. I said, 'This is wrong. Turn it all off. I can't stand it.' As the lights were turning off, it started to make sense to me: It's a silhouette. It's black and white. And that's how it developed. It was just an intuitive thing—it just happened. I lit their faces, and it just really worked."

ELECTRICAL BEST BOY

The electrical best boy, also called a second electric, is in charge of the electrical crew and is the gaffer's key assistant. This person is in charge of everything electric. He performs the tie-in or generator hookup, cable runs, load balancing, and selection of electrical equipment. He will supervise the crew in terms of selecting and scheduling electricians, and makes sure their time cards are filled out properly. He also checks that all the equipment requested is available and accounted for.

ELECTRICIAN/LAMP OPERATOR

The job of the electrician/lamp operator is to maintain the equipment and place the lights. The electrician must make sure that every piece of equipment is ready and working. When the gaffer calls for a light, it is the electrician who actually brings the light, hangs it, and focuses it. The gaffer directs where he wants it focused, and the electrician scrims or dims it.

THE KEY GRIP AND THE GRIP DEPARTMENT

Like *gaffer*, the name *grip* also comes from early Hollywood. The workers on a set used to carry their tools in a sturdy bag, similar to what a doctor would use, called a grip bag. Although such bags are no longer used, the name stuck, and the workers became known as grips.

The key grip is the head of the grip department. It is this person's job to gather a crew, including the department's best boy, or second grip, and as many additional grips as needed to get the job done. The key grip attends planning meetings during pre-production. He must determine what special support equipment (dollies, cranes, mounts, etc.) is needed for filming. He will go on a location scout to determine the need for special equipment, such as a helicopter or a boat, that may be required to transport the filming equipment to the location.

On set, the key grip works with the gaffer and is responsible for rigging all lights hanging from the set or from vehicles; setting flags; rigging and adjusting diffusions; placing sandbags; tying off and leveling tall stands; hoisting and rigging any heavy equipment; helping out with any heavy units or hard-to-reach areas; providing ladders, lifts, and cranes; and providing rain protection for the lights. This key person always must be planning ahead for what will be needed in the next shot.

Katz has worked with some outstanding grips over the years. "I've seen [a grip] take a bow and arrow to shoot rope through trees to support microphones. Whenever we're in the swamps, [my key grip] is behind me with his .45 shooting water moccasins and guarding me. They really protect me and make sure the rigs are safe. I'm hanging off buildings and out of helicopters, but with my guys, I never feel insecure."

THE BEST BOY GRIP

The best boy grip is to the key grip what the best boy electric is to the gaffer. The best boy grip is also the link between the key grip and the other grips in the department. Essentially, this person acts as a foreman, delegating responsibility to the other grips and following through to make sure tasks are completed. The best boy grip also is in charge of all the grip equipment and expendables, such as tape, gels, and nails on the grip truck.

THE DOLLY GRIP

The dolly grip actually pushes the dolly or moves the crane that holds the camera. He figures out how to get the camera from point A to point B. "He is an artist in his own right, because he may have a shorter way or a better way of getting there," Katz says. "It's like a dance. The actors are dancing to their marks, and the camera's dancing to its mark, and they have to meet at the same time, everywhere."

THE GRIPS

Grips are the handymen of the film set. They do most of the rigging of light-support equipment, securing the lights and mounting the cameras in every place imaginable. They must know how to rig things securely because they are ultimately responsible for the safety of the equipment. Basically, they deal with whatever equipment needs to be lifted, moved, and rigged.

Grips build the track on which the crane or the camera moves. They also flag the lights once the gaffers and electricians mount them. Flags are pieces of cloth or metal that diffuse the light to remove shadows from the walls. "There's a real art to setting a flag," according to Katz.

Grips and electricians can have a lengthy wrap every day, especially if the company is on a move. They're rolling cable and packing the trucks before the trucks move out to the next location.

GET A GRIP, CLIMB THE LADDER

"I was working in Santa Fe when a woman came to me from Los Angeles. I didn't know her from Adam," remembers Katz. " She said, 'I really want to be your apprentice.' I said, 'OK, first thing to do is make me a cappuccino.' " She graciously got the cinematographer his beverage.

"Then she schlepped the video around," recalls Katz. "Then the loader starts teaching [her] about loading. Doesn't let [her] load but can show [her] how. Then I watch them and there's a point where I said, 'Let her load a magazine.' She can do it. She can do more than that, I find."

On the next movie, she's with the crew as their loader. Today she's a major DP. "She stuck it out. I knew it from the very beginning," says Katz. "We bring apprentices in, and every once in a while I see that in them, and I move them along fairly quickly."

Typically, climbing the ladder from loader to DP might take seven to ten years. "It's a difficult thing," admits Katz. "Someone starting out, they can have all the schooling possible, but until they're on the set, it just doesn't come together. They have to really be passionate about it. It's hard to get that little door open, but when it opens, they have to go through it."

10

Picture Perfect

You buy a Picasso because you like his look, and somebody hires me because they want a certain looking film.

GARY WISSNER, production designer

Production designer Gary Wissner had built four period sets in the middle of a vast El Paso, Texas, desert for the action film *Last Man Standing* (1996), which starred Bruce Willis. The desert ranch was approximately 90,000 acres. "It felt as if you were on the moon," recalls Wissner of the beautiful location. "I placed the sets in such a way that if you were standing at one, you couldn't see the other ones because they were over a hill or beyond a bend, yet they were all within five minutes of each other for ease of building and shooting."

One of the sets was the skeletal structure of a two-story roadhouse café that had been painted to look burned. While shooting at one of the other locations, Wissner heard the location manager's screams come over the walkie-talkie: "One of the sets is on fire. Call the fire department."

"I looked to the horizon and saw a trickle of smoke arching over the hillside," says Wissner, who jumped into his car with the construction coordinator and raced down the dirt road to their "burned" set that was not supposed to actually be burning.

They arrived to find their beautiful set engulfed in flames. "My heart sank," says Wissner. "We unrolled a hose from a nearby water truck and tried to put the fire out, to no avail." The fire trucks did not arrive for another thirty minutes, and all they could do was watch the set burn to the ground. Fire inspectors later discovered how the fire had started. A set dresser was burning a couch with a blow torch to achieve a special scorched look. "Unfortunately, he didn't put out all the embers before he placed the dressed couch into the set," explains Wissner. "Once the wind picked up, the set was a goner."

A construction crew was flown in from Los Angeles to rebuild the set. The job was completed in eight days. "It was terrible to watch a piece of art you worked on for so long be destroyed by one careless mistake," Wissner sighs.

THE ART DEPARTMENT

Movies are a visual medium, and a great number of factors contribute to their look. Some of these include costumes, makeup, visual effects, and lighting. All of these elements are integral to the visualization of a film. It's the art department, however, that gives birth to the look of a picture. The art department is responsible for every aspect of the film decor and set construction. This includes designing and preparing all sets, and acquiring all props and set pieces with which to decorate the set.

When you watch a movie, everything that you see on screen has been carefully preorchestrated and scripted. Take, for instance, the famous shower scene in Alfred Hitchcock's *Psycho* (1960). What kind of shower curtain should be used? Is it the right length and texture? Is the material translucent enough to see the killer's shadow, yet protective enough to conceal a supposedly naked leading lady?

THE PRODUCTION DESIGNER

The production designer (PD) is responsible for the total visual design of the movie. "Production design is like the visual architecture of the movie, and the script is really your client," says Wissner, whose credits include *I Know What You Did Last Summer* (1997), *8mm* (1999), and *Detox* [2000]. "You look at a film like *Gattaca* [1997], where you were totally drawn in and believed that those characters lived in that world. That's [about] picking out locations, the doorknob design, the wardrobe design, where the light sources are coming from. It's all part of the production design right from the outset."

THE PROCESS Wissner works closely with the director to conceptualize how the feature film should look. "I will spend days researching the 'look' that I want to achieve," he explains. This may include visiting bookstores and libraries, surfing the Internet, and scouting and photographing specific locations and establishments outlined in the script. "[Director] Joel Schumacher and I scouted real underground private sex clubs—with our clothes on, of course—in Manhattan and L.A. to get graphic ideas and details for *8mm*."

Wissner brings back visual images for the director and organizes them into categories of color, light, texture, form, size, architecture, and so forth. This provides the basis and foundation of the illustrative map, or visual color "script," of the production design of the film. Collages of everything from fabric samples to foliage are mounted on exhibit boards and displayed in the art department.

"I'll assign those collages to a character or to a scene, and it gives me a sense of starting with the big picture of the movie and slowly breaking it down," Wissner says. This allows him to track the progression of the film visually and give the director a sequential, stylistic consequence of the production design over the course of the 120-page script.

According to Wissner, "Throughout my painting and building schedule I can refer back to my established and approved visual principle to choose specific materials like paint, plaster, fabric, and wallpaper." In addition, every member of his team, from set decorator to art director, now has a chart to adhere to throughout the process. This forces them to be uniform in their combined procedures and techniques.

For example, the costume designer refers to Wissner's collage board that incorporates everything about a specific character and pulls off a swatch for the character's clothes or shoes. The set decorator does the same for the couch or the drapes. "There's a visual icon that everybody can refer to," says Wissner. "No one on my team makes random, arbitrary, or aimless choices that affect what I'm trying to accomplish visually."

In *8mm*, he divided the script into zones. "Once this character went from one locale to another, the colors changed, the lighting changed, and the geometry of the spaces changed. As he sinks deeper and deeper into this hell, tracking these killers, and is really in the middle of this world that he never really wanted to be in, things are closing in on him, the ceilings become lower, the sets become redder and darker and more saturated." As the film is stitched together after being shot out of continuity, the filmmakers see the vivid path that they all agreed to months earlier.

Sometimes there's just not enough time or money in the budget to build an entire film's design from scratch. "When I did *I Know What You Did Last Summer,* I only had about ten weeks. We weren't building a lot, but we took locations in North Carolina and totally repainted them, took walls out, put new doors in, and painted the faces of buildings. It was mostly decorating and paint jobs. You have to spend more time making sure the locations work. When you have less money, you have to think of more creative solutions. If you only have money to build one set on a movie, you may have thirty other locations in addition to that one set, but those thirty other locations have to be as visually pleasing as that one beautiful set. When you have a complete stage show, like *Batman* [1989], you're going to need six to eight months of construction time before you even roll camera."

THE ART DIRECTOR

In the old days, there was no such thing as a PD. There was only the art director. When the Civil War epic *Gone with the Wind* (1939) was made, William Cameron Menzies did so much work above and beyond the scope of normal art direction that producer David O. Selznick gave him the credit of PD. "The union is actually a couple of years behind the times in that they have never made a classification of production designer, and they've never set a minimum wage for the position," says Wissner, who was an art director before he became a PD. "It's been an ethereal position that's intangible and isn't on the books officially, but it's been created over the years. The art director is a very powerful position on a film. In fact, being an art director is an essential step to becoming a designer. "I always saw myself as a bodyguard when I art directed. I would open the doors for the designer to just come in behind me and create and take all of the unneeded pressure away from the designer," says Wissner.

This job is really about management, budgeting, and scheduling. The art director will speak directly to the construction coordinator, who is the foreman on the construction site. She also is responsible for staying within budget and for delivering a look. However, she is not the person who creates the look—that's the PD's job.

The PD will sketch, paint, do research, and have meetings with the director and the DP. "I'll come up with the mood of what the texture is, the gloss, the architecture, whether a set is period, modern, tech, sci-fi, or whatever it is, draw it up and present it," explains Wissner, who then sends his rough designs to the art director. "He will take my creations, which could be verbal, research, paintings, or drawings, and turns them over to his drafting room so that they can actually be translated into hard scenery."

The art director is like a PD-in-training. All future PDs must have background in art direction to be effective in their field. "There's more management in terms of scheduling and how long it takes to build a set," says Wissner. "He'll work with the construction coordinator to come up with a budget for the actual set. And if I have 100 sets, I do that 100 times. And if 100 of those sets are at eighty-seven locations in and around Los Angeles, for each single location that art director will sit down with me and say, 'What are you doing here? What are your designs? What do you plan on for set dressing and paint?'"

Making the leap from art director to PD can be difficult. Like any other transition in Hollywood, you need another career break. The first step is to get an agent. Most art directors do not have agents until they're ready to make the leap; then the agent pitches them as a PD to help them reach the next level.

"I knew it was time to get an agent when I woke up as an art director and I said, 'I just don't like going to work anymore,'" recalls Wissner. "I was chomping at the bit to break out of the more technical/managerial end of the art department."

Wissner designed his first movie, *Graveyard Shift* (1990), when he was twenty-six years old. However, he spent another four years art directing after that. Eventually he got enough of a résumé together as a good art director and felt it was time. "*Seven* [1995] was the last movie that I art directed. That held a lot of weight on my résumé. On bigger movies like *Hoffa* [1992] and *Wyatt Earp* [1994] and *Seven*, art directing paid off in the long run because those résumé items still get me work. I learned more, and I worked with top people [Danny DeVito, Lawrence

Kasdan, David Fincher, et al.]. If I had just said, I'm a designer now, I never would have gotten to work with those people."

In 1996 Wissner re-emerged as a PD on *Last Man Standing* and has been designing ever since. He continues to take classes to this day. "I take directing classes; I take classes at Panavision, just to keep learning. I take computer classes, because we all know that the technology is always expanding, and I embraced it right away. I design all my sets on computer now even though I continue to draw."

THE ASSISTANT ART DIRECTOR

The title of assistant art director is a bit misleading, because the job is a lot more complicated than simply assisting the art director. In fact, the assistant art director really is somebody who is training to be an art director. His duties range from surveying locations and running the drafting room, to supervising the art department coordinator or assisting the designer if the art director is not present.

Because so much work needs to be done by the art department in preparing for a film, the assistants are given a great deal of responsibility. Wissner recalls, "The toughest thing for me as an assistant art director was, Am I making the right decision for the designer? You have to trust your instincts. As an assistant art director, you may have a million dollars' worth of sets staring you in the face, with a bunch of construction guys looking over you, saying 'what do you want me to do here?' and you've got to know what you're doing even though you're down on the food chain."

THE ART DEPARTMENT COORDINATOR

The art department coordinator is the office manager of the art department. This person's main responsibility is to organize legal approvals, called clearances. Every real name on a sign or actual product that is created for a film has to get cleared through the legal department of the studio.

The coordinator tracks the labor budget within the art department. There may be a room full of draftspersons, two model makers, and two assistant art directors. The coordinator assures that everyone has his or her supplies, everyone is getting paid, and everybody has access to the PD or the art director. In other words, the art department coordinator basically keeps the machine running.

THE SET DESIGNER

The entry-level position in the art department is a set designer. The senior set designer has an overall design ability and more control over the physical drafting of a set. It's his job to draw plans as described by the art director. He might hand off more of the detail work to the junior set designer, or draftsperson.

THE MODEL BUILDER

Model builders are an offshoot of the draftspersons. They are responsible for designing study models, architecture models, and pre-visualizations that the director can use to see a set, space, or location in scale. If there is a spaceship in the film, for example, the director needs to know what it will look like before hundreds of thousands of dollars are spent to make it, so a study model is built. However, it's not the same model that's used for principal photography; those models will be made by the construction department, or visual-effects team.

THE SET DECORATOR AND CREW

Movies today just don't look like they used to. Perhaps this is merely indicative of a simpler past. When you look back at many old black-and-white films, you'll notice that there are only about six things on the set. It almost looks like a cartoon. Today's sets are infinitely layered with many items. It takes a lot more time to acquire one hundred things for a scene versus six things, however. As a result, the role of the set decorator has grown increasingly important over the decades.

The set decorator is the person who "dresses" the film set with appropriate furnishings such as furniture, lamps, drapes, and paintings. She is an interior designer of sorts. She reads the script, envisions what is needed for each scene, and then locates it.

This includes the obvious items like sofas and chairs. It also encompasses all of the lighting fixtures, the art on the walls, the cigarette butts in the ashtray, the mail that's piled up on the counter, the clothes in the closet, even the pair of soiled underwear lying in the corner of the bedroom. "If the floor is dirty, we get dirt for the floor," explains set decorator Maggie Martin, who has worked on *Reality Bites* (1994), *The Truth About Cats and Dogs* (1996), and *Out of Sight* (1998). "If the set is an alley, we get the Dumpster, garbage, and rats."

For that matter, if the scene calls for a Dumpster, not just any Dumpster will do. If there is a stunt, the stuntperson must not be injured when she lands in the Dumpster. It's also imperative that the Dumpster works within the color theme. If there's no blue in the movie, the Dumpster cannot be blue. In addition, the container must look natural. For instance, a brand-new Dumpster probably needs to be aged.

Many directors have a difficult time conceptualizing what they see on paper. They can see that the set decorator is planning to have a sofa and a chair, but unless they can see the actual furniture in a room, it's often difficult for them to imagine the finished results. Showing them pictures and giving them samples of material are sometimes the best approach to help them visualize the decorator's ideas.

According to Martin, "Directors may have very specific ideas of what they want, but oddly enough they're not often very capable of articulating those ideas. They'll know it when they see it. Or they might not have a vocabulary that includes technical furniture talk, so they may know what they want is a Windsor chair, but they don't know it's called a Windsor chair." In such cases, the decorator will bring back pictures of every chair known that resembles the director's limited description until they find the one he has in mind.

Set decorators open, or *ready* the sets in the morning, making sure that everything is in order, that the director is happy with the dressed sets, and that any last-minute changes are handled properly. Once filming begins for the day, however, they're off preparing everything else that needs to be done for the remainder of the shoot. The actual dressing of the set generally is done on the day of shooting or the night before. "I may come in at three o'clock in the morning in a frenzy, go in and get the set ready, and do everything we need to do in a few hours before the shooting crew shows up at 6 A.M.," Martin explains.

The set decorator reports to the set designer, art director, and PD. As the head of set decorating department, this person usually hires the leadman and any shoppers, both of whom are described below.

THE LEADMAN The leadman is responsible for managing his crew of swing gang, or set dressers, and planning the logistics of the set decorating department. This includes making certain that everything gets picked up, taken to the set, and put on the set according to the floor plan. Then the decorator will start placing smaller items, adjusting furniture, and hanging art.

SET DRESSERS/SWING GANG Swing gang and set dressers perform the same functions (as opposed to an on-set dresser, which is explained below). They do all the lifting, moving, and rigging. They pick up the furniture and other set pieces that the set decorator has selected, bring it to the stage or the location, and put it in place. They must be organized about putting things away, and be able to pack objects without breaking them. They have to be able to correctly rig and hang art or decorative lamps. When finished, they take everything back, put it into storage, and inventory what remains. Rentals are later returned to the rental houses.

THE ON-SET DRESSER The on-set dresser is responsible for maintaining the set continuity between takes so that the set looks the way it should. For instance, if a coffee mug is on the right side of a table for the entire length of a master shot, the on-set dresser must make sure that the mug remains on the right side of the table during subsequent takes for coverage. Sometimes the camera operator might not notice that something on the set is out of whack. The position of on-set dresser was initially created to have one dedicated person ensuring the continuity of the set pieces and that everything remains intact.

"When you come in to a set, we have it all dressed up pretty. It looks like you've walked into somebody's house, or a bank. It looks just like the real thing," says Martin. "There's about five minutes when the set looks like a set, and then it's totally demolished. Everything gets piled in a corner and they fill the room with equipment, and all that's left is just whatever is seen by the camera. If the camera is not seeing it, it's moved."

Once the master shot is finished, the camera crew will go in to do coverage. One take they'll do is a reverse shot to see the other side of the room. This necessitates taking out everything that they just shot, putting the wall back in, and redressing the other side of the set with everything that's sitting out in the hallway. This is a job for the on-set dresser. She enlists the help of the prop people, the grips, and others who are sitting around on the set.

Sometimes a director will want to move things around on set once it already has been established. "We'll have these arguments . . . the lamp can't just disappear, and that's a pretty hard conversation to have with a director. They don't always want to hear it."

You might shoot for a long period on the same set, but the plot line action taking place may occur over several days, months, or even years.

The on-set dresser must create subtle changes to denote the passing of time. For example, one day the dish towel may be hanging on the refrigerator, the next day it may be hanging on the stove, or it's a different dish towel. "I can't stay there all day to do that," says Martin. "So I'll give them a little pile of things and say, "One day I want you to have some fruit on the table, another day I want the table to be empty, or there's mail and they're paying their bills. Nobody's house looks exactly the same every day.""

To help maintain continuity, on-set dressers take many Polaroids or digital pictures. The script supervisor also takes Polaroids and keeps accurate notes about what the actors dealt with on the set. The on-set dresser will refer to these pictures if reshoots are necessary.

THE SHOPPER OR BUYER   Imagine a job that pays you to spend your days shopping at malls, antique stores, and flea markets. Better yet, you're spending somebody else's money. If this sounds like a dream come true, perhaps you should consider a career in the film industry as a shopper or buyer.

A set decorator often hires people to help shop because she cannot cover enough territory alone. Technically, the position of shopper is a job that does not exist because it's not an official union position. Sometimes a shopper will be hired as swing gang, but he'll still do the job of a buyer. The position is somewhat controversial. "Some decorators don't like it because it implies that anyone can do our job," says Martin. "Others say that they're not doing our job, they're doing something else."

While it sounds like a great deal of fun, finding the right set pieces can be brutally difficult. "A sofa is not a sofa is not a sofa. I'm not just looking for a sofa. I'm looking for a sofa that has really specific character," explains Martin. "I'm looking for a sofa that says something about the person that has it. I'm looking for that certain sofa. It's a certain color, it has round arms or square arms, it's this length because somebody has to lie down on it, it's got this kind of a texture because we're trying to create this kind of a feel. It can be like looking for a needle in a haystack. I can't tell you how many sofa hunts I've been on. You look at eight hundred sofas and none of them are right and you think, *How can this be?* But it's true. This one's the perfect color, but the arms are the wrong shape. This one's a little too short. So you have the sofa manufactured. Or you buy something that's got the right shape, and you have it reupholstered and then you have it aged because it's supposed to look old."

Detail is integral. What bothers Martin most about poor set decorating is a character who doesn't look like he or she belongs in that apartment. "How can a poor person have really expensive furniture?"

READY, SET, GO

There are basically two ways one can become a set decorator. One is to work as a set decorator on a non-union project that gets organized by the union so that you're grandfathered in, or unionized. The other is to earn 720 hours as a leadman and pass a union test. "The problem inherent in this is that the skills required to be a good leadman and the skills required to be a good decorator have pretty much nothing to do with one another," explains Martin. "Once a leadman takes a [union] decorator card, he can't work as a leadman or swing gang anymore." However, when he's a leadman, he can work as swing, so if he doesn't have a lead job he can work on other projects as swing gang.

THE STORYBOARD ARTIST

A storyboard is a series of sketches that outlines the narrative progression of a film or a sequence of a film. The storyboard is a general production tool to help the editor learn what the pace, or camera angle, should be; to help the DP understand potential production problems; to convey the scope of the film to the art department; and to explain trick shots to the visual-effects team. It also helps all of these departments in their budgeting because they each don't really know how many setups, or shots, or cuts it might take to make a sequence come alive.

Even though the use of storyboards in live-action films is a relatively modern convention, they've been utilized in animation for years. For the most part, they are used for the big production sequences, effects sequences, and action sequences, because it helps those involved to foresee potential production problems. Depending on their level of experience, directors work with the storyboard artist in different ways.

Directors with a strong point of view, a strong visual sense, and a good cutting sense know what they want to do with a sequence. They tell the storyboard artist how to draw a sequence or what they want to see. The storyboard artist then visualizes what the director has in mind. The less seasoned director may have less experience with a camera and may not know what the lenses do or what the cutting pace should be. For the most part, these directors want the artist's own take on it.

While the role of the storyboard artist on union films is a union position, additional work is available that does not require a union card. Storyboard artists often play a pivotal role in the development or preproduction of a film by helping to visualize different ideas and concepts. Once a movie is greenlighted, however, any storyboard artist working on the project must be in the union.

CONSTRUCTION

The film's construction crew physically builds the sets. They are led by a construction coordinator who must meet both the artistic and budgetary demands of the production.

Carpenters and members of the construction team must be in the union if they are building union projects. There are two possible ways to become a member of the union. The first is by working for thirty days on a non-union project that becomes union. Alternatively, you can place your name at every studio personnel department. If Local 44, the construction union, cannot fill a call, they will hire names from these lists.

THE PROPERTY MASTER AND CREW

The property master (or propmaster) is responsible for acquiring, maintaining, and distributing all of the props for a film. A prop can be any item that moves, is handled by an actor, or is specifically identified in a script but not physically handled.

"Actors use hand props in order to give them action and character in the scene," explains Bruce Mink, propmaster on *The Mask* (1994), *Austin Powers: International Man of Mystery* (1997), and *Sunset Strip* (2000). "They may be flicking a lighter to light their cigarette in a certain way that gives them the style they're seeking."

When the propmaster is hired, he highlights all of the hand props identified in the script. "Then I start thinking about what I don't see in the scene that I know is going to appear via background actors or just things that will complement what these actors are doing," explains Mink.

Next, he transfers the information into a computer program to organize the needed props. From there, the propmaster determines what props will be purchases, rentals, fabrications, graphics, photos, or food—the basic classifications of props. Classification is determined by whether these items can be found in a prop house and rented, whether it's more cost effective to buy them, or whether they will need to be specifically created or re-created for the movie. Obviously, most props in a futuristic sci-fi film will need to be fabricated because they don't yet exist. Vendors will manufacture props based on designs or photos that the property master provides. With a period movie, the propmaster must research what things looked like during the specific era being depicted on screen. He must determine if these items are available from a prop house, or if they're more likely to be found at a garage sale or flea market.

"I actually had to fabricate the magazine that shows JFK being killed in 1963," reveals Mink about a prop in *Sunset Strip*. It is usually the job of the production office and studio legal department to get clearance for such items, but on some smaller movies, propmasters have been known to personally write letters and make phone calls to ask for permission and authorization to use certain images.

Preparation on an average picture generally takes between four and eight weeks. During this time, props are secured. The propmaster places hold tags on props at the rental houses two to three weeks before they are needed, so he must study the schedule to decide when to rent these items. Certain props are rented for the whole duration of the movie depending on the size of the budget and scheduling needs. The preparation process continues throughout the shoot as there are always last-minute changes.

THE PROP MAN

The assistant to the propmaster is called the prop man, or assistant propmaster. This person's primary job is to work the set. Mink explains the differentiation: "I will be there to open the scene up and to establish the props. Then I will let the assistant work the continuity of running those props [i.e., working the set]. The propmaster hands over the props, the prop man runs the props, and then I get them returned to the prop houses once they're used." There are some propmasters who prefer to work the set and the functions are switched.

The prop department probably has the most crossover with other departments. For example, if an actor is putting on lipstick in a scene, the propmaster will try to obtain the lipstick from the makeup department so that the color remains consistent. If the actor is brushing her hair in a scene, the propmaster will obtain the brush from the hair and makeup department, because actors are particularly fussy about what goes in their hair. At times it is necessary to coordinate with the wardrobe department. Props such as eyeglasses, sunglasses, wedding rings, and watches need to be coordinated with the rest of the performer's outfit so that everything matches and flows.

THE PROPMAKER

While the propmaster may do some of his own building, he generally works through a prop manufacturing company that employs propmakers. Propmakers are usually among the finest craftspeople in the business. They create unique items that cannot be found in stores. A PD or propmaster will come up with an idea, and the propmaker brings this idea to life.

There are also graphics houses where everything from the cover of a video box to a reprint of a newspaper or magazine can be created. Other specialty divisions of propmakers include drapery, upholstery, carpeting, and floor covering.

THE SPECIALISTS

Food stylists prepare and style any food needed on camera. The food stylist not only prepares the actual food, but also determines the look of the food, prepares backups so that it can be eaten in each take, and ensures the quality and quantity of the food needed. Food can be purchased or prepared by the propmaster or even the production's caterer.

Weapons specialists are responsible for providing and overseeing the use of real guns and weapons when they are used on set. Certain licenses are required to handle various guns, like assault weapons. Any propmaster can get state certified to handle the different types of guns, or specialists can be brought in as needed.

If the set has grass, trees, shrubs, flowers, or plants, these items are dressed by a greensman. Greens are used to subtly enhance the look of a scene, such as a plant in the corner of an apartment, or a vase filled with fresh flowers at a restaurant. Other times, greens become one of the most important facets of the movie, as with *George of the Jungle* (1997), or

Tarzan and the Lost City (1998). Greensmen work with both real and artificial plants, sometimes in combination.

Sometimes grass is painted green to make it look more vibrant. This may be the job of the scenic department. The scenic department also paints backdrops, murals, figures, portraits, freehand decoration, fine art painting, and stained glass. In addition, they also perform set painting, sign writing, and prop aging.

11

GETTING DRESSED

*Costume, makeup, and hair are the final coat of
the painting, which brings the actor and actress to
life on the screen.*

TOM BRONSON, costume designer

My first exposure to the hair, makeup, and wardrobe departments of a studio came when I was working as an assistant to Marty
Katz while he was producing *Mr. Wrong* (1996), with Bill Pullman in the
title role. It was Ellen DeGeneres's birthday, and she had just signed on
to star in the dark comedy as a youngish "old maid" named Martha. At
that time our office was located on the Disney lot in Burbank, the same
place DeGeneres's TV show, *Ellen* (1993–98), was being taped. Katz
wanted to send something special to the actor-comedian for her birthday,
and he wanted to somehow tie his gift in with the upcoming film.

There is a scene in *Mr. Wrong* in which Pullman's character dresses
as a clown and shows up at Martha's house in the middle of the night
bearing gifts. Katz thought it would be funny if I dressed as a clown and
went to the set of *Ellen* bearing birthday presents.

Tom Bronson, head of the studio's costume department, sent me to
his costume shop to be measured and fitted. While Bronson gathered the

clothes, I headed to the makeup department, where white liquid was applied to my face. I was made to look like a clown, complete with a red prosthetic nose. From there I went to the hairstylist to get a funny-looking wig. Finally, I arrived back at wardrobe, ready to put on my outfit. In less than an hour, I had been transformed from a producer's assistant into a clown.

After picking up the gifts I was to deliver, I quickly made my way over to the sound stage where DeGeneres's sitcom was taping. The cast had just finished rehearsing a scene when I arrived and gave DeGeneres her presents. The comedian was thrilled, and everyone on her show thought it was a funny stunt. Best of all, I got to "clown around" with Ellen.

What I found amazing was the cumulative effect that hair, makeup, and wardrobe had in transforming me into a clown and helping me become that character. I felt free to dance around, do silly things, and move my body in ways that I just normally wouldn't have. It helped me understand how integral hair, makeup, and wardrobe are to assisting actors in finding the essence of their onscreen characters. Like the art department, these professionals also contribute to the cumulative look of a picture.

STAR REQUEST

One thing all three departments have in common is the *star request* (when a leading actor asks to have his or her own specific hairstylist, makeup artist, or costumer work with them on a film). This is a common practice. The bigger the star, the more likely such demands will be granted. The artists requested by the star works only on that one actor, while the remainder of the department supports the rest of the cast.

With multiple stars, there may be several star requests for each department. For instance, on *The First Wives Club* (1996), Diane Keaton, Goldie Hawn, and Bette Midler each had her own hairstylist, makeup artist, and costumer. Midler's hairstylist was Robert Ramos, who has built his career on star requests. In addition to Midler, he's worked with Sharon Stone on *The Muse* (1999) and Jennifer Love Hewitt on the TV biopic *Audrey Hepburn* (2000). Ramos also owns his own salon, Estilo, in Hollywood.

Ramos moved to Los Angeles in 1984 and didn't know a soul. He did, however, know exactly what he wanted to do professionally. "I specifically moved here because I wanted to work with actors," he says. He quickly enrolled in a local beauty school, where he made contacts and found out what salons would be best to work at to get ahead within the industry.

Once Ramos got his certification, he started working at a salon in Hollywood where an occasional actor would come in. The first actor whose hair he cut was teen star Corey Haim. "I would tell my clients [who were actors] that I would love to do TV and movies," explains Ramos. Eventually, Ramos was given his big break by Pamela Bellwood (TV's *Dynasty*), who hired him to work on some of her TV projects. One celebrity led to the next, and soon he was cutting his way to his Hollywood dream.

A HEAD FOR BUSINESS

The jobs of all members of the hair department are union positions on union films. To get into the union, hairstylists must have a current cosmetology license. The head of the hair department is called the key hairstylist. This person has been hired by the director or the film company to set the whole movie with regards to hair. By talking with the art director, costume designer, and makeup artist, he helps figure out what each character is going to look like. "I read the script and figure it out," says Ramos. "This is a night scene, so she should wear it up. It shouldn't be too fashionable. It should be more like a woman at home would do it."

The key hairstylist hires a staff, which usually consists of one or more stylists and occasionally an assistant hairstylist. The stylists will break down the script day by day. What are they doing? Are they waking up in the morning? Are they getting ready to go to work? Are they at work? Are they on their way to work? Would this person leave her house with her hair wet? "You have to understand the character and figure out who she is," says Ramos. "Is she the type that would bathe in the morning, or

> **Letting Your Hair Down**
>
> "The most challenging film for me was *The First Wives Club* because I had to make Bette [Midler] look frumpy," says stylist Robert Ramos. "When I started working with her, it was to make her hair look beautiful and glamorous, but when *First Wives Club* came around, she had to look dowdy. And I couldn't get it. I kept making her look too good. Her hair was too styled. I had to relearn how to do a normal, everyday hairdo on a woman."

would she bathe at night? It says a lot about a person. Bed-head hair and freshly washed hair are completely different."

GOOD HAIR DAY

When the actors arrive on the set, they have to visit the hair, makeup, and wardrobe departments. The order in which this is done is important. For example, if the costume must fit over an actor's head, it would not be a good idea for that actor to have her hair done before going to wardrobe.

Once the actors are on set, the hairstylist must ensure their hair is not mussed. "I make sure the hair is the same from the beginning of the scene to the end of the scene," explains Ramos. "If the hair was behind the ears when the scene started, it's got to remain the same. If I were to not pay attention and just let it go, there would be no continuity."

The stylist needs to consider an even greater continuity issue when prepping for a film. If someone on camera has to be blond and dark within the same movie, the shooting schedule must take this into consideration. Often, all the dark-hair scenes will be shot first, and all of the blond scenes will be shot last. Sometimes, however, there may be a need to shoot the dark hair first, the bleached hair next, and then the dark hair again. This could be caused by a number of practical reasons, such as limited availability of a location or an actor.

At the end of the day, the hairstylists remove any wigs that were worn by the actors. The wigs used are very elaborate. They're hand woven and made with human hair. They're very expensive and extremely fragile. If it's a big-budget movie, there will be duplicate wigs. If it's a low-budget entry, there may be only one wig per actor, so it's especially necessary to keep it clean and not put too much styling gel in it; otherwise the stylists will be washing that wig every few nights. Every evening the wigs must be brushed and reset for the next day.

MAKING THE CUT

Ramos advises aspiring hairstylists to attend beauty school to get their license first. "Try and hook up with someone like myself and become an assistant," Ramos suggests. "Call the union and get a list of the hairdressers. Call them up and say you want to assist them. Tell them you want to learn and you'll start by sweeping hair. When you come into this business, you start at the bottom. You don't start at the top."

Because so much non-union work exists (commercials, print ads, photo shoots, personal appearances), there are many opportunities to get experience assisting a professional hairstylist until you earn enough hours to get into the union and work on films. "My assistant goes with me everywhere," says Ramos. "She goes on commercials, she goes on photo shoots, she goes to the stars' homes with me to help color their hair. My assistant is my right-hand person. You'll get an idea of what it's like. Sometimes it can be a lot of fun, and sometimes it can be really hard, strenuous work with long hours and a lot of pressure."

For those who already have experience working in a salon, but want to come to Hollywood to do hair in the film business, independent movies and student films are a good start. Most of the people on these films work for free. This is a necessary step in an effort to build up credentials working in film. There's always some young producer who needs someone to do hair. Just call around and ask.

A hairstylist must work on non-union movies and commercials until he accumulates sixty hours to become eligible to apply for union membership. Or there's always Ramos's way: "I've always been a star request. If you work with a big enough star, they get a pardon slip from the union. I [eventually] got in the union because it's easier for me to work [and less] problem for the producers."

A FACE IN THE CROWD

When he was just thirteen years old and living in New York, John Caglione Jr. started making himself up. Don't get the wrong idea. He was a huge fan of monster movies, and he transformed himself into some of his favorite big-screen monsters, as well as creatures from the depths of his own vivid imagination.

At fifteen, Caglione saw *The Exorcist* (1973), and it made a deep impression. He wrote a letter to Linda Blair's fan club in Hollywood. Somehow the letter reached Dick Smith, the film's makeup artist. "It was like a note in a bottle thrown out to sea," recalls Caglione. "One letter made it to him, and he sent me a letter back, and I started a correspondence with Dick."

Through their letters, Smith explained different special-effects makeup techniques to Caglione like making molds. Smith even recommended the teen to the NBC network in New York when he graduated from high school, helping him land a job on *Saturday Night Live* (1975–present) where he put his learned techniques to work applying coneheads to Dan Aykroyd and Jane Curtin.

"It was all on-the-job [training] for me," admits Caglione, who never went to college, but has gone on to win an Oscar for makeup for *Dick Tracy* (1990). "I really learned for the first five years working on *Saturday Night Live*. I started cleaning the mirrors and worked my way up."

Many aspiring makeup artists enter the film industry through salons around the country. This may be a good way to learn general makeup technique, but it does not teach anything about the special requirements for working in film. Salon graduates also should take film classes to learn about continuity, design, and other important elements of movie makeup.

The main difference between everyday and movie makeup is that for film, there are many additional factors to consider: Hot lights, color gels, and various film stocks all play a role in determining the type and application of makeup. "There are different consistencies of makeup," notes Caglione. "Actresses and actors may have skin problems and [as a result] coverage is heavier. It just takes a keen eye and experience with certain film stocks and lighting conditions."

Caglione works as a key makeup artist, who is the department head, as well as a special-effects makeup artist, who is responsible for out-of-the-ordinary makeup effects. "I think you should be able to do everything," he advises. "It's like a good actor. The more characters you can play, the more you're going to work. I'm still trying to do everything—the sculpture, the mold making, and beauty makeup too. I don't think there's any separation."

Usually there are only two makeup artists per film production, not including star requests. For large crowd scenes, additional makeup artists are hired as needed. Also, for certain unique visual sequences, a special-effects makeup artist may be brought in if that type of makeup is not the forté of the department head.

SPECIAL-EFFECTS MAKEUP

Although Caglione is versed in all types of makeup, he especially enjoys special-effects makeup, which ranges from full prosthetic foam-rubber appliances to mold making and sculpture. One of a special-effects makeup artist's most difficult tasks is properly aging an actor. In *Chaplin* (1992), for example, Caglione made lead actor Robert Downey Jr. look sixty-five years old at one point. "He was in the chair for about three and a half hours, because for that age he required a bald cap, a foam latex forehead, and a full wrap around neck appliance with gels on the side of his face, and a wig and fake eyebrows—it was a big deal."

Getting made up is not always as much fun for the actor. Sometimes it means sitting in the chair for hours while oily substances are applied to the skin. In fact, some actors are quite apprehensive about the whole process. As a result, the makeup artist has to be a bit of a psychiatrist. "They feel a little claustrophobic," says Caglione. "You hang on for dear life and try to get them through it, help them to relax."

On *Dick Tracy*, some of the actors wore their masks and appliances fifty or sixty times during the shoot. They would start at three-thirty in the morning and work on the set until nine or ten at night. "The actors were submerged under rubber, and it's not the greatest thing for your skin," says Caglione. "You really have to be careful in cleaning and maintaining an actor's skin so that they can endure a [production] schedule like that."

MAKEUP ENCOUNTER

The first thing the makeup artist needs to do, as a department head, is determine how much it's going to cost to do the makeup on the entire shoot. More money is obviously needed for those films that rely heavily on special-effects makeup. Next she does sketches and drawings of what the makeup and special-effects makeups will look like. Once the initial conceptual work is completed, the head makeup artist shows her ideas to the director, and they discuss how to proceed.

On *Dick Tracy*, the original comic strip by Chester Gould was used as a bible. "But it was our responsibility to translate it and make it three-dimensional," recalls Caglione. "I think in the beginning [director-star] Warren [Beatty] thought that these characters were going to be big rubber heads. It was our suggestion, through sculpture and little three-dimensional mockettes, that you could really put these characters next to him with no makeup and it might work."

To produce molds, impressions are taken of the actors' heads. The makeup artist must determine how many days each character in the script will be needed to figure out how many different sets of appliances will be required each day of filming. When character makeup is made of foam-rubber appliances, you can use them only once because they're destroyed during the removal.

Ideally, the makeup artist will run tests in front of the camera during pre-production. On *For the Boys* (1991), some scenes called for Bette Midler to be eighty-five years old. Several tests were done to see how the makeup would appear under the different planned lighting sources: outside, inside, in broad daylight, in the dark, in nightclubs and bars, on stage, and so forth. "That makeup went through every condition you can go through. So you're constantly adjusting for each environment," says Caglione.

During production, makeup artists are on their feet nonstop. They do every actor's makeup early in the morning in a span of about two hours. Then, throughout the day, it's basically maintenance before every shot. When it comes time for close-ups, the makeup artist stands right behind the camera to make sure the actors look their best. Then after lunch, the actors come back to the makeup trailer for touch-ups.

When the shooting day ends, the artists help the actors remove their makeup. In addition, all the typical "glamour" work needs to be done, such as cleaning the trailer, filling out time cards, labeling the backs of Polaroids they may have taken during the day, putting them in continuity books, and keeping everything organized for the next day. The head makeup artist also will go through the call sheet with the second assistant director to determine the next day's call times for the actors so that sufficient time is allowed for makeup application.

CLOTHES MAKE THE ACTOR

Costume designer Tom Bronson and actor Sylvester Stallone used to play practical jokes on each other during the making of *First Blood* (1982). Bronson remembers one scene in which several state police officers and military types are looking for Rambo. Two days before they were to shoot that sequence, the production brought in one hundred extras and gave them all buzz cuts. When Bronson walked into Stallone's motor home that night to change him into another costume, he noticed a bag in the shower area. Out of curiosity, he looked inside and discovered all the hair from the haircuts.

"I decided that the hair must mean he's trying to get me," says Bronson. "So I took it out and I stuffed the ends of his boots full of hair." The entire next day, Stallone complained to the costume designer that his feet were itchy. Bronson told him it was probably nothing.

By the end of the day, Bronson was trying to conceal his laughter. "I went into his motor home, and I keep looking at his feet. He kept saying, 'What are you looking at?' And I said, 'I'm just looking at your feet. They look kind of strange today.' " So Stallone looked down at his feet, and sees about four inches of hair protruding from his toes and realized what had happened to him. "If he had caught me, he probably would have killed me," says Bronson. "I thought it was funny and we all got a big laugh out of it."

THE COSTUME DESIGNER

Once the costume designer is hired on a film, she has an initial concept meeting with the director to get an understanding of what the director wants to achieve through the use of costumes. Generally, the production designer (PD) also will be at this meeting, which is separate from the concept meetings of hair and makeup.

The costume designer works closely with the art department to conceptualize ideas for wardrobe. In determining the look of a costume, she will closely follow the color progressions and design themes that the PD has established for characters and scenes throughout the picture. It's sometimes helpful for the costume designer to meet with the principals in the cast to discuss their screen roles. "If there is a specific character [trait] that you can help the actor find through the costume, or make that character believable to the audience, it can be important," says Ingrid Ferrin, costume designer for *The Client* (1994), *A Time to Kill* (1996), and *Batman & Robin* (1997).

The designer must devise garments for every wardrobe change that each character makes throughout the movie. Costumes can be designed, but they also can be bought and rented. Most budgets today don't allow for a costume designer to completely build from scratch. Sometimes shopping for costumes is even more difficult to accomplish, because to make the characters believable, it is necessary to coordinate the entire look, and that may mean shopping until each outfit is fully complete.

Often, there's a certain degree of product placement involved in costuming. A clothing manufacturer will pay money so that characters in the film wear its brand of clothing. Of course, in such cases one must follow certain restrictions. "Why should a mad killer be in Nike from head to toe?" offers Ferrin.

Once the director has approved the designs, the costume designer will go about having the costumes made. Either the work will be sent out to established costume shops or to freelance workers who make costumes at home, or the costume designer will set up her own costume shop. When a designer creates a costume shop, the first step is to hire a cutter/pattern maker. This person is in charge of physically manufacturing the costumes. He will hire one or two people, called stitchers, to do the sewing. There also may be a draper, who helps set the patterns. All of these jobs are union positions on a union film.

If a costume designer does not draw her own sketches, she works with a sketch artist to help put the ideas down on paper. They may even use a computer to design their sketches. These costume illustrations are presented to the cutter/fitter with the selected fabric to manufacture the actual costumes. The actors visit the shop to be measured. Once the costume is made, the actor comes back for a fitting. If alterations need to be made, the actor must return for additional fittings.

On costume-intensive movies, such as a period piece or science fiction film, the costume designer might have six to eight months of preproduction time. However, most movies allow the costume designer only six to eight *weeks*. As a result, the designer is still prepping the movie as it is filming. "You're prepping the whole way through," Ferrin confirms. "Things may change. The director's concept may change. They may even write a new scene."

Once the costume designer has made sure that everything is ready for a given shooting day, she then starts working on the next big scene. "You never know when an actor may get sick, or when they decide to shoot the scene that was originally [set for] three weeks from now, tomorrow," notes Tom Bronson, costume designer for *Beverly Hills Cop* (1984), *Man of the House* (1995), and *The Waterboy* (1998). "You always have to be ready and stay on top of the shooting schedule, and preparation." As such, Bronson likes to have his costumes ready prior to shooting.

The costume designer evaluates the necessity for duplicate costumes. Duplicates are needed when an actor is going to be wearing the same costume for most of the film, for photo doubling (if an actor is unavailable or her face is unseen), and anytime a stunt is involved that will soil the costume, such as blood hits when someone gets shot.

On a typical production day, the dry cleaning arrives (by the Teamsters, delivery, or production assistant). The wardrobe department organizes the dry cleaning and sets up for the first change of the day by placing the stars' clothes in their trailers before they arrive on set.

The designer is always present for the first change of the day and stays on the set until the actors are dressed. "If [the director] has any comments or questions, I'm right there to answer them," notes Ferrin. Once filming begins, however, the costume designer is off to another fitting.

The costume designer often has a vision for the production's costumes well before the roles are even cast. Once the actors are cast, elements may change. "The actor is the one who is going to be wearing the clothes," says Bronson. "If they're not happy and comfortable in the clothes, they're not going to be giving a good performance. The audience goes to see the actors; they don't go to see the clothes."

THE WARDROBE SUPERVISOR

Because the costume designer spends most of her time at the costume shop, the wardrobe supervisor is the main costume representative on the set. This person is hired by the costume designer and is a day-to-day link between the producer, the designer, and the rest of the department. He solves any problems that arise, helps track the budget, and keeps everyone crucial on the production in the loop.

The supervisor makes sure that the costumes work within the context of each scene, maintains the continuity, and cleans and maintains the costumes. He usually has an assistant who helps handle computer work and paperwork, such as ordering supplies and keeping continuity logs.

Wardrobe supervisors also may spend time at the shop, perhaps while the costume designer is away creating or in meetings. On set, the supervisor oversees the costumers.

COSTUMERS

The costumers are the official set persons in the wardrobe department. In the morning, they're the ones who set up the clothes in the actors' trailers. At the end of the day, they collect the worn clothes from the cast, make sure they're in good condition, and have them cleaned. Sometimes the costumers help an actor get dressed. Some actors actually may have their own personal costumer. Others may get dressed on their own. Frequently, personal costumers function as star requests.

On set, during filming, they take pictures and keep notes and descriptions for continuity. The costumers are also on the set at all times with a kit in case anything needs to be stitched, cleaned, nipped, or tucked. They accompany the actors whenever the actors are on the set.

BEAUTY TIPS

Ingrid Ferrin went to art school, where she learned graphic design, ceramics, and jewelry making. "I finally figured out what I liked to do was design things, whether it was fashion, furniture, or costumes."

Ferrin advises future costume designers and wardrobe staff to familiarize themselves with the film industry in any way possible. They also should fax résumés to the costume departments at the major studios. "In the beginning, you have to be prepared to do whatever it takes," she says. "Don't give up. It's a process. It takes so many people to be part of a team. I couldn't do my job if I didn't have my supervisor, my set people, my sewing room, and everyone else. It took me a long time to understand. I'm lucky that I started as a set girl because there's just so much that makes it work."

In the meantime, Ferrin recommends reading as much as you can. She scans every magazine possible, looking at their visuals for ideas. She also studies music videos, album covers, artworks, and other films and TV programs. "I'm constantly looking at every image that's out there. My eyes are wide open. I just take it all in."

12

CUT AND PASTE

*I think books on writing and storytelling are the best
things for an editor to be reading because that's what
you're doing. You're the final storyteller.*

MARY ANN SKWERES, editor

The last cut had been made and the movie was ready to be
screened. Director Bryan Singer knew there was still a structural problem with the final sequence of his complex new thriller, *The Usual
Suspects* (1995), but he didn't know how to fix it. "That was actually the
worst scene in the film and we were very depressed about it," recalls
John Ottman, the picture's editor (and composer—an unusual combination), who felt the scene didn't work. "All I had [to work with] was some
bulletin board coverage and [the shot of Kevin Spacey] walking out of
the [police] station. I'm like, how am I going to make this [ending] really
amazing?"

Since there wasn't enough time in the shooting schedule, they were
not able to get a shot of Kujan (Chazz Palminteri) standing on the sidewalk as the camera craned up. Instead, they had to settle for a less interesting shot of him standing on the sidewalk as Verbal (Kevin Spacey) gets
away in a car. Early on, editor Ottman added the bulletin board scene

into his cut, which stayed intact through the entire editing process. Still, something was missing from the sequence.

"I didn't do the audio montage [of the voices] yet, and the music I put on the temp score [sounded] like getaway music and just made it totally expected," Ottman remembers. Then in the eleventh hour, he went through all the original footage, watched all the alternate takes of every scene, and wrote out a script on his own of all the lines. He was using a flatbed editing system, which allowed him to hear only two soundtracks at one time, so he had to imagine the third line of dialogue being staggered. He started building soundtracks of all the different voices, trying to put them together in interesting ways, like audio commentary on what was being shown in the scene.

Things were starting to come together. "Originally when I read the script," says Ottman, "I had thought to myself, in that sequence we're going to have to hear all the things that Verbal's been talking about, but that's dumb and expected, so I'm probably not going to do that. But that's exactly what I ended up doing, and the last element was the music, which was still making all of that not work.

"I suddenly had this epiphany. Don't make it suspenseful; make it magical. Make it almost euphoric that this bad guy's getting away, and that will make it interesting." He found a piece of music by the French composer Camille Saint-Saëns called *Carnival of the Animals*, and he put that on at the last minute.

"We had the screening for Bryan [Singer] and some friends. Bryan wasn't expecting this at all; he was just expecting the typical scenes we'd

The Plot on the Cutting Room Floor

While enrolled in the film program at USC, Ottman became known as a good editor, but it was not what he really wanted to do. He had met Bryan Singer while working together on a student film, Ottman as a boom operator and Singer as a sound recordist. The director ended up dismissing the editor and asking Ottman to re-edit the movie. Ottman disassembled the entire film and edited together a new story because the original cut did not make sense. The film ended up winning the Student Academy Award. Remembering that, Singer asked Ottman to edit his feature directorial debut, *Public Access* (1992), as well as his subsequent features, *The Usual Suspects* (1995) and *Apt Pupil* (1998).

been watching with the crappy music on it." Needless to say, he was pleasantly surprised.

"Hearing that magical music with these visceral lines, and watching people being shot in this montage, created this bizarre sequence. That is a scene in a movie that is utterly constructed from just stuff in the editing room," explains Ottman. "The basic story was that he sees the bulletin board, he sees stuff on the bulletin board, he sees the coffee cup, and he leaves the station. But it had to be done in a whole bizarre way. That's where things happen—in the editing room."

SPLICING 'N' DICING

Ephraim Katz's *The Film Encyclopedia* defines *film editing* as "the process of selecting, assembling, and arranging motion picture shots and corresponding soundtracks, in coherent sequence and flowing continuity." It describes the process as one that is both laborious and exacting, which may be why John Ottman jokes, "It's a dreary, horrible, depressing plight I would never wish upon my worst enemy." Perhaps that's how they coined the term *negative* cutter.

THE EDITOR

The editor comes onto a film just before shooting starts. A meeting is held to discuss the movie from an editorial point of view to see if the filmmakers can save any time or money by eliminating scenes that the editor thinks are not going to work, or integrating these scenes into other ones through a montage, or some other convention.

As the editor goes through the editing process, she seeks to repair certain elements, including making good performances out of bad performances or solving story problems through editing. "There may be thirteen takes of one actor. You may use an eye blink of one take, then go to the other actor for another take. You construct all of these performances that never really existed on the set," Ottman points out.

"A scene that's cut on its own may seem good, but when you put it in between two other scenes that are part of the whole movie, it may change the pacing," notes Mary Ann Skweres, assistant editor on *Maverick* (1994), *Mr. Wrong* (1996), and *B*A*P*S* (1997). "You just might decide to take a different performance, because [although] you've decided that you liked that performance the best, when it's now in the bulk of the picture, you see that the performance is too high or too low for the character arc at that point."

The physical editing of the film begins the moment shooting starts. The editor is given the footage—known as dailies—at the end of each workday. She feverishly tries to keep up with the production while the shoot continues. That way, shortly after the picture wraps, the editor will have ready a rough assembly, or editor's cut, of the movie.

Most film editors have their own philosophies on how that assembly is going to be accomplished. Many editors intentionally make that assembly fat; they do not cut out anything. "Unless you've worked a long time with the director and you've been given very specific instructions to do so, you won't be overtrimming," notes Skweres.

Ottman does the opposite. "After I edit a scene for that day, I want to believe that that's exactly how it's going to be forever, so that when I present my editor's cut, this is my version of how the film should be. So I err on the other side, and I figure if Bryan [Singer] doesn't miss it, it should be out of the movie. If he asks about it, then we put it back in."

The editor's assembly generally is finished a few weeks after production of the film wraps. The majority of the remaining post-production schedule is used to tweak the film by trimming down, refining, and reshaping the material to achieve the desired content, construction, and rhythm within each sequence and throughout the overall movie. Contractually, the director is given ten weeks from the date of the editor's assembly to do a director's cut. This is a fine cut in which the director works closely with the editor to get the film to a point where he feels comfortable showing it to the producer and studio.

Few directors have the contractual right to the final cut. This cut usually is not determined until notes on creative issues from the producer and studio are considered and implemented. In addition, results from test screenings performed by the marketing department may affect the final cut. If a majority of screening audiences are unsatisfied with the ending, the editor may have to recut the end of the film differently. If footage to make the suggested changes does not exist, reshoots, or additional photography, may be necessary. This may be feasible only if costs and cast availabilities do not deem it prohibitive. Of course, once a new ending is created, it will then be retested with new audiences.

It is also the editor's responsibility to indicate transitional effects such as fades, dissolves, and wipes. Traditionally, this was done by marking the corresponding symbols onto the film itself with a grease pencil. Today most of this is done digitally.

THE ASSISTANT EDITOR

The size of the editing crew depends on the budget and the amount of footage that's being shot. There is always at least one assistant editor, though often there are two, the first assistant editor and the second assistant editor. The assistants' primary function is to create and maintain an environment that allows the editor to work without having to worry about any of the messes she creates. They also keep track of everything for the editor, including the hundreds of little pieces of film.

The first assistant editor is similar to an office manager and keeps everything running smoothly. This editor manages the cutting room. "The editor is busy editing, and that's a very creative process whereas assisting is much more organizational," Skweres says. "It's sort of like the difference between a director and an assistant director. The first AD has to run the set and make sure everything is on time and on budget. To some degree, the first assistant editor does that [in the editing room]."

The second assistant editor supports the first assistant editor. On a studio project where dailies are printed on film, the second generally syncs the dailies for screenings, which involves aligning the picture with the sound, since these two are originally separate elements. The second assistant editor also does most of the coding (correlating scenes to the edge numbers printed on the film) and logging of the film. When the film comes in, the assistants prepare it for the editor by taking the film, digitizing it, organizing the shots, and labeling everything. Once this is accomplished, the editor can now edit the footage. "It's important for the assistants to be good, because if you screw up and you don't check all these numbers that are going into the computer, you can start getting weird things [in the cut]," says Skweres.

Today most editors work on digital computer systems. The two most popular systems are Avid and Lightworks. One is Macintosh based, the other DOS based. Courses on these editing systems are offered, but expertise comes with experience. And although this method is becoming the standard in

---

Digital Domain

"I didn't know Avid until midway through *Apt Pupil*," editor John Ottman confesses. "We edited *Suspects* on a splicer out of my living room. We started *Apt Pupil* that way, and for two months I was on a splicer and flatbed. Bryan [Singer] was shooting a [large] amount of film. I finally waved the white flag and said, 'I'm never going to finish this cut on time if we don't go over to a digital system.' So we did a really bizarre thing where we changed over midstream from film to digital, which is the opposite of what is normally done." Editing usually is done in the digital system; then the film is conformed to what has been edited in the computer.

"As it turns out, the film ironically became the kind of movie that had a lot of dissolves and weird effects in it, and I could never have rendered all that with a grease pencil. No one would ever have known what I was trying to convey," says Ottman. "When we first went over to the Avid, because dissolves and effects are expensive, the [producers] were very concerned because we had a low budget. They said, 'If we give you this Avid, you're not going to go crazy with dissolves and stuff, right?' I go, 'No, I never use dissolves. I think they're a crutch.' I think they're way overused to solve problems."

In the end, the movie required several dissolves and unusual effects. "Their optical budget ended up going through the roof."

Hollywood, some editors still prefer to use the traditional moviolas (motor-driven editing machines that run the film at sound speed and slower).

The assistant editor conforms all the raw footage to the Avid or Lightworks cut. This is done by referencing the key numbers, which are microscopic-sized numbers written on the sides of the film. A lot of the assistants' time is spent on this monotonous but essential process.

As the editor makes additional changes in the computerized cut, the assistants must make corresponding changes to the raw footage. They must constantly keep track of all these alterations and prepare what are called *change notes*. If the editor makes any changes, the assistants have to be notified so that they can change the print, otherwise the sound is not going to match up with the visuals when the finished movie is projected.

THE APPRENTICE EDITOR

Many editors allow their assistants to cut a few scenes of a film so that the assistants can have material to include on their sample reel. This may enable them to land an editor position on a small, low-budget movie. Frequently there is a position on a film crew known as apprentice editor.

This entry-level job is a learning position. The apprentice does a majority of the film handling, delivering the film to screening rooms, and syncing the dailies. "They don't always do the conforming," notes Skweres. "You might have them pulling the pieces, but you might not have them putting it all together. It depends on how much experience they have."

The apprentice position is a union position. The guild has a roster of available apprentice editors. Editors must go through this roster to see if anyone is available to work on a film. If no one from the list is available, a non-union apprentice can be hired. This could be a great way in for someone who wants to learn the craft of editing.

The film shipping department at some of the major studios also hires apprentice editors. This might be another place to route a résumé. Film shipping is the studio department that receives and dispatches the film to and from the set, lab, and screening rooms.

Bryan Forbes's *The Naked Face* (1985) was the first feature Mary Ann Skweres worked on that had an open dailies policy, which allowed anyone on the crew to attend. Dailies are roughly assembled prints of scenes that were shot the day before and processed overnight to see if any retakes are necessary. "For the first time, I actually got to see raw footage," remembers Skweres. "I'd been on set during the day, seeing what they had been shooting. Then I got to see it on film. Then I got to see it afterwards as the project progressed, edited. I found that whole process very interesting."

The experience inspired Skweres to become an editor. Less than a year later, she found her opportunity. "My first editing experience I did for free," she recalls. "When I decided on editing I was just looking for a way in. I found an ad in *Drama-Logue*. There was an editor who needed an assistant and was basically willing to take somebody without any experience and train them on the job."

Skweres worked for this editor for about three months on a low-budget film. When that person got his next project, he brought her on as an assistant. This time, she even got paid.

THE NEGATIVE CUTTER

"I'd rather stick bamboo under my fingernails than cut the negative," jokes Ottman. Negative cutting is an unbelievably monotonous job. The negative cutter sits in a lab, wearing white gloves, with thousands of feet of film and literally cuts by numbers. He looks at the work print, reads off the key number, goes to a box, pulls out the corresponding film, and splices it together. And he has to do it right. If he makes one mistake, it's all over. He can't make any false cut because he's cutting the negative. "It's a nine-to-five job that people have on a regular basis as part of a company," says Ottman. "But to me it's very assembly line. There's nothing creative in it at all."

SOUND AND MUSIC

Music is the soul of the film. Once the editing, and the lighting, and all of the other conventions of filmmaking have done their best to create a certain reality on screen, sound and music bring the audience across the line to make you believe the illusion of the movie because it finishes off the filmmaking process.

JOHN OTTMAN, composer

Clearly, film is a visual medium. If you have any doubt in your mind, though, about the importance of sound and music to a motion picture, try this exercise. Watch a video of any movie with the sound turned off. Now view the same movie again, but this time keep the sound on. Enough said.

In today's world of motion pictures, theaters are equipped with the highest quality sound systems available. THX, Dolby Digital, Digital Sound, and Sony Dynamic Digital Sound were not available when the first (partial) sound feature, *The Jazz Singer* (1927), was released. Sound has become such an important component of the filmgoing experience that director George Lucas at the time of the film's release allowed his *Star Wars: Episode I—The Phantom Menace* (1999) to play only in theaters that had installed the most state-of-the-art sound systems. Interestingly enough, the visual aspects of filmmaking have remained virtually unchanged since Georges Méliès made *Le Voyage dans la Lune* [A Trip to the Moon] in 1902 in France.

"Quiet on the set" is a phrase you're probably familiar with. Sometimes it's impossible to get it completely quiet on the set. Such was the case during the filming of a scene in *Deep Impact* (1998) that took place in a space capsule. Actor Robert Duvall, as Spurgeon Tanner, was inside the capsule, but because of the noise from some of the electronics onboard the craft, Duvall's dialogue level was very low. Mark McNabb, the production sound mixer, asked the veteran actor if he could raise the level because the distracting background sound was so high. McNabb remembers Duvall getting upset and leaving the sound stage abruptly.

Production sound is the recording of all of the dialogue and a good deal of the sound effects on the set. It's important to capture the dialogue as clearly as possible so that the actors do not have to redo it later in post-production. This is because the audio performances are generally much better when they're done in front of the camera than when they're corrected later on a looping stage. This is why McNabb asked Duvall to speak up.

THE PRODUCTION SOUND MIXER

In pre-production, the sound mixer breaks down the script, looking for shots where more equipment will be required. Most sound mixers provide their own equipment, for which they receive a rental fee. On an average production day, the sound mixer sets up and tunes all of the equipment, then aligns the tapes on the equipment that will record the dialogue. Once the director yells "Roll it," everything on the set starts.

While the cameras roll, the sound mixer adjusts all the levels of the mix. If there are two actors in a given scene, and one speaks more softly than the other, the mixer can pull the volume of one up a little and drop the other down. "You try and make as good a mix of it as you can on the set," says McNabb.

The mixer also needs to make sure no equipment or vehicles are operating outside on the periphery to cause noise interference. On location he's always sending somebody around to stop cars from driving by. "If you're in somebody's kitchen, turn off the refrigerator," McNabb suggests. "You don't want any kind of sound other than the dialogue. If the actors are loud on their feet, you try to put carpet down to stop them from putting foot noise over their dialogue. They can put the footsteps in later."

Syncing the sound is done by using a clapboard or by using time code. Keeping track of these time codes makes paperwork a critical part of the job. The mixer writes down as much information as possible about what has been recorded, including what happened in each scene, the types of microphones used in each take, and whether or not it was a good, uninterrupted take.

At the end of the day, the tapes are dispatched to the sound transfer department at the studio or audio lab, where they are transferred for dailies. This means that the sound and picture are matched for a sync sound screening of the day's work. The master soundtracks are digitally input into the computer system (Avid or Lightworks) for the picture editors to use when cutting the film. Later, during the pre-dub, the sound editors go back to the original production masters and edit from there.

Mark McNabb began his career as a producer and singer of rock-and-roll music. After a while, he learned engineering because he didn't like the engineers he was using. From there, he segued into movies, easily transitioning his mixing knowledge from the music industry to the film business. When he got into the union (after working 100 days on non-union films), he had to start again at the bottom. He worked his way up the ranks, first as a cabler, then as a boom operator, and finally as a mixer once again. McNabb has worked as a mixer on *The Mask* (1994), *Deep Impact* (1998), and *Blast from the Past* (1999). As a department head, he is responsible for hiring his own crew. Ideally, he tries to work with the same team if they are available and not employed on another film.

For new people looking to break into film production sound, McNabb says the best way to learn is as an apprentice. If classes in motion picture production sound are not available at your local college or university, he suggests taking classes in studio recording because there are many similarities between recording and mixing sound for the film and music industries.

THE BOOM OPERATOR

"I think the boom operator is probably the best job on the set," says McNabb. "He works only a few feet away from the actors all the time." The boom operator has to have a great deal of diplomacy because he's dealing not only with the actors, but also with the cameraman, the gaffer, the key grip, and the director.

The boom operator must know a lot more than just sound and where to position the microphone. He must be familiar with lighting so that he can ask somebody to put a flag in (to block the microphone's shadow) or ask the gaffer to move a light so the booms don't bump into them. "The sound department always gets nailed for that," McNabb says. "So it's basically the boom operator's job to make sure that doesn't happen."

Despite their physical appearance, boom mikes really are not that heavy. In fact, the entire rig weighs only about two or three pounds. Of course holding the boom mike out all day can be rather taxing when the days are eight to twelve hours long. "It's just a mind-set," says McNabb. "You finally relax with it and it just works." It's an extremely important job; if the mike's not in the right place, there will be no sound.

SOUND UTILITY

Sound utility, also known as a cabler, is the entry-level position in the sound department. Cablers keep everything plugged in, run the cable out to the mikes, and place miniature radio mikes on actors when needed. They learn by observing, watching, and helping out wherever they're needed. As in most entry-level positions, offering help before being asked is a great way to get noticed.

When the cabler gets to know the equipment a little better, he'll tone up the machines in the morning and maintain them throughout the day. If there's a second microphone needed on the set because two people are speaking at a distance and both need to be heard, the cabler controls the second boom.

THE PLAYBACK OPERATOR

Anytime a scene requires a dance sequence, live music, or singing into a microphone, audio playback is employed. This is where the actual music that will be used in the film is played on the set for the benefit of the actors. Essentially, if an actor needs to hear the music in order to make her performance work, playback is involved. Normally, the music is pre-recorded during pre-production well before the particular scenes are shot. This is because music rights must be cleared prior to filming to ensure the producers have legal permission to utilize the music in their movie.

Recording can become complicated if a lot of dialogue is required during a playback scene. Because the music cannot be played loudly while recording dialogue, a tape called a room loop is created. This enables the actors to hear the music through earpieces while the sound mixer hears only the dialogue being picked up by the boom microphones. The music itself is generally pre-recorded on minidiscs because of their nonlinear, instant queuing ability, which allows for instant song selection.

Because audio playback is not required for every scene, the person who handles this task is hired only for the days he is needed. There are people who specialize in audio playback, and they are always in demand.

THE COMPOSER

When he was a youngster, composer John Ottman watched the original *Star Trek* (1966–69) to study how the music was used on this TV series. "It was scored very traditionally, and they could only afford to score every fifth episode," he recalls. "What they had to do was reuse a lot of the music and themes, which gave the series a continuity. So I learned, through watching the show, how the same piece of music was used in different ways, and that kind of taught me the shape of film scoring."

Growing up, Ottman had always been interested in music, but most of his musical knowledge came through being a fan of the art. Ottman attended USC's film school to study production, and he never seriously considered making a living as a composer. While at USC, as a hobby, he built a makeshift studio out of secondhand equipment. For fun, he would score his friends' student films.

Ottman soon began thinking about writing music for pay and shortly thereafter began scoring training videos and industrials (instructional or promotional films made by and for corporations). "My philosophy was find something that you have fun doing and don't be obsessed with being *successful* at it. I just did this because I enjoyed it. I had no expectations. I thought to myself, *If this takes off some day, great.* But if I'm still working at a hotel and doing this on the weekends, then I'm still at peace with that. That enabled me to just have fun and not feel the pressure of having to have it work for me professionally."

Director Bryan Singer, whom Ottman had met and worked with while both were attending USC film school, was working on his first feature, the eerie *Public Access* (1992). "The composer wasn't working—he dropped out—and Bryan's back was up against the wall," recalls Ottman. "I said, 'Bryan, I'd be the perfect person to score this movie,' and he knew I'd give [anything] to score the film. So it was a grand experiment to see what would happen, and we saw the symbiosis that developed and I proved to Bryan that I could do something other than flowery industrial music. His fear was that everything I'd done was so sweet and saccharine. The irony now is that all I get hired for are sinister, dark movies because that was the tone of the first feature I did."

KNOWING THE SCORE

The composer is brought on to the film as the editing process is being completed. Because the movie is not yet locked (i.e., finalized), he's working with a film that is somewhat in flux. If a composer scores a scene that is then recut, he will have to rework the score. It's a difficult and challenging position.

Even before being officially hired, the composer studies a rough cut of the project to get an idea of the scope of the movie and start thinking of musical themes. Before he actually starts writing the score, though he attends a spotting session in which he and the director go through the film and decide where music should come in and where music should fade out. Usually the composer guides this process. The spotting session lays the groundwork as to what the composer is going to do so that everyone on the project has the same expectations.

The director places a great deal of trust in the composer. Because not many people are that musically inclined, most directors actively consult the composer for his ideas and point of view. "It depends on the director," notes Ottman. "I'm sure Steven Spielberg is somewhat musically inclined. He has definite ideas he wants [his frequent collaborator] John Williams to follow, but he's also coupled with a very good composer who has his own ideas. Then there'll be a director who has absolutely no idea musically and completely trusts the composer. "The funniest question that I always get from friends is, 'Have you seen the movie?' And I answer sarcastically, 'No, I haven't seen the film, I just wrote the score.'" Obviously, the composer has to watch the movie repeatedly to determine what the goal is musically. Then he creates a game plan for composing the score.

"The best composers have an overall story they're going to tell with their score from frame one of the movie to the end," reveals Ottman. "They don't really start in the middle; they have to have a plan."

In writing the score, the composer surveys a scene and catalogs each event or action that needs to be emphasized with music. He marks down the measure number and the beat at which the door opens, or the beat at which someone screams, and then uses this map to guide him as he writes each piece of music or cue.

When the composer is finished with the entire film, the scoring session is scheduled to record the music with a live orchestra. Contractors hire the musicians, who will spend the next two to seven days, depending on how much music there is, on a scoring stage. The stage has a big mixing console behind glass, and video projection to display a reference picture of the film as the musicians' playing is recorded.

"The picture really is superfluous," Ottman notes. "Hardly ever do I look at the picture to make sure it's matching—I'm listening to the orchestra. With today's digital editing systems, you can be off a frame here or a measure there and still work miracles in the editing. It gives you a great comfort level."

Once the score is recorded, it's mixed together to the composer's satisfaction. Then it's delivered to the final mix stage, where it's integrated into the soundtrack.

So how do you go about becoming the next Jerry Goldsmith or John Williams?

A director has a reel. A costume designer has a portfolio. What, then, is the calling card of the film composer? If you write music and dream of scoring a movie, put samples of your work on tape or CD, and use this demo as your audio business card. Try sending your tapes to below-the-line agents who represent composers. You can find this information in the *Hollywood Agents & Managers Directory*. You also might try sending your demo to producers of student films and independent features, who might be willing to give you a break if you'll score their movie for free or inexpensively.

POST-PRODUCTION SOUND

Re-recording sound mixer Andy Nelson was working on the final mix for director Ken Russell's film *Gothic* (1986). Throughout the thriller, it is implied that a strange creature lives in the attic. It is heard but never seen. The sound editors had come up with ideas for what this creature might sound like, but Russell was not satisfied with what he had heard so far. "They came in with all these weird tracks, and Russell would say, 'I don't know what I want, but I don't like this,'" recalls Nelson, an Oscar nominated re-recording mixer on such films as *Braveheart* (1995), *Evita* (1996), and *The Thin Red Line* (1998).

After lunch one day, the group returned to the dubbing stage to continue working on the mix. Nelson poured coffee into a Styrofoam cup. That gave Russell an idea. He had Nelson set up microphones. Russell put one in front of his face and another one near the floor. He got a piece of wood onto which he placed the cup. He then put some mints in his mouth. "We started running the tape," recounts Nelson. "All in one go, he mashed up these mints and squeezed this cup around on the wood, which made this awful scraping sound. I then put it through echo and delays. We played it in the room, and it sounded like this creature was just up there slurping and scraping."

After the sound editors had spent weeks bringing Russell all sorts of wonderful, bizarre sounds, the director created it himself with just his mouth and his hands. "It wasn't that his sound was any better or worse than what these guys had done," says Nelson, "but to him, this was the sound he was looking for."

DUBBING

Dubbing is a general term used to describe the process of sound mixing. In sound mixing, all of the different soundtracks of a film are combined into one master soundtrack. The main soundtracks are the dialogue track, the music track, and the sound-effects track. Because there are multiple takes of each scene and, therefore, multiple tracks, it is necessary to divide the mixing process into two parts. The first part is called the pre-dub; the second part is called the final mix.

THE PRE-DUB

During the pre-dub, all of the various soundtracks are organized and prepared. Generally, this is done by three sound editors: the dialogue editor, the FX (sound effects) editor, and the music editor. Each editor tends to work individually during the process.

One of the sound editors, usually the FX editor, is also the sound supervisor. He hires additional editors and oversees the pre-dub process. The music editor falls under the category of music rather than sound, and is hired by the composer and music supervisor rather than the sound editor. The sound supervisor usually allocates the work to the other sound editors, reel by reel. The supervisor works closely with the re-recording mixer, although he generally comes on to the film earlier than the mixer. He also has many discussions with the director to get a good idea about what the director is looking for.

THE DIALOGUE EDITOR

The dialogue editor handles the production sound that comes from the shoot. She takes the tape from the production sound mixer and lays it up against the picture. This editor cleans up clicks and pops wherever she can, and occasionally listens for alternate takes in which the sound may be cleaner. Those tracks are then sent to the re-recording mixer and spread out across a dozen different channels of the mixing console. The re-recording mixer makes sure that the tones of the voices are good, verifies that there's enough high frequency and low frequency, and checks the overall clarity of the voices. Keeping tracks separate allows the mixer more flexibility.

As the dialogue editor and re-recording mixer analyze the quality of each recorded line, they decide which lines need to be looped by re-recording them. "We'll talk about looping this line and have it on standby, to cover ourselves just in case," says Nelson. "Other times we say we should definitely loop this thing. I may get two or three choices of the same line, but I'll always have the other couple of takes ready for the director if they don't like our choice. But I've got to have selections made just to make my final mix go smoothly. I can't have the same line coming up all across different speakers. I've got to get it condensed into a manageable form. And then if they say, 'OK, everything's great, but I don't like that line. Do you have any alternates?' then I can replay my tracks and get a different take."

LOOPING Looping is done when an actor needs to be called back to re-record dialogue because the existing lines are unclear and unusable.

The system used to do this is called the automated dialogue replacement (ADR) system. The ADR supervisor deals with all issues relating to looping. This includes scheduling the actors on the looping stages, covering the lines that need to be looped, and having them cut, ready for the mix.

When the artist is in the studio reading the lines, the ADR supervisor watches to see if the words sync to the movement of the lips on screen. "They'll look at the screen and say, 'You've got to go again because it wasn't a very good sync,' " notes Nelson. "If it's very close to sync, but not quite, they might accept it because they know back in the editing room they can move stuff around and make it work."

THE FX EDITOR

Sound effects are natural or artificially created sounds other than speech or music. These sounds may include a gunshot, a door slamming, glass breaking, thunder rolling, and so forth. They may be recorded during filming, separately ("wild sound"), or borrowed or rented from a library of stock sound effects.

The FX editor helps prepare the dialogue track for dubbing and adds sound effects to the film. He coordinates the creation of sound effects or their retrieval from the library. He also helps solve problems on the dialogue track such as unwanted background noise, clipped words of dialogue, and differences in recording levels.

"On a film like *Forces of Nature* [1999], there are lovely moments where the romance has magical areas," explains Nelson. "That's the sort of thing that the [FX editor] and the director will have discussed, and therefore the tracks that they bring to mix will have the design element done to them. What we then do is bring our own sensibilities to it and hopefully enhance what they've already started to prepare. We can then take it to another level."

FOLEY A Foley artist creates certain sound effects heard on the effects track, particularly those sounds made by people rather than by machines or natural objects. These may include punches, footsteps on different surfaces with the appropriate footwear, and movement on fabrics. The process was named after Jack Foley, who created the very first sound effects for film. The Foley artist stands on the stage in front of a screen. Say the actor in a particular scene walks into an underground garage, is hit, and falls to the ground. As the artist watches the scene unfold onscreen, she creates the necessary sounds, matching her footsteps to the actor's, then throwing herself to the floor at the right moment.

The FX editor hires someone to procure the Foley stage and the Foley artists, or walkers. Sometimes the Foley walkers actually come with the stage; other times they're independent. A Foley supervisor cuts and prepares all these tracks under the supervision of the FX editor.

THE MUSIC EDITOR

One of the music editor's first tasks is to create a temporary score for the movie. This is done by digging through old soundtrack albums and editing things together seamlessly to create a temporary "score," often called a temp track, so that the studio can test the film. This is done because the final score is not yet ready when the studio begins its research screenings. Since the studio doesn't want to show the film to test audiences without any music, a temp score is created.

The music editor stays on after the composer is hired. She goes to the spotting session, takes notes, and basically becomes the composer's assistant. In the recording session, the music editor has an oracle, a time-saving device that enables them to count off what measure they're at and start recording midway through a cue. She is also present during the mixing of the music.

Essentially, the music editor takes the music (songs and score), edits it into the editing system, and syncs it to the film. She brings the editing system onto the final mix stage and operates it. "In the middle of a mix, the director might say, 'That cue is not working. Can you take the cue from the other scene and merge it together with that cue? Can you change the head of that cue, but fade it in with bells from cue number four?' The music editor sometimes has to do editing on demand," explains John Ottman.

THE FINAL MIX

The final mix is where all of the individual, cleaned-up, and edited tracks are combined. "On the first day of the final mix, we run the reel through, listening to all the work we've done in terms of the preparation," notes Andy Nelson. "At that point, we're really narrowing the choice down for the director in terms of 'Do you like this particular sound here, do you like the swoosh of this car, or would you prefer a different type of car sound?' It's really a big shaking-down process.

"When you put everything in, it tends to be a bit overwhelming for the first time. Generally, having listened to the whole reel once in a kind of cacophonous way, you then start to go through and say, What do we have to do within this scene? What I'll tend to do is switch the music off, and concentrate on getting the final touches on the dialogue. [The FX mixer] will be working the sound effects in and around the dialogue, making sure that they don't tread on top of the dialogue too much, but that they fill in the stereo aspect and make a great big feel in the room, because now we're creating an illusion. We have six channels of sound to play with, so we can now make this start to sound like a movie. Then I'll start to work in the music and listen to the sound of the orchestra."

Nowadays, with digital recording, it's much easier to conform the mix to a new edit because it's being recorded on a tapeless recording system. The editors literally can pull the hard drive out and plug it into an editing machine, and conform and cut the reel internally.

THE SUPERVISING RE-RECORDING MIXER, MUSIC MIXER, AND FX MIXER

Normally the supervising re-recording mixer is also the dialogue mixer. "I don't stand and supervise the mix and not do anything," explains Nelson, "I'm actively mixing all the time."

When leading the mixing process, this person needs to understand what the director wants in terms of ideas and style. The technique is learned over time. "I made plenty of mistakes when I was starting out, and you learn by your mistakes," Nelson says. "I can't say that there's really any technical aspect that you look for. I'm not a very technical person. I didn't have an engineering background. When I work on a console, I can make the console do what I want it to do, but when it breaks down I call the engineers, because I have no clue [how to fix it]. But that's good, because I can then relate to the director, and the director can relate to me. If the director saw me pull a screwdriver out and start repairing the console, they'd probably lose confidence in me, because they'd be thinking I'm more of an engineer than somebody who is in sympathy with them as a filmmaker. I think it's 50 percent bedside manner and 50 percent ability to do the job."

The music mixer is in charge of controlling, balancing, and blending the film score and songs into the final mix. The FX mixer mixes in any sound effects and Foley, including both mechanical and physical sound effects.

GETTING INTO THE MIX

The traditional route to a job in post-production sound is to start working in the back room where the actual recording equipment is located. Apart from those sitting at the mixing console, three other people work on the mix who are part of the crew. The recordist is in charge of making sure that what is being recorded is of the right quality, and that everything is loaded correctly in the film machines. The loader is in charge of running the projector and all the different soundtracks that need to be loaded to make the mix. Finally, the engineer is responsible for operating and monitoring all the equipment.

"Generally teams form and stay together," Nelson says. "If you want to get into mixing, you have to get on to a crew on a mixing stage." One possibility is to apply to the sound transfer department at one of the major studios. Also, some sound houses, such as Todd AO, have their own training programs. Nelson's FX mixer started that way. "It's generally on a first-come basis, so the longer you've been with the company and the more potential you have, the more chance you'll have of going through that program," explains Nelson. "[My FX mixer] worked in the back room at Todd AO as a loader, then became a recordist, then was given the opportunity at Todd AO to go on to that program, and she's survived it and become a great mixer."

14

EFFECTS

*Being able to help a director tell his story without
the images getting in the way and overpowering
the story is what I like to do.*

MICHEAL McALISTER, visual-effects supervisor

SNOW PROBLEM

When Joel and Ethan Coen made *The Hudsucker Proxy* (1994), they
envisioned a sequence in which Tim Robbins's character jumps out of a
building and falls fifty floors to the ground—during a snowstorm.
Micheal McAlister, visual-effects supervisor on such effects-driven block-
busters as *Indiana Jones and the Last Crusade* (1989), *Demolition Man*
(1993), and *Waterworld* (1995), knew he could accomplish most everything in the shot because they were all cinematic tricks he had done previously. However, he had no idea how he was going to engineer the
snowstorm.

"I didn't know how to have a very interactive snow effect with this
falling body," recalls McAlister. "I jokingly kept trying to convince them
to write it out of the movie."

Although McAlister was an expert in his field, this was still in the
early days of using computers to create certain effects. After attempting

a variety of tried and true methods of making snow, the ultimate solution proved to be particle system animation created on a computer, combined with traditional ways of making movie snow using mashed-potato flakes dropped through the air. You can see the realistic results for yourself when you screen *The Hudsucker Proxy*.

"In my role as a visual-effects supervisor, I tend to take more of a directorial approach to the work rather than feeling the need to know everything technical," explains McAlister. "It becomes overwhelming at a certain point to stay current on everything. So I know the people to call when there's something specific about an effect that I don't know. The effects industry is filled with 'computer rocket scientists' who know so much more about the ins and outs of the technology than I do; however, in most cases they don't know much about filmmaking. As the supervisor, the most important thing to know is filmmaking, because you can [always] call on the rocket scientists to fill in the blanks."

Special effects are artificially devised and used to create a particular illusion in a movie. Physical, or mechanical, effects take place on the set during the shoot and include explosions and bullet hits (when someone is shot). Visual, or photographic, effects are achieved through manipulation

---

Types of Effects

Computer generated imagery (CGI): Any image created with the help of a computer.

Digital video effects: Video effects including zooms, reductions, flips, tumbles, page turns, morphing, and so forth, are produced by manipulating images that are stored in binary form on a computer.

Makeup effects: A transformation of a human face into another character using prosthetic and traditional makeup techniques.

Mechanical effects: Special effects performed during principal photography without the use of photographic tricks. For example, robotics, rock slides, collapsing walls, explosions, bullet hits, flood effects, rain, and snow are examples of mechanical effects.

Optical effects: Visual effects traditionally achieved with the help of an optical printer. These effects generally involve the combination of two or more images onto one piece of film. Freeze frames, fades, dissolves, wipes, and optical composites are examples.

Pyrotechnic effects: The use of smoke, fire, or explosives to achieve a desired effect.

of the film image and generally are done during post-production. These include an inanimate object that moves and a person flying through the air, like Superman. Obviously, physical and visual effects are made to work in harmony with each other.

THE VISUAL-EFFECTS SUPERVISOR

The visual-effects supervisor is responsible for working with a film's key creative team to determine what special images are needed to help tell the story onscreen. Once a certain sequence, or group of images, is decided on, it is the supervisor's job to make those images appear effectively in the final product. That involves figuring out how to accomplish it technically, getting help from other experts, hands-on directing the process of making the effect, and creatively supervising the effects on behalf of the director.

It does not matter how big a budget a film has; all films are low budget when it comes to visual effects. "I've never had more money than I needed, even on the biggest movies," McAlister admits. "So you have to make decisions at some point as to where you're going to spend the money and where you're going to save the money. The first thing that you do is figure out where the money needs to go in order to best make a great movie."

Next, the visual-effects supervisor separates the required effects into broad categories. Say the film takes place in outer space, and a lot of space shuttles are needed. There are two very viable approaches one can take. In the past, everything was clearly a physical model shot against a blue screen. A blue screen is, literally, a blue backdrop that when filmed upon can be digitally replaced by alternative background footage. These days that option still exists, or a computer model can be made. The costs of building the different types of models are similar. The disadvantages of a physical model are that it has to be physically lit and shot, and once shooting is finished, the set must be struck and the model put away, probably never to be used again. With a computer-generated model, one can create new angles and new shots with little effort or expense. It also can be stored easily for future use or reference.

The process for many effects begins in pre-production, such as visualizing creatures or models that are going to be computer generated. The visual-effects team is generally in place and working prior to principal photography and, in many cases, the research done in advance of pre-production actually contributes to the feasibility of the script itself. For instance, on *Jurassic Park* (1993), Industrial Light & Magic (ILM), under Dennis Muren's guidance, worked for two years before the picture was ever greenlighted simply to determine how far they could go with the available computer technology in making dinosaurs.

Once the plan is in place, everything else takes a secondary role to executing correctly the principal photography in the movie. In some cases, the visual-effects supervisor knows exactly what the shot should be, and he controls the scene in such a way that it will ultimately yield the kinds of effects on set that will tie into the visual effects. For instance, if there are to be lightning bolts striking, or explosions that will be added to a sequence after filming is completed, the visual-effects supervisor must make sure that the set is "blasted" with the appropriate interactive lighting to reflect such lightning bolts rather than manufacture that interactive lighting after the fact, which never looks as good. The gaffers, the lighting people, and the camera operators can all help determine how much interactive lighting will be needed, the direction and source of the interactive lighting, and its duration. When the effect is ultimately put into the film, it's tied into the overall shot, not just tacked on.

The visual-effects supervisor must pay attention to the performance of every single person who is on frame during a visual-effects shot. "My job on the set is to allow the director to do whatever he needs to do creatively with his actors to get the performance from them that he wants, because ultimately none of the visual effects matter if you don't actually believe the human beings in the movie," says McAlister. They all must be reacting properly to the effect that eventually will be onscreen. Unfortunately, very few of the actors have an opportunity to see the effect that will be sharing the screen and must rely on their imagination. That is one of the principal jobs of the effects supervisor—to know full well what the final image is going to look like and communicate this to the actors and crew. The director doesn't have the time to do this, nor does he necessarily have the effects supervisor's expertise.

Most of the work for visual effects occurs during post-production. Like filmmaking itself, the entire process is actually three-tiered. During pre-production, the visual-effects supervisor works with the production

designer, physical effects coordinator, and cinematographer to decide
(1) what can be done in camera and on the set, (2) what has to be
accomplished after the fact, and (3) what can be done partially on set
but must be finished after the fact. All digital effects and any other alterations to the filmed image itself must be created during post-production.

OTHER VISUAL-EFFECTS CREW

The visual-effects producer and supervisor are the counterparts to the
film's producer and director. While the effects supervisor handles all
things creative, the visual-effects producer handles all things business oriented. Of course, there is a great deal of overlap and a lot of consulta-
tion and cooperation between these two positions. Both are considered
key positions in a visual-effects department.

The visual-effects art director works closely with the production's art
department in designing the effects. She generally is an art director with
a lot of experience in visual effects, especially computer-generated
effects. This person must possess good problem-solving abilities and constantly bring fresh ideas to each situation. The job involves determining
what can be built as a physical set versus what the visual-effects department can create as a miniature, a matte painting, or a digital matte painting on computer.

The visual-effects editor knows the inner workings of visual effects
and can therefore solve problems pertaining to specific effects. (This is an
ability most editors and assistant editors do not have.) This person is not
involved in editing the movie, but rather takes the visual-effects
sequences and constantly updates them into a Lightworks or Avid computer system. He takes the count information from the editor of the
movie and supplies the editor with all of the essential information, such
as how long a shot is and where it falls in a particular sequence.

Every decision that the effects supervisor makes inevitably ends up
affecting a sequence in the movie, and therefore he must be kept
informed of what is happening on the movie in the minds of both the
director while shooting and the editor while cutting. The visual-effects
editor is responsible for the transference of cut information between the
effects supervisor and the editor.

In the visual-effect arena, there are people who are model builders and
companies that specialize in making models. "One of the great surprises of

Extra-Special Effects

"I worked on *E.T. The Extra-Terrestrial* [1982] and helped make the bikes fly," recalls Micheal McAlister of one of his most fulfilling moments in visual effects."At that particular time, *E.T.* was one of two Steven Spielberg movies within ILM. The other one was *Poltergeist* [1982].

"*Poltergeist* was big and loud by comparison and grand in the scale of visual effects, and was getting all the attention from within and without the company. Those of us who were working on *E.T.* were a handful of people by comparison. We were sort of quiet and tucked away and doing our thing, knowing that we were working on a really cute little movie, which at that time was called *A Boy's Life*. As the productions of these two movies progressed, we began to slowly get a sense that someone was really on to something with *E.T.*

"*Poltergeist* by comparison was another really good visual-effects movie, but *E.T.* was going to be something that could conceivably affect people in a whole different way. It wasn't until the movie came out and we all saw it that we realized, for the first time, what a special movie we had been contributing to. And I don't think that anybody, including Spielberg, had the wildest imaginings that *E.T.* would affect as many people as it did."

my adulthood was that people actually got paid for doing the things that we wanted to do for fun when we were kids," says McAlister. "That was one of my greatest delights when I first got involved in visual effects, the realization I was actually going to get paid for doing some of this stuff."

The special-effects coordinator is responsible for organizing and overseeing all of the physical effects on the set. These can range from the simplest of tricks, such as a fire in a fireplace, to very complicated storm sequences.

15

EVERYTHING ELSE

While producing my low budget short film, I found myself juggling many different jobs. Not only was I the producer, but I was also the casting director, location manager, post-production supervisor, and even a gofer from time to time. It gave me a whole new respect for each department's responsibilities and their distinct significance to the moviemaking process.

YVETTE TAYLOR, vice president of production,
All Girl Productions

If you have read through this book and considered all of the various production jobs in the Hollywood film industry, and you still have not found your niche, that's OK. There are plenty more positions out there that might be right up your alley. This chapter focuses on several of the remaining popular movie business opportunities. Each one is integral to a motion picture's success.

CASTING

When casting director Amy McIntyre Britt was a junior at American University studying international public relations, she had read an article on casting directors Jane Jenkins and Janet Hirschenson in *People* magazine. Britt had always been a tremendous fan of movies and a huge enthusiast of actors. When she read the piece, she thought, *How fun—it's not really a job*. It didn't enter her mind again until her senior year in college. She had started interviewing for positions and really was not excited about any of the prospects. "I started thinking that people go to Europe for a year or do whatever they want after graduating from college," she recalls. "I decided to go to L.A., where I don't know anybody in the industry and I really don't know anything about casting, but why not just give it a shot?"

Britt relocated to the West Coast. Once settled, she literally picked up the Yellow Pages, looked up the Casting Company—where Jenkins and Hirschenson are partners—and phoned them. She connected on the phone with Michael Hirschenson, the firm's head of business affairs, and set up an interview with him. "He didn't have any positions open, but he said he'd give me a call when they did. I thought I would never hear from these people again." Three months later, however, she landed a job at the company.

Starting as a receptionist, Britt quickly learned the names of the important players in the casting business, mostly actors, talent agents, and directors. She proved to be a motivated employee and was quickly promoted. Within a year of moving to Los Angeles, Britt was working as a casting assistant on her first movie, *Little Giants* (1994). "I remember going over to Amblin [Entertainment] one day and sitting next to Steven Spielberg on his terrace reading [i.e., auditioning] all these kids. It was a surreal experience. You grow up, and at ten years old you watched *E.T.* in the theater ten times and bawled every time. Now I'm sitting there and I kind of turn my head and realize, 'Wow, he's practically an idol, and he's sitting right next to me, and I'm working with him.' It's pretty humbling."

THE CASTING DIRECTOR

The casting director is responsible for selecting actors to play the various roles in a movie. If you are a huge fan of actors and you always seem to know everybody's name when you see a film, then casting just might be the field for you.

Britt, a partner in CFB Casting, says, "You know you have a knack for it when you watch a movie and you pick somebody out that has one line and you say, That guy has talent. Then, five years later, he's a star. It happens all the time. Look at Hank Azaria in *Pretty Woman* [1990]. One line."

The casting director's main relationship on a film is with the director. Once the director is hired onto a project, the casting director is brought in.

On independent productions, the casting director is usually brought into the fold from inception. This is because they are involved in packaging the movie with a star so that the project can get proper financing. Without monetary backing, there is no production, so the casting director's role is essential.

On a studio film, one or more pieces of star talent are usually already attached. It is the casting director's job to cast every other speaking role in the movie, from the major parts all the way down to the minor parts that consist of one line of dialogue.

For the major roles, the casting director starts by putting together a series of lists. Each consists of the name of the character and the names of all the available actors who could play the part. With the input of the director and producer, this list is put in a preferential order.

Next, the casting director checks on the availability of these actors. This is done simply by confirming the actors' status with their agents or managers. See chapter 6 to review how to find out who an actor's agent is.

If the actors being considered are major stars, many of them won't audition. In fact, many of these actors won't even look at a script unless a monetary offer is made. If the director wants to offer a big role to an actor, the two usually will meet before either side commits to working together. Assuming the conference goes well, the offer becomes official and the casting director negotiates the client's fees and perks with the agent.

If the actors are not huge stars, they generally will come in for a reading. Sometimes major actors will read for a role if the character is different from anything else they've ever played. A reading is an audition that is videotaped. In addition to the casting director, the director and producer also may be present at the reading. Sometimes the project's star will be on hand so that the actors can be taped reading together to observe the chemistry, or lack thereof, between them.

Not all auditions are taped. For the smaller parts that will be played by lesser known actors, casting directors hold general auditions. Numbers of candidates will read sides (i.e., a few pages from the script) for the casting director. The best of these will be called back and their next audition may be put on tape.

BREAKDOWNS The standard way to find actors for a movie is by listing the production with Breakdown Services. This company distributes daily breakdowns (listing all the films that are currently casting) to agents and managers throughout Hollywood. They include a description of the film, the roles being cast, and the people involved with the upcoming production. Talent agents then submit to the casting director, in the form of a head shot and résumé, those clients who they feel are right for each part. The term *breakdown* derives from the process of breaking down a script. (See page 191 for a sample breakdown.)

GETTING STARTED Breakdown Services also publishes the best available book of casting directors in Hollywood. If you want to find work in the casting industry, I suggest picking up a copy of their directory and sending résumés to each casting director listed.

The Casting Society of America (CSA) also can be a helpful resource for someone just starting out. CSA is a professional organization of casting directors working in the entertainment industry that lobbies for the work needs of casting directors. The next time you see a movie, pay close attention to the casting director's credit. Many have the initials CSA after their name.

This organization keeps résumés on file for people who want to find work as a casting assistant. Periodically, casting directors call the CSA when they need to hire an assistant or require an intern. Many of today's successful casting directors got their start in this field simply by submitting a résumé to the CSA.

EXTRAS CASTING While there are casting directors who work specifically with extras, most of the extras casting on the production of a film is handled by the assistant directors (see chapter 8). Extras casting directors usually are the heads of agencies whose main function is to recruit and catalog extras for their files. When an assistant director calls looking for extras, the extras casting director pulls pictures from their files and sends them to the assistant directors. If the pictures are approved, the extras casting director calls up the extras and gives them their assignment. No talent agents are involved, as extras are not represented by an agent. The production pays the extras casting company, who then pays the extras for their work.

LOCATIONS

In today's Hollywood, most films are shot away from the studio, on location. In fact, more and more movie production is leaving Los Angeles

(File 0228f07-lk) L
TOUCHSTONE PICTURES
"MR. WRONG"
FEATURE FILM
DRAFT: 3/2/95

Exec. Producer: David Hoberman
Producer: Marty Katz
Director: Nick Castle
Writers: Chris Matheson/Kerry Ehrin/Craig Munson
Casting Director: Jane Jenkins/Janet Hirschenson
Casting Assistant: Amy McIntyre
Start Date: May, 1995
Location: L.A. & San Diego

WRITTEN SUBMISSIONS TO: THE CASTING COMPANY
7461 BEVERLY BLVD.
PENTHOUSE
L.A., CA 90036

MARTHA: CAST—ELLEN DEGENERES
WHITMAN: CAST—BILL PULLMAN

WALTER: The Production Assistant for "It's Morning," the morning local San Diego show Martha produces; he's a cute guy of about 25–28, with long hair, a kind face, and smart eyes. He and Martha are having a clandestine affair, and though he's obviously head over heels for her, he realizes that she's lukewarm about him. Funny, endearing and fairly sensitive, he has dreams about his future and he valiantly tells Martha that he won't be in this job for long. He is heartbroken but resigned to her relationship with Whitman, and like everyone else, believes that she's madly in love despite her protests to the contrary. However, when Walter finally realizes that Martha's serious about getting un-entangled with Whitman, he quickly leaps into action—and proves to be the hero she's been waiting for...LEAD [Copyright 1994, Breakdown Services, Ltd.]

MRS. CRAWFORD: Whitman's wealthy mother; she's in her 70s and wizened, but with eyes that are still keen and intelligent. She's thrilled to meet Martha, feels she's good breeding material ("you have birthing hips and an adequate bosom") and proves to be an odd mixture of the profane and the stately. A relentless, insensitive woman, she encourages her son in his overbearing, dogged, blindly insane pursuit of his beloved, even though the beloved has no interest in—even an active hatred—of him. She accompanies Whitman when he kidnaps Martha to take her to their nuptials in Mexico, and never lets her out of her sight for an instant...LEAD [Copyright 1994, Breakdown Services, Ltd.]

INGA: A lean, wiry, wild-eyed woman of 30, almost striking looking; she's Whitman's former girlfriend and is insanely jealous of Martha, to the point of doing her physical harm—like slapping her, slashing her sofa, and putting gum in her hair. Foul-mouthed, intense, and obviously nuts, she pursues Martha with her obliging boyfriend, Bob, who assists Inga in her crazy schemes to keep Martha away from Whitman. When her bizarre plan to finish Martha off is thwarted by Whitman, she eventually shows up at Whitman and Martha's wedding—where she accidentally shoots Whitman instead... LEAD [Copyright 1994, Breakdown Services, Ltd.]

and traveling around the world in search of exciting, fresh backdrops. As a result, the role of the location manager has become increasingly crucial to the filmmaking process.

THE LOCATION MANAGER

The location manager or location scout is one of the first people hired on a movie. She reads the script to gather information about where each scene takes place. After considering budgetary restrictions, she then consults with everyone from the studio executive and director to the producer and production designer to gain a better sense of the requirements for each location.

Mark Indig began his career as a location scout on *Body Heat* (1981) and *The Big Chill* (1983). "Ideally, you talk to the director and try to get inside his head, because if you have the same script and two different directors, 'Exterior Suburban House' would mean a clapboard Victorian to one guy and a split-level seventies house to another guy."

Once the location manager has a good idea of what is needed, she grabs her camera and goes in search of locations that match the script. "They have to be locations that are controllable and affordable," advises Indig. If the film is not going to be shot locally, the location manager is part of the decision-making process as to where the film will be made.

"It's a process of narrowing down," says Indig. "You contact a number of film commissions and broadcast what you're looking for. They start sending you things from their files to get you focused. Maybe you contact twenty film commissions, and ten of them give you something that you like, and the director only likes five of them. Then you go scout five different states. You bring back the pictures, and now maybe it's narrowed down to two or three."

When scouting locations, the location manager drives around, finds a house she thinks may work, and knocks on the door. "If you're out of town, it's probably a house or a business that's never had filming before," explains Indig, "You try and explain why you're there, why they shouldn't call the police, why they shouldn't sic their dog on you, and why they should let you go into their unmade bedroom and take pictures of it."

The director examines the photos of the suggested location. If he likes what he sees, he'll look at the sites in person. If the director approves, a deal is negotiated with the home or business owner for use of that locale.

The Perils of Scouting

Mark Indig was scouting a Broadway theater in New York City for *The Fan* (1981). They needed a real Broadway theater. If you shoot at a legitimate Broadway house, however, the cost is a small fortune, and the stage union matches you person for person for your union film crew. As a result, the operation becomes cost prohibitive.

Indig did a lot of research. "There were hundreds of old vaudeville theaters that were built in the New York area that were painted over and turned into movie theaters. One of them had been turned into a pornographic movie theater. They had taken the proscenium and painted it all white. It was unrecognizable, but the bones were there."

Indig explained his task to the theater manager and asked if he could take photographs. The manager told him to go right ahead. However, the show wasn't yet over, and there was only one minute between performances, clearly not enough time to take the necessary pictures. If that wasn't bad enough, the shows were continuous, twenty-four hours a day.

"You have to understand, it's a dark theater," Indig explains. "I have to use a flash. There's people sitting there. They're going to get pretty upset." The manager said not to worry, just go on in.

Indig went into the auditorium. "There's a movie running. I stand up on the stage. There's an act of fellatio going on [i.e., being projected] on my shirt. I take my camera, aim it toward the audience, take one flash picture, and the guy in the front row jumps up with a knife."

Indig sprinted out the side door of the theater and never looked back.

Finding the location is just the beginning. After a location has been approved, the location managers deal with everything from negotiations and contracts, to permits, police, fire, parking, and bathrooms for the extras, among other things. And that's for *each* location. Generally about eighty locations per film are used.

"It's become so complex," says Indig, referring to the permit process and the contracts. "It's a reflection of our litigious society." As a result, a production's location department is much bigger than it used to be. There's a real need for assistants to do legwork and secure permissions. Hence, it's a good form of entrée into the business.

"It's very rare for a big studio film to have less than three or four people in the department," says Indig. "For a film like *Armageddon* [1998] that travels from South Dakota to Washington [D.C.] to L.A. to who knows where, you can have three or four location managers and a handful of assistants. Then there are the films where there's chaos—the director doesn't make up his mind and they're rewriting all the time. You literally can have twenty people working on the same movie."

The job of the location department is not over until the location wraps. They are responsible for restoration, cleanup, and generally keeping ordinary people affected by the shoot happy. "If it's a house, you can be impacting blocks and blocks of neighbors with the trucks and the noise. Everybody has to be happy," Indig emphasizes. "You have cleaning crews on standby. You make payments to make people happy—and they're justified a lot of the time. Crews do damage. If you're good, you go and talk to people. You make the time. You don't just abandon."

In the thirteen Western states (California included), location managers must be part of the Teamsters union. In New York, they're part of the Directors Guild of America. In the remaining states, they don't have to be union—for now. The studios will hire only unionized location managers, who, in turn, if necessary, will hire a local location manager at the site of the shoot. So until you become a union member, you may be working on smaller films and commercials.

THE SCRIPT SUPERVISOR

Remember the moment in *Pretty Woman* (1990) where Julia Roberts's character picks up a croissant, and then in the very next cut she's forking a pancake into her mouth? Or how about the scene in *Twister* (1996), in which the windshield of the hero's (Bill Paxton) red pickup truck is smashed by a grain combine, but is in one piece moments later when he drives through an overturned house? And in *Good Will Hunting* (1997), while Stellan Skarsgård's onscreen professor is lecturing to his students, did you notice the chalkboard keeps changing position between takes?

The script supervisor's job is to try and prevent, while in production, all those mistakes that could end up on the screen. "To accomplish that, your job is somewhat masochistic in that you have to bring up things that people don't want to hear," explains Karon May, a script supervisor on *A Perfect World* (1993), *Fear and Loathing in Las Vegas* (1998), and *Cruel Intentions* (1999). "You have to know when to be diplomatic and how to bring things up.

"It's not your movie. The director can do it however he wants. But if the wineglass is in the left hand on one printed take, and you're doing coverage and the wineglass is now in the right hand, it's your job to bring it up so that everybody is aware [of the problem]. If they don't want to change it, that's fine, but cutting between those is going to be difficult."

The position of script supervisor is extremely demanding. For starters, the script supervisor is the smallest department on a film—just one person. In addition, she is working right alongside the director and his key people. Also, the script supervisor has so many responsibilities that the job does not warrant a lot of downtime.

The script supervisor has two main functions during pre-production. The first thing is to break down the script for matching purposes. "I call mine my cheat sheet," explains May. "It's a little synopsis, in chronological order, of the movie. If the dog dies in scene fourteen, and for some reason we're shooting scene sixteen and somebody says, 'Is the dog in this scene?' it's a quick reference: 'No, because he died in scene fourteen.'"

The breakdowns also can be helpful to the actors. If it's a complicated narrative, there may be many questions about who is where, and the script supervisor's breakdown is used as a quick reference: "Where was I immediately before this? Where am I going to be right afterward?"

Sometimes several different breakdowns are needed for the same movie. It depends on how complicated the story is. Generally, there will always be a day/night breakdown to get an accurate count of the number of days a movie spans. Other breakdowns may vary depending on subject matter. When May worked on *Rough Riders* (1997), a TNT miniseries directed by John Milius, the subject was war. She did an entire breakdown with regard to rank, and another with regard to injury.

The script supervisor's other prime responsibility during pre-production is pre-timing the script. She literally acts out the script and assesses how long the finished movie is going to be in its final form. It is obviously just an estimate, but it is more accurate if the script supervisor has worked with the director and the actors before.

Many other timing issues arise during production. A script supervisor clocks the rehearsals when scenes are being blocked. That way, she knows exactly how long a rehearsed scene runs. She also keeps track of the time from the call of 'Action' to the direction 'Cut,' to record the actual time for the length of the shot.

It's also necessary for the supervisor to estimate the running time during filming. If someone wants to know how the day's shoot is progressing, the script supervisor gives an answer based on how many pages have already been shot and what the estimated running time is. The supervisor's most important tool is, naturally, a reliable stopwatch.

DID SHE SAY WHAT I THINK SHE SAID?

Another duty of the script supervisor is to verify dialogue during shooting, making sure the correct words are spoken. Notes are made of any deviation in scripted dialogue. Some filmmakers are much more particular about exact wordage being said than are others. If it's a picture in which the words are extremely important, another person whose only job is to watch the dialogue may be brought in, because it's quite difficult for a supervisor to do this and the rest of the job simultaneously.

The dialogue also must be matched with the oncamera movements. If, on various takes, an actor sits down or stands up on a different line, or turns to look over his left rather than his right shoulder, all sorts of problems may occur. It's a very common cutting point to do so when the actor is making that turn. If the actor switches directions in the middle of a turn, the editor will be unable to cut the scene together properly.

The most important aspect of script supervising is to preserve continuity, making the story line match from one scene to the next, whether it's matching the words that are said, the temperament, or the action. "If you have an actor who whispers his lines when he's off camera, but when he's on camera he's screaming, then the other actor's performance isn't going to be the same when you cut them together," explains May. "You bring that up, but usually the director is already aware of it. He might say, 'But I loved that performance. It was the best one.' " In a case like this, the script supervisor would make a notation to the editor that they're aware that the two parts don't match, but the director likes the performance in this take, and the editor should cut it as best as possible.

TAKE NOTE

With so many elements to keep track of, it's important for the script supervisor to maintain a detailed set of notes. "There are forms that you use for your daily log, so if they're syncing up dailies, they know what your print takes were," says May. A print take is the shot footage that you actually want developed. "Then there are forms in the actual script itself. You have a lined script. You have coverage lines on the actual pages of your script which show each shot, where it started, where it ended, who was on camera, who was off camera. Then, facing that is a set of notes that give the specifics about the shot: what the take was, whether it was good or bad, what camera roll it was on, what film roll it was on, how long it was, and then a description of the shot. And, more importantly, if there were any problems in that shot. Things you want the editor to know. 'In take four, we liked it but he forgot to take off his hat, so the part after that wouldn't be any good.' " Every night, that day's notes are typed up and sent to the editor.

Finally, the script supervisor must keep a list of pickup shots and a wild soundtrack [scripted sounds or dialogue not recorded] that are still needed. The shot might be an insert of a computer monitor that the characters are looking at, or a close-up of an actor that can be filmed later in the schedule. "If there are any little bits and pieces left as you're going along at the end of the movie, you've got the list to make sure that nothing gets left out," May says.

BEING A SCRIPT SUPERVISOR

"I love my work, but it's a job that I think requires some real life experience first," says May. Being savvy about the business world gives one a practical advantage.

For aspiring script supervisors, there are quite a few classes you can take. Some are taught by individuals and others are in a more traditional classroom setting. Some script supervisors will take on individuals to mentor on a one-on-one basis.

The script supervisor is a union position. To join the union, one must provide proof of 100 days as a script supervisor on non-union work within the immediately preceding two years, or be tapped in on a project that goes union.

THE UNIT PUBLICIST

Publicity is the process of selling a person, place, or thing to the news media. It is an integral component of both the moviemaking and marketing experiences. What most people do not realize is that the publicity machine starts up on the set as the film is being shot. In fact, sometimes it begins the minute a script is sold.

In the film business, the actual movie is the product that is being sold. Actors and filmmakers also are being sold, which is the job of the personal publicist (see chapter 17). The unit publicist is the person responsible for all publicity while the film is being made.

"Most films that don't have publicity while they're filming usually regret it once they wrap because the publicist on the set of the film coordinates the electronic press kit [EPK], as well as shooting the B-roll," explains publicist Jimmy Dobson. An EPK is a series of interviews with the actors and filmmakers that is put together during principal photography. That way, when the film is released, if the actors aren't available to do publicity (perhaps because they are out of the country shooting another movie), the interviews from the EPK can be used on TV shows like *Entertainment Tonight* and *Access Hollywood*. The B-roll is a look at what's happening behind-the-scenes on the film. Essentially it's footage of the movie being made. This is also highly in demand by entertainment newsmagazines on television.

THE STILL PHOTOGRAPHER

The job of the still photographer is to take photos, or production stills, that the unit publicist can use to promote the production in the media. These photos generally are used in the press kits that are put together by the studio publicity department.

Even though the still photographer's primary function is that of publicity, this person is actually part of the International Photographers Guild, the same as the director of photography. Since he is technically the only person on the set allowed to take photographs, he has several secondary functions. These include taking detailed documentation of the sets in the event that they may need to be rebuilt at a later date, making historical documentation of the production such as the crew at work, recording famous guests who visit the set, and shooting photos for inclusion as props in the film, such as a family photo on the mantelpiece in a character's home. While most of the departments that monitor continuity take their own Polaroids to assist them in this task, this too is technically the job of the still photographer. As long as a still photographer is employed on a set, however, the union does not bother the other departments about who is taking the photos.

Amateur photographers wanting to break into motion picture still photography should first develop a portfolio of their work. The next step is to start working on non-union films. Beginning in any entry-level camera position, such as a camera loader, also can provide an opportunity to move into stills.

CRAFT SERVICES

The history of craft services goes back to the beginning of the film business. Like laborers, this position originally serviced all of the crafts of the basic bargaining agreement. They did everything from moving editorial equipment and makeup tables, to sweeping all the stages and taking care of a variety of other service-related work.

While some of the service tasks have remained, today the main focus of the craft services department is providing food between meals for the crews. Some craft services workers may be expert chefs, but it's not a requirement or a necessity. "I'm pretty good on a telephone," says craft services worker Jim Wills, who orders snacks from vendors who deliver to location, as well as entire meals when no caterer is budgeted for the film.

Working in craft services is an excellent opportunity for someone with limited education and/or specialty skills. "It's a chance to make a decent living," notes Wills. "We have members [in the local] that are doing well into six figures."

PART FOUR

EXECUTIVES

16

THE STUDIO SYSTEM

*I don't think anybody's job on a movie is done
until well after the film is released because if it's a
movie you really care about, you want to make
sure that the movie gets a good release, that your
marketing people are as much in love with the
movie as you are, that you deal with the studio in
such a way that the studio gets what they want,
and that the filmmakers are happy with the way
you're releasing the movie.*

JONATHAN KING, president of production,
Laurence Mark Productions

When I moved to Los Angeles, I was always fascinated by
what lay beyond the studio gates. I longed to walk on to a lot and wit-
ness the magic of filmmaking, but I had no way to gain entry. I quickly
learned that if I acted like I knew what I was doing and where I was
going, I could sneak on to a studio lot without too many complications.

There is a Hollywood legend about how Steven Spielberg got his
start. Allegedly, the future director was a guest on the Universal Studios
Tour when he jumped off the tram and started wandering around the
backlot. He found an empty office and literally set up shop. On his way
out that first night, he made a point of waving to the security guard so
that the next day, when he returned, the guard would recognize him and
let him on to the facility.

It didn't quite happen that way for me, but I did spend one summer
as a Universal Studios tour guide. (Repeat after me: "Part the waters.")
I also have fond memories of sneaking on to the Sony lot and having

lunch at the executive commissary, getting lost amid the New York street sets at Warner Bros., and finally, legitimately, coming to work at the Walt Disney Studios for more than four years. What has always struck me about all the studios is the relaxed atmosphere that exists, one that is reminiscent of a college campus. It's a vibe that makes you want to go to work every day!

Today I'm always going to the different studios for meetings. It's quite a change to drive up and have my name waiting at the security gate. When I attend these conferences, it's usually to pitch a project to one of the creative executives in hopes that they'll like it enough to buy it and put the project into development.

This chapter discusses the roles of various studio executives. First, it is essential to have a basic understanding of how a studio operates. The best way to understand this is by examining the basic structure of a major motion picture studio. Many of the mini-majors (Miramax, Good Machine, etc.) and several of the larger production companies (Mandalay, New Regency, etc.) operate with a similar, yet somewhat smaller, corporate structure.

SWIMMING WITH SHARKS

In today's world of mergers, takeovers, and entertainment conglomerates, it is important to note that most of the major movie studios are just a small part of much larger business organizations. The chief executive officer, at the very top of the corporate ladder, usually reports to a board of directors or a group of stockholders and is held accountable for the success or failure of each of the company's divisions. This includes the motion picture division. Although it's not something you generally think about while enjoying the newest film release at the local multiplex, Hollywood is very much a bottom-line business. Thus, profitability affects all moviemaking decisions, even creative ones. It does not matter that a script is great or that the project's director just won an Oscar. Unless a film will see a return on investment, the studios will not want to make it.

Of course, that is the high and dry point of view. If you have a great script, an Oscar-winning director, an A-list actor, or any other magical pieces of the movie puzzle, odds are that the film will make money. But what if a movie in production is budgeted at $20 million and goes over the planned cost? Who is accountable for this overage? If the project goes over budget but ultimately makes a profit, does the end justify the means?

Case Study: *Titanic* (1997)

It's no secret that *Titanic* is the most expensive movie made to date. James Cameron's epic was initially budgeted at around $120 million. Cameron was the director of such megasuccessful entries as *Aliens* (1986) and *Terminator 2: Judgment Day* (1991). Thus, *Titanic* was a divergence from the science fiction adventure movies in which he excelled. To make matters more complicated, this project was a period drama (the least commercial type of film) and featured no major stars at the time.

Twentieth Century-Fox acted responsibly by bringing Paramount Pictures in as a partner to absorb some of the huge financial risk. At the time, the deal they struck made a lot of sense. Paramount would provide half of the production budget and distribute the film domestically. Fox would put up the other half of the money and control foreign distribution. What ultimately hurt Fox in the long run was a clause in the contract with Paramount stipulating that Paramount would cap their spending at $60 million. Any overages would be absorbed by Fox.

It is not uncommon for films to go over budget. In fact, on special-effects movies and projects where new technology is being created for the specific purpose of the picture at hand, it is difficult to accurately assess a price tag on something that does not yet exist. However, nobody ever imagined that *Titanic* would go as far over budget as it did. Industry analysts suggest the production cost in excess of $200 million by the time it was finished.

Paramount seemed to have made one of the smartest deals in town. They had no further financial obligation after their $60 million investment, so Twentieth Century-Fox was responsible for the $80 million plus in overages. News Corp., the parent company that owns Twentieth Century-Fox, surely was not thrilled by the situation.

As we all know, *Titanic* went on to become the highest grossing movie of all time, grossing close to $2 billion. In addition, it practically swept the Oscar race in every category, including Best Picture and Best Director. The money spent on overages, as extraordinary as it was, was ultimately recouped. The movie that was doomed to sink before it set sail became the most profitable motion picture ever made.

But does that make going over budget OK?

A few years before *Titanic*, another film faced a similar situation by going way over its budget. The final results were far different. This movie was neither a financial nor critical success. That movie was *Waterworld* (1995).

Hollywood is a risky business. Without risk, however, there is no reward. No one sets out to lose money on a project, but sometimes it is not easy to accurately predict how a movie will do in actual release. Some films that are made for very little money go on to greater success than ever anticipated. Take, for instance, *The Full Monty* (1997) or *Good Will Hunting* (1997). In contrast, other films that seem to have all the right elements just do not perform well at the box office. Consider *Last Action Hero* (1993) or *Fathers' Day* (1997).

The easiest way to understand a studio's corporate structure is to look at it visually. The organizational chart below outlines the hierarchy of a studio's motion picture division.

In today's business world of conglomerates, motion picture studios are only one of many businesses in various industries owned by a corporate parent. Other allied firms that these corporations tend to control include those involved in television production and distribution, music, on-line services and interactive products, consumer products, publishing, sports teams, theme parks, and legitimate theater.

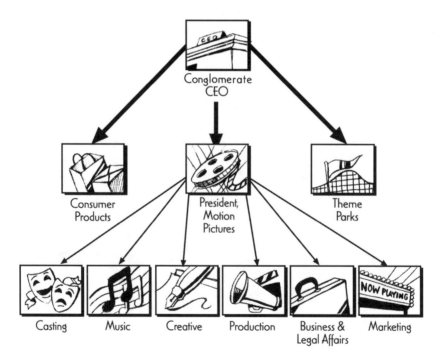

Chart by Eric M. Davis

One common attribute that these corporations share is synergy. *Synergy* is defined as a combined or cooperative action. In this context, synergy pertains to a marriage of ancillary industries. For instance, the Walt Disney Company produced a series of feature films about hockey called *The Mighty Ducks* through its motion picture studio. A few years later, when they acquired a hockey team, they named it after these comedies. The Disney Stores, operated by the consumer products division, sells Mighty Ducks merchandise related to both the films and the sports team.

THE CREATIVE EXECUTIVES

Being a creative executive at a studio is similar to being a development executive at a production company—but on a much larger scale. Instead of acquiring material directly from agents, for the most part screenplays are submitted by producers. Each creative executive oversees a slate of projects in different stages of development and production, but they do not physically produce the individual movies.

Jonathan King was a creative executive at Miramax Films before his current position as president of production at Laurence Mark Productions. At Miramax, he read scripts, held meetings with writers and producers, and looked for projects for the company to develop and produce. He also oversaw several movies that were already in production. "I would be the on-set executive, making sure that we were getting the movie that we wanted," says King.

"You don't have a specific job," King adds. "You're making sure that the producer, director, and everyone [else] is giving you the movie that they said they would give you in terms of quality and in terms of remaining on budget and on schedule. You're making sure that the director is getting all the coverage you're going to need to cut the movie together. You're making sure they're shooting what they said they were going to shoot [i.e., the approved script]. You're making sure that you're making your days, and that the number of pages you said you were going to get on any given day is the number of pages that you got, and that you're not going to come to the end of your twenty-eight-day shooting schedule and still have ten pages left to shoot."

Development executives at a studio and at a production company perform similar tasks. "You're reading material, and you're working

---

Studio 54, Where Are You?

One of the projects Jonathan King developed while at Miramax was *54* (1998). Mark Christopher had made two short films before *54* that King had seen and liked. He had run into Mark at a party and told the director that he was a fan of his work. They had lunch the next day. Christopher informed King that he wanted to make a movie about the late, lamented Studio 54 disco club in Manhattan. King had always hoped to make a disco movie and thought this was a great idea.

"He had been working off and on on this project for years," recalls King. "Various producers had been attached to it, and he'd been developing the script, and it had been through huge changes. He showed me a draft of the script, which I thought was pretty good, so I got [Miramax] to buy that.

"Mark and I developed the script together for quite a while. I was in Chicago working on a movie, and we were sending pages back and forth to each other. He went away for a little bit [to work on the screenplay] and the script took a huge leap forward. [That's when] it really picked up momentum at the studio and became a high-priority development project. When [actor/comedian] Mike Myers said, 'I want to do it,' then it became an actual movie. I think until you have cast attached to most movies, at most studios, it's [just] a development project. Then when you get your cast, you set your start date, and it's a movie."

---

with the writer to make the script good," says King. "You're trying to give good notes and make the script the best script it can be."

THE STORY DEPARTMENT

The story department is a service adjunct for the studio's creative executives. When material is submitted by producers, the executives forward it to the story department for coverage. The story department itself is strictly administrative, but they have a staff of readers who do the actual script analysis. Most of these readers work out of their houses and come in only twice a week to pick up or return scripts.

One of the most accessible jobs for people entering the film industry is as a script reader. Every studio, production company, and agency uses readers to evaluate material and cover scripts. In fact, this is what King first did when he moved to Hollywood. "Get a job as a reader immediately, and start familiarizing yourself with material and writers. Call everyone in the *Creative Directory*, and ask if they're looking for readers. Call the agencies and offer to do it for free until someone will pay you for it. Then, if you're so inclined, get a job as an assistant at a company whose films you respect and would want to move up at. Connect yourself to people who are working. Everyone knows someone who knows someone who is looking for an assistant."

Studio readers are union positions, but it's a Catch-22 to get in to the union. First, the hiring story department has to approach the union to see if any member is available. Once everyone in the union is working, then they can hire a non-union person for the open spot. If that reader works for thirty days, he is put into the union.

Most story departments keep track of new drafts of scripts that the company is developing. Some story departments also have video libraries that they maintain. Additionally, they may handle research assignments and obtain books and other material for executives. In many ways they function as the studio librarians.

ACQUISITIONS

At Miramax, Jonathan King was in the unique position to work not only as a creative executive, but also as an acquisitions executive. Looking for projects to acquire is similar in many ways to searching for projects to develop. The main difference is that acquisitions projects have already been developed and are either already partially or fully packaged, possibly partially or fully financed, already in production, or already finished shooting.

As an acquisitions executive, King tracked movies that were in production, read scripts, visited sets, and went to many screenings to find product for Miramax to distribute. He also attended many of the major annual film festivals, looking for product.

When considering a film from an acquisitions standpoint, you first must ask yourself, do I want to spend the company's money to buy and distribute this movie? And if I buy it, is there anything I want to do with it before it is distributed? For instance, you may want to re-edit, shoot a new ending, or add songs to the soundtrack.

"Oftentimes, if you see a movie at a festival, the music in the movie is licensed only for festival play," King points out. "So you have to figure out, are you going to pay the licensing fees for all of the music in the movie, which can turn your music budget on the movie from $40,000 to $250,000, or are you going to replace some of those songs? Oftentimes you'll see a movie at a festival or a screening, and because the filmmakers rushed to finish the movie, the movie isn't as tight as it should be. You can go through and re-edit some stuff, making sure the filmmakers are comfortable and that the studio is getting what they want."

King says there are two questions he always asks when looking at a film. "First, do you like the movie? Second, can you sell it? Can you get people into the theaters? Do you like it—that's subjective. Can you sell it—that's a little more objective. Is there a cast that you can get people interested in coming to see? Is this a movie that will appeal to critics? There's no one factor. It's an endless combination of things."

Acquisitions executives like to look at packaged material as early as possible because there's always the chance that the script will be great, the cast will be great, and they'll be familiar with enough of the director's work that it is worth the risk of pre-buying rights to it. At Miramax, King wanted to pre-buy *The House of Yes* [1997]. "I loved the script. I believed in Mark [Waters] as a director, though he had never directed a feature before. People knew who [actor] Parker Posey was. [But] it was too risky. They said, 'No, go finance it elsewhere.' Then we saw it at Sundance and bought it. A lot of times you take a wait-and-see attitude. Who knew what Mark was going to do with that movie?"

The more senior-level acquisitions executives are involved in the actual negotiating of deals and figuring out how much of the company's money they should be spending on a given film. "You want to get it for as cheap as you can," says King. "If there are other people bidding on it, the price can go way up. The price went up on *Swingers* [1996] because other people were bidding on it." That movie was acquired for $5 million.

THE PRODUCTION EXECUTIVES

Production executives represent the studio's interests with regard to how individual productions operate and spend their money. When a studio hands over millions of dollars to a filmmaker, the production executives monitor the movie as closely as possible so the studio knows how the money is being spent.

Once the studio's creative department is interested in a script, they need to know how much it will cost to make the movie. In addition, they want research done to determine such things as where the movie will be shot. The production executive does the research and creates a schedule and budget. The studio can then use these tools as a basis to decide whether they want to proceed with the project.

The schedule and budget are next presented to the producers. If they agree to move forward and the movie goes into production, the production executive will oversee that film.

"As an executive, you have to make sure the script matches what you have to spend," says Mark Indig, a former production executive with Walt Disney Studios. This may mean making changes, such as cutting out certain stunts or shooting in a less expensive location.

A production executive may handle as many as six or seven films at once, all in different stages of production. "You're trying to anticipate trouble before it happens, to deal with trouble when it comes, and to keep the filmmakers on track budgetarily," reports Indig, who worked as a production executive on *Encino Man* (1992), *The Distinguished Gentleman* (1992), and *Unstrung Heroes* (1995). "You are the bottleneck in the hourglass. You're reporting to the studio the status of the film, in terms of the budget and the schedule, and you're also being a facilitator to the filmmakers in dealing with the studio."

As a resource to filmmakers, the production department keeps an updated database of crew people that the studio has worked with before and whom they recommend. They also track information like the going pay rates and changes in union rules. Dealmaking is also a big part of their job, as they establish and enforce rate structures, review location contracts, and make sure the company is not exposed legally in any way. "You're trying to protect the studio brand name," says Indig.

Production executives visit the set on occasion. According to Indig, "You have to try and make the filmmakers understand and accept your presence as a friendly face so that they keep you in the loop on everything they're doing."

In the meantime, production executives review the daily paperwork, including call sheets, production reports, and cost reports, monitoring the movie on a macro level. When a film is spending more than what's budgeted, the production executive starts working with the filmmakers and creative executives to determine what can be trimmed to save money.

The most typical background for a production executive at a studio would be as a production manager.

BUSINESS AND LEGAL AFFAIRS

In today's highly litigious society, the major studios employ their own large stable of in-house attorneys. These lawyers are housed in two departments: business affairs and legal affairs.

For the most part, business affairs handles the broad-strokes deals, while legal affairs handles more of the detail work. Not all studios differentiate between the two departments. In many cases, they are one and the same. The division of labor is divided by seniority. In companies where business and legal affairs are separate, business affairs prepares a deal memo, then sends it to legal affairs to prepare the more elaborate contract.

Legalese 101

It's no surprise that legal contracts in general are difficult for the average person to understand. Contracts in Hollywood are no exception; in fact, they're probably worse. They are hard to comprehend, and they also are notorious for covering every possible contingency—not only the ones that exist, but any that may exist in the future! Take a look at the following sample from a standard option agreement.

1.1　*Option; Rights Granted.* Joe Artist ("Artist") hereby exclusively and irrevocably grants to Joe Producer ("Producer") the option ("Option") to acquire all right, title and interest, including without limitation, the exclusive copyrights (and renewals and extensions thereof), motion picture, television, radio, videocassette, videodisc, computer-assisted media (including but not limited to CD-ROM, CD-I and similar disc systems, interactive cable, and any other devices or methods now existing or hereinafter devised), character, remake, sequel, sound record, novelization, theme park, stage play, merchandising, all allied, ancillary and subsidiary rights and all other rights of every kind and nature, now known or hereafter devised, throughout the universe and in perpetuity, in and to the screenplay, *Portrait of a Starving Filmmaker* ("Screenplay"), written by Artist (the "Rights").

As most contracts are more than twenty pages long, you can see why attorneys are generally necessary to interpret the wordage for others without a legal background working in Hollywood.

"For all the hoopla about it, entertainment law is really just the same thing as anything else. You're doing contracts and making agreements," explains attorney David Steinberg. "It's more difficult [to get into], but only because of the perception that it's glamorous."

To add to the difficulty of obtaining an in-house legal position, studios generally do not hire attorneys straight out of law school and fresh from passing the bar exam. This is because they want law firms to train their future counsel. "The law firms, both the boutiques and a lot of the big corporate firms that do studio work, are the farm system," explains Steinberg, who himself started at a full-service law firm that had a substantial entertainment practice. He worked in corporate securities, handling normal tax-finance transactions that just happened to be for a studio.

As a result of his hard work, Steinberg kept getting assignments from the studios and ultimately transitioned into the studio system. He has since worked in business and legal affairs at First Look Pictures/Overseas Film Group, where he advised on *The Secret of Roan Inish* (1994) and *Party Girl* (1995), and has served as vice president of business and legal affairs at Miramax Films, where he was involved with *Scream* (1996), *The English Patient* (1996), and other films.

Steinberg feels that gaining experience outside of the studio system is invaluable. "You don't develop the best habits when you're working in-house at a studio because you tend to do things quickly. It's OK to cut corners once you understand what the corners you're cutting are, but if you only learn how to do a shorthand deal and you've never negotiated a sixty-page profit definition, there are a lot of stumbling blocks."

Steinberg's advice is to get experience in contract and employment law, because essentially that is the bulk of what entertainment lawyers do. On top of that, network with entertainment attorneys and other studio people so you will hear about opportunities to become a studio attorney.

LET'S MAKE A DEAL

"I don't get the phone call until they say, we want to buy it and we've talked to the producer and the producer has agreed to take X number of dollars," explains Steinberg. "The broad strokes of it are generally done by the creative people with business affairs. Business affairs can say, how much are you, creative person, envisioning for this? Is this going to be a $200 million major motion picture or one of our little indie throw-aways? What kind of attachments do you already have? And that's how you can figure out how much you're willing to pay. There are parameters. The whole puzzle has to fit together."

In addition to negotiating salaries and purchase price, a slew of ancillary perks must be carefully bargained. "A lot of the deal points are going to be significant for the creative people," explains Steinberg. "Credit is going to be significant. If I agree to give somebody a star trailer and it turns out nobody else is getting one and they haven't budgeted for it, you can wreak all kinds of havoc."

And in Hollywood, being what it is, there will always be those unique clauses that most lawyers would never dream of negotiating. "It's always amusing to negotiate nudity riders," Steinberg acknowledges. "OK, she has to be completely naked, but in the final cut you won't see anything."

Just some of the perks of the business—or not.

MARKETING

Marketing a film has become just as important as making the film itself. This is evident by the amount of money allocated to marketing expenses, which can sometimes be half as much as the cost of making the actual movie.

The marketing division at a studio oversees several different departments that, together, contribute to the selling of a film. These are advertising, publicity, promotions, and product placement. The marketing director comes up with a strategy involving each of these departments as to how to best market the movie.

Callie de Quevedo was attending graduate school, studying public relations, and interning at Artisan Entertainment. A few months into her internship, a job in the publicity department opened up, and de Quevedo was suddenly promoted from unpaid intern to junior publicist because she was in the right place at the right time.

She was thrilled with the prospect of working for a company she admired. As to finding your niche in the world of film marketing, she advises, "Learn who the big players are, who is initiating those marketing ideas, and try to put yourself under them and work with them either in an internship or as an assistant. Follow their example and learn their tricks."

RESEARCH

One of the functions of a studio marketing department is to conduct test screenings of a film before it is released. This is often done before the movie is finished, and frequently the results of such surveys can affect the outcome of the completed picture. For example, if the majority of test audiences do not like the ending of a film or the way a certain character comes across onscreen, they will note this on their survey. The results of such opinion polls are tabulated, and the filmmakers consider making changes to address the noted problems.

ADVERTISING

Advertising is so important that a movie will not be made unless the studio has a clear idea of how they will advertise it. The main marketing tool used in advertising is the one-sheet, or movie poster. I've been in pitch meetings with creative executives who have asked me what the poster will look like.

The advertising department designs the ad campaign and allocates the money spent for each campaign among television, radio, and print media. Today, print media includes not only newspapers and magazines, but also the Internet, billboards, ads on park benches, and even the sides of buses. To help differentiate advertising from other marketing techniques, it is best to remember that advertising takes place when you are directly paying for the media spots.

PUBLICITY

Whereas advertising is direct payment for media coverage, publicity is poised as generating media coverage for free. Of course, the studio is still paying for the coverage, just indirectly. Their expenses include the publicists, and the costs of screenings, junkets, and premieres that will all hopefully garner useful media attention.

Publicists generally handle all the screenings of new films before they are released to the public. Not every movie has a big, glamorous premiere. Those that do, however, have them for one purpose. "The only reason you do a premiere is for publicity," concurs entertainment publicist Jimmy

Dobson. Celebrity arrivals at the opening of a movie make international headlines, and it's great buzz for an upcoming release.

Also on the publicist's slate is setting up media screenings for film critics to review the movie, and industry screenings to give industry professionals (who were not invited to the premiere) an opportunity to preview the new release. They also run acquisitions screenings of independent films for possible distribution.

Publicists distribute press kits to the media to assist reporters and critics with their coverage of the movie. Both the press kit and the electronic press kit (EPK) are prepared with the help of the unit publicist while the film is still in production.

Press junkets and interviews are also the responsibility of the publicist. A press junket is when the cast and filmmakers are on hand for a day's worth of interviews with a succession of reporters. In addition, separate interviews and photo sessions may be coordinated by the publicist, as well as promotional appearances on such TV programs as *Good Morning America*, *The Rosie O'Donnell Show*, or *The Tonight Show with Jay Leno*.

PROMOTIONS AND PRODUCT PLACEMENT

People often think that promotions and publicity are the same thing, but they're not. As publicist Dobson explains, "Promotions is actually printing flyers and making product to sell in conjunction with a film. So if I'm working with a film, like *Child's Play* [1988], there's Chucky, which is the scary doll. The marketing people would create this doll. They'd create promotional tools based on that doll. Then they would market the doll to the public. Publicity would get the articles about the doll and articles about the movie. Promotions is product placement and creating an image through a product."

Product placement is how other products can market themselves through films. For example, you have a pizza delivery franchise that you want to publicize. There is a picture being made about a pizza delivery guy. Imagine the publicity if the delivery man in the movie worked at your pizza place!

The Reese's Pieces in *E.T. The Extra-Terrestrial* (1982), the BMW Z-3 in *GoldenEye* (1995) and the Ray-Ban sunglasses in *Men in Black* (1997) are three examples of product placement you might readily recall. Although a film cannot be financed on product placement revenue alone, it's certainly a way for a movie to offset costs.

MERCHANDISING

Product merchandising is an entire industry unto itself. The major studios have their own consumer products divisions that oversee the merchandising and licensing of their films.

For *The Lion King* (1994), Disney created stuffed animals, books, games, clothing, and other toys based on characters from this full-length animated movie. Some of these items were created by Disney. For others, the studio licensed out the right to use character names and images to established companies. In either case, *The Lion King* merchandise not only brought in direct sales revenue, but it also helped in the marketing of the film in its initial theatrical release and later on pay TV, home video, and DVD sales.

RELEASE PATTERNS

Several strategies are commonly employed in the distribution of a motion picture. A wide release literally puts the film in as many theaters as possible at the same time. A movie like *Batman & Robin* (1997), which has huge audience appeal, would call for simultaneous wide release. In contrast, a limited release starts off very small. Films may be placed in only a handful of theaters. Often they premiere only in Los Angeles and New York outlets. If the film plays well, the distributor may slowly increase the number of theaters in which it screens. Independent productions, such as *Love and Death on Long Island* (1997) are generally put out with a limited-release pattern. *The Full Monty* (1997) is a great example of an entry that began in limited release, but because of its big success early on—credited mainly to the brilliant marketing campaign—the movie ultimately went into wide release and became one of the highest grossing movies of the year.

THE SOUNDTRACK ALBUM

"The soundtrack album used to be an adjunct to the movie," says Dean Pitchford, Oscar-winning lyricist of *Fame* (1980). "If you saw the movie, maybe a few thousand people would go out and buy a reminder. There's a lot more at stake with regard to soundtrack albums these days. What has happened since *The Graduate* [1967] is that the soundtrack has become a total stand-alone industry. When it gets married well, you have a hit movie combined with a hit soundtrack, like *Footloose* [1984] or *Dirty Dancing* [1987] or *The Bodyguard* [1992]." In such cases, they cross-promote each other.

THE MUSIC DEPARTMENT

The music department at the studio supervises all of the music elements on a given film, from the soundtrack to the score. In pre-production, the department may help the production choose a composer who will be able to creatively service the film while remaining within their budget range. They also will be the middlemen between business affairs and any music-related vendors such as licensers and music agents.

THE CASTING DEPARTMENT

Most of the major film studios have a feature casting department. While there are hundreds of independent casting directors in Hollywood, there are only about a dozen casting directors employed today in these studio positions. As a result, getting one of these positions can prove challenging. See chapter 15 for information about independent casting directors.

Christian Kaplan currently serves as one of two vice presidents of casting at Twentieth Century-Fox, where he oversees casting for all four of the Fox film divisions. "We are there to service the filmmakers, service the studio, and work as productively and effectively as possible to get the best movie made," says Kaplan about the function of the studio casting department.

WHAT'S THE DIFFERENCE?

Ideally, an independent casting director starts work on a project after it has already been through development. She comes on once a director or, at the very least, a producer is attached. From there, she packages the movie, and then casts it.

The studio casting department works with the studio to attach a star to a project, sometimes even before a producer, director, or casting director is associated with the film. According to Kaplan, before casting directors Priscilla John and Lucinda Syson came on board *Ever After* (1998), the studio had already attached Drew Barrymore to star in the romantic epic.

Sometimes the studio casting department does the job themselves. Such was the case with John Woo's *Broken Arrow* (1996). "It varies project to project, depending on the filmmaker, who we want to work with, and whether or not they want to work with us," says Kaplan.

"Sometimes there are people who already have relationships." For instance, James Cameron has consistently worked with casting director Mali Finn.

Independent casting directors tend to work on one or two projects at a time. Studio casting directors work on many projects simultaneously. And while independent casting directors can make a lot more money than studio casting executives, they do not have the stability and security that comes with a studio position (e.g., benefits, weekly paychecks, contracts). Even for casting directors with established director relationships, a given director can do only so many films each year.

When an independent casting director is on a movie, the studio casting department provides support to that person. They might suggest talent the casting director has not thought of, they may introduce them to new actors, and they may be able to solve problems that arise during the casting process. Frequently, the studio casting department is called in at crunch time if the casting director has not found an actor for a key role. Sometimes casting needs arise after an independent casting director has already moved on to her next project. For the studio casting department, the job isn't over until the movie is released. There may be reshoots and dubbing, which require additional casting or recasting.

Another area the studio casting department manages is talent deals. A talent deal is a commitment the studio has with a particular actor to appear in a certain number of movies. This type of deal is commonly made with a TV actor appearing in a series produced by the television department at the same studio. For instance, Disney made the comedy *The Santa Clause* (1994), which starred Tim Allen. At the time, Allen had a talent deal with Walt Disney Studios stemming from his starring role on the Disney-produced sitcom *Home Improvement* (1991–99). It's mostly about synergy within the studio.

INTERACTION

To get a clear idea of how the different departments within a studio interact, consider the following scenario.

Peter Producer submits a script, *Dennis the Phantom Menace*, to Cathy Creative, a creative executive at M&M Studios. Cathy sends the script to the story department for coverage. Positive coverage comes back from the reader, who describes the screenplay as "a cross between *Dennis the Menace* [1993] and *Star Wars: Episode I—The Phantom Menace* [1999], with huge commercial potential." Cathy reads the script herself and agrees with the reader's comments. She puts the script on weekend read so that the entire creative department looks at it before Monday.

On Monday morning, the creative group meets to discuss weekend read. Everyone agrees to move on *Dennis the Phantom Menace* immediately. They get business affairs on the phone and strategize an offer to buy the script. Business affairs works out the broad strokes of the deal with the agent representing the script. The final forty-page contract, however, is output by legal affairs incorporating every detail known or hereinafter invented. A deal is also struck for Peter Producer to produce the picture.

The script is sent to Pamela Production, a production executive at the studio. She evaluates the material with regard to costs and locations, even going so far as to create an initial budget and schedule. Carla Casting, the head of the studio casting department, reads the script and puts together lists of possible actors for the major roles. Her assistant might even check on the availability of the leading candidates.

While the casting lists are being compiled, Cathy and Peter are making their own wish lists for directors. Once a director and stars are attached, and a budget and manageable schedule worked out, the studio greenlights the project.

Throughout the production of the project, the different studio departments service and support the film in any way possible. This may include the production department recommending crew, the creative department providing notes based on dailies, and the music department identifying soundtrack opportunities. All departments closely monitor the pace of filming and the level of spending, making sure that the production is meeting its schedule and staying within the parameters of the budget. If any problems arise, the studio executives come to the set to resolve them with the producer.

When the creative executives screen the rough cut of the film, they make notes that they would like to see incorporated into the next cut of the movie. This is also an opportunity for the marketing department to screen the film so they can begin to plan their marketing campaign. The marketing department works closely with the music department on the soundtrack, an important marketing tool. They also conduct test screenings with recruited audiences to make sure the film is well received before its release.

Once the film is locked (i.e., no other changes can be made to the print), the marketing department works with creative affairs to determine a release date and strategy for distributing it. *Dennis the Phantom Menace* gets a wide release and goes on to become a financial success. Peter Producer wins his first Academy Award for Best Picture.

Granted, this is a simplified example, but it gives you a general idea of how the well-oiled studio machine operates.

17

Handlers

*Jim Gosnell [president of Agency for the
Performing Arts] told us, and he hit it on the head,
'Let's put all the glamour aside, we're an employment agency. That's what we do. Let's not sugar-
coat it.' We have actors who want jobs. We have
producers who want actors. We try to put them
together and make a match, and that's what it's
about. It couldn't be simpler.*

JOEL DEAN, talent agent

Faye Dunaway and Bette Davis were making a TV movie
called *The Disappearance of Aimee* (1976). The two big-name actors got
into a dispute on the set. At the time, Joel Dean was Dunaway's agent.
"Bette Davis would not come out of her dressing room because Faye had
insulted her [Davis's] hairdressers," he recalls. "I had to fly down to Den-
ver because I was the only one who could talk [Faye] into apologizing to
Bette. I couldn't do it on the phone. I had to do it in person."

Herein lies a typical day in the life of a Hollywood handler. Whether
it's an agent, manager, lawyer, publicist, or personal assistant, there's a
reason most stars travel with an entourage. In keeping talent out of trouble, getting them work, or just helping them manage their complex lives,
handlers more than earn their keep.

For Dean to drop everything and fly to Colorado might sound a bit
dramatic. However, for every hour of every day that the production is
halted, hundreds of thousands of dollars are being lost. Luckily, Dean

was able to resolve the problem and convinced Dunaway to apologize. "She sent [Bette Davis] flowers and said, 'I've been a naughty girl. Will you forgive me?'" Davis did, filming resumed, and Dean returned to Los Angeles and the everyday frenzy that is the talent agency business.

THE AGENCIES

Many people consider the talent agencies to be the hub of all business in Hollywood. More than anywhere else in the industry, the agency is considered the best place to start a career in film, especially if you are not exactly sure where your focus lies.

The number one responsibility for an agent is to procure work for clients. Agencies represent above-the-line talent including actors, writers, directors, and occasionally producers, and key below-the-line talent, including directors of photography, production designers, editors, production managers, composers, hair and makeup artists, and costume designers.

There are only a few full-service agencies that represent all categories of talent, above- and below-the-line. It is more common for firms to strictly handle either above-the-line or below-the-line. Above-the-line agencies that represent only actors are called talent agencies. Above-the-line agencies that handle only writers and directors are called literary agencies. The *Hollywood Agents & Managers Directory* features a complete list of agencies, contact information, and the types of clients on their roster (see appendix A).

"I acted for eight years before I was an agent," says Carl Bressler, an agent specializing in below-the-line talent. "I promised my clients when I started that I would be the agent that I never had. I knew what the job was and I knew who didn't do it for me. And I was going to take on the business of agenting in the way I always wished, and hoped, and prayed that someone would [have done] it for me."

Debbie Deuble, a literary agent at Don Buchwald & Associates, feels as though she has the greatest job in the world. "I'm reading things, so usually it's entertaining. If I don't like it, I throw it away. I talk on the phone all day with my friends. My friends are development executives, studio executives, and story editors. I go out and I have a free lunch and dinner at a fancy restaurant every day. I make movies. And I get paid too! It's the greatest job ever."

For Angela Cheng, a literary agent at the Writers and Artists Agency, it's the commitment to wanting to work with writers that gives her fulfillment. "You really have to be in love with the written word and also with writing," she offers. "If you are emotionally engaged by really good writing, then being an agent could very well be for you."

TALENT AGENTS

So you want to work with actors? Attend parties with Tom Cruise? Go skiing in Aspen with Julia Roberts? Hang out at the Improv with Chris Rock? Don't let the glitz distract you from reality. First of all, Cruise, Roberts, and Rock already have well-established representation. Second, being an agent for one of these megastars comes with a great deal of responsibility. One right or wrong move can affect their careers and subsequently turn your own livelihood upside down in a flash. On the other hand, if you're representing Tom Cruise, everyone in town will take your calls. But if you're representing a brand-new actor without any screen credits, you may be dialing a lot of numbers before you book one business meeting for your client. "This industry takes you, swallows you up, chews you up, and spits you out," says Dean. "I'm not being cynical. That's the way it is."

The first thing you need as a talent agent are actors to represent. At a larger agency, you may inherit certain clients or be added to a team as one of several agents who handles a specific actor. You may know about an actor who is unhappy with his current representation at another agency and be able to bring him over to your firm. Or you may be out and about town when a fresh new face with star potential catches your eye. You approach him and ask if he's an actor and if he has an agent. "I'm fearless at that," says Dean. "'Here's my card, I think you're great, call me.' You can't be shy."

One of an agent's main tools in identifying casting opportunities for their clients is the *Breakdowns*. See chapter 15 for a sample. The *Breakdowns* are pages that outline the upcoming film's story, a description of each character (the leads and the supporting players), and the names of the director, producer, and casting director. They are published every workday and detail what films are casting. Every agency subscribes to the *Breakdowns*, and every agency submits its clients for the same roles.

Actors are submitted in the form of a head shot and résumé. Casting directors get hundreds of submissions, and some of the envelopes probably do not even get opened. "There have got to be over one hundred agencies in town, so you have to keep after them and be aggressive," Dean explains.

The agent's objective is to have his client audition for the casting director. It is the actor's job to win the role.

THE DREAM TEAM At most of the bigger agencies, the agents work as a team. Each agent handles his own set of clients. In addition, each agent handles one or more territories. For instance, one agent might cover Universal and DreamWorks, while another covers Paramount and Warner Bros.

The first thing Joel Dean does when he receives his copy of the *Breakdowns* is pull out the casting notices for the territories he is directly responsible for. "I think about the entire agency, rather than the small group of actors that I have," he explains. The other agents send Dean their copy of the *Breakdowns* marked with the clients that they are directly responsible for and who might be right for a role in the projects he's covering. He also may get a call from an actor's manager who has read the *Breakdowns* and wants to make sure Dean is submitting their mutual client for the part, though chances are he's probably already done it.

"Then I go through [the other territories' *Breakdowns*] that's come in that day for my [clients] specifically, just like the other agents have done for me," notes Dean. Similarly, the other agents have probably already thought about Dean's clients when preparing submissions for the projects they cover, but by doing it this way nothing will be missed.

Let's say you see a part that the actor you are representing might be right for. It isn't a project at a studio that you are covering, so you call the agent who's covering it and tell him that your client is perfect for this part. The covering agent makes his initial submissions that include your client to a casting director. He comes back to you and says the casting director doesn't think your client is quite right. You pick up the phone and call the producer or the studio executive and pitch your client directly to them. They think it's a good idea, so you tell the covering agent to tell casting to bring the actor in to read for the part. You want to go through the proper channels first, which is why you don't bypass the casting director initially. Of course, the studio exec may agree with the casting director, in which case you're simply out of luck this time around.

At smaller or solo agencies where team agenting is not in play, the agents are individually responsible for submitting their clients to all territories. This may seem like an awful lot of work for one person, but remember, they are responsible for a smaller number of clients.

While many agents rely strictly on the *Breakdowns* to get their clients work, creative agents do a little more legwork to see what projects are in the pipeline that their actors may be right for. This is done by talking to people they know at the various studios. They call and ask what is coming up on their slate. Is there a director yet? What's the story about? They keep notes and read the trades to find out about forthcoming projects. "You have to be proactive rather than reactive," advises Dean.

GETTING TO CHECKMATE Once an actor gets cast in a role, the agent must negotiate the deal. "That to me is where the fun begins," says Dean. "I love the chess game that goes on." The agent works with the actor's attorney to negotiate a deal with the studio, or producer.

Part of the negotiating process requires being familiar with the rules set forth by the Screen Actors Guild (SAG), since this is the union that covers actors. These rules incorporate provisions such as the number of consecutive hours an actor can work and the method of travel to and from location. "I'm not professing that I know all the SAG rules by heart," Dean allows. "You have to know the general parameters and investigate on a project-by-project basis."

Like every other aspect of becoming an agent, you learn negotiating skills through osmosis. "You work with good agents and watch how it's done," he adds. "There's no handbook that tells you how to negotiate a deal. With a film, you're talking about how much money, how many weeks, if it goes over, how much, if there's a percentage involved, what the percentage involved is, how is that broken down, when does it kick into profits, billing, artwork, dressing room, et cetera. There's a whole litany of things you can go through.

"The worst thing that a client can say to an agent is, 'I love the project. I want to do it. Negotiate it, but don't lose it. Get me more money, but don't lose it.' That's an impossibility, and I tell them that. 'You can't have both. They've offered you $5,000, let's just take it. Don't ask me to get you $10,000, because if you're willing to take $5,000 now, we may as well just close it.'

"It's a pleasure when someone says, 'I'm willing to walk away from this. I won't work for less than $10,000 a week. If you can't get it, that's fine.' Then it gives me some strength because what I do then is ask for [more]. And if he tells me he won't take less than $10,000, I'll say the guy wants $20,000. What can I do? He's crazy. Then they offer him $10,000, and they think they got a bargain. They never know. So you have to work with your actor and you have to know how much they're willing to bend."

LITERARY AGENTS

Literary agents represent writers, directors, producers, and anyone else who works above-the-line, with the exception of actors. Although the jobs of literary agents and talent agents are similar, the very nature of the clients each represents makes for a difference in the daily responsibilities and duties the agents perform. Still, the objective remains the same—secure work for their clients.

"If you have writer clients, the goal is to sell their original material," explains Debbie Deuble. "If you have novelist clients, it's to get somebody to pick up the film rights. With directors, we try to fill open directing assignments."

Deuble, who has been in the business for six years, looks at her role as an agent as much more than just getting her clients the job. "I'm your mother. I'm your therapist. I'm your writing partner. I'm your business manager. I'm hoping that you're going to hand me a script that I think is commercial, has enormous potential, and is going to sell for a lot of

---

Literal Difference

Literary agents in Hollywood, and as discussed in this book, deal specifically with material for film and television projects. However, literary agents are also prevalent in the publishing world, where book deals are made. Although the two worlds are quite different, some agents do handle both publishing deals and film deals. It is more common that a publishing agent, who is probably based in New York since that's where the publishing industry is centered, would team with a film agent in Hollywood to exploit the rights to their client's published or soon-to-be-published material. In cases where team agenting is involved, the agents generally work together and split the commission.

Signing Spielberg

Signing Spielberg

"I got Steven [Spielberg] because he was my next-door neighbor," says Joel Dean. "He took a liking to me, I took a liking to him, and we became very good friends. He hadn't done a motion picture yet. I was covering Universal, and I found *Duel* [1971] and told him about it." Dean described the film as an interesting story—mostly action, with very little dialogue.

"George Epstein, who was the producer of it, didn't know Steven Spielberg from Joe Schmoe. I literally used to park myself on George Epstein's bungalow doorstep almost three times a week until he would see Steven. He finally did, and he hired him just from that."

money. If the script is not there yet, I do rewrites with you until we feel that it's ready to go out."

Like producers, agents can't just accept a script from anyone who walks through the door. Clients are signed mainly through referrals from other clients, managers, lawyers, and development people. The great thing about referrals for a writer is that there is already someone on your team who believes in your material.

Not all writers have an "in" with an agency. Another way agents find clients is through query letters. "Even through a query letter, I can tell the caliber of writing," says Angela Cheng. "I can tell whether or not this person is engaging enough to make me want to read their stuff." See chapter 4 for more information on how to write a great query letter. Of course, it also helps if your next-door neighbor happens to be an industry agent.

SPECS When a client writes a new script on *spec* (short for *speculation*, or without being commissioned), the agent strategizes a plan to sell the screenplay. This generally involves assigning a different territory to each production company. Because there are many more production companies than territories available, the agent carefully plans the submissions. In doing so, she considers the following factors: Which producers are the biggest fans of the writer's previous work? Which producers will "get," or best relate to, the material? Which producers have a deal at which studio? Whose relationships are strongest at each lot?

"Every company has a reputation for doing a certain type of movie," explains Deuble. "Kopelson [Entertainment] does big, action-packed, explosive $100 million movies. I'm not going to send them a period drama starring two forty-year-old women. They're never going to buy that movie."

When a spec script is sent out, the agent usually requests a response the next day. This is because if a production company doesn't like the script, the agent can then send it immediately to the next choice on their list for the same territory. For instance, let us say that International Creative Management has a comedy spec script. On their list, they've determined that the Robert Simonds Company (*Problem Child*, *Happy Gilmore*, *The Wedding Singer*) is the best production company to take this property to Universal because this is the type of movie they do best, Bob Simonds is a big fan of the writer, and Simonds's firm has a deal at Universal. Let's say Simonds passes because they have a similar project already. The agent immediately sends it to her second choice, Northern Lights Entertainment (*Beethoven*, *Ghostbusters*, *Space Jam*). Northern Lights may have never read this writer's work before, but is still a good candidate because they also have a deal at Universal and they have made comedy movies like the script they are about to receive.

Alternatively, agents make simultaneous multiple submissions and assign territories on a first-come, first-serve basis. This helps elicit a speedy response.

The spec market is a great way to get a young writer introduced to the town because twenty-four hours after a script goes out, everybody knows the writer's name, is familiar with the writing, and hopefully thinks it's great. If the script sells, the writer could earn anywhere from Writers Guild minimum to a high-six/low-seven-figure deal. In addition, if everyone likes the script, the writer will schedule a slew of meetings that could lead to additional writing jobs.

WRITING ASSIGNMENTS Generally, writers can only obtain work once they are established. In Hollywood, that means the writer has sold a script. Sometimes it means that the script has been produced. There are exceptions, however, like the spec script scenario described above. A script goes out and gets a favorable response but does not sell. Maybe it wasn't commercial enough. Maybe it was too similar to another project already in the pipeline. Whatever the case, if the writer takes a good meeting, he could land a writing assignment.

Writing assignments come in several different forms. Book adaptations are when a studio has purchased an unpublished manuscript or a published book and needs a writer to adapt it to a screenplay. Rewrites are another form of the open writing assignment. A project is having problems, and the studio blames it on the screenplay. They decide to ax the original writers and bring in a fresh new perspective. Maybe the characters need work. Maybe the jokes require punching up. Different writers may be brought aboard for different reasons. Sometimes a production company requests a meeting with a writer because they have an original idea and are looking for someone to come up with a story. The agent arranges such a conference. If the writer responds to the idea, he may work up a pitch, telling the story beat by beat. If the production company responds, they bring the writer to the studio to pitch the idea there.

DIRECTING ASSIGNMENTS Getting jobs for directors is similar to getting rewrites and adaptations for writers. Instead of submitting a script, the agent submits the director's reel. Obviously, more established directors don't need a reel as a method of introduction. If the studio executive responds positively to the reel, the agent sends the script to the director. If the director responds positively to the material, the agent sets up a meeting between the director and the studio.

BELOW-THE-LINE AGENTS

It used to be that a producer would call up his favorite cinematographer and put him on a film with a director he has probably never worked with or even met before. Nonetheless, the cinematographer would show up on the set ready to do the job. "The way the business is now, with all the budgets being up and the competitive nature of the game, and with so many film schools in so many countries pumping out art directors, cameramen, et cetera, it has changed," says Carl Bressler, owner of Montana Artists, an agency that represents below-the-line talent.

For a long time, below-the-line agenting was strictly a booking business wherein the buyer would call up and ask who was available for this rate on these dates. Those résumés that fit the simple criteria were sent over to the producer, and that was the end of it unless an offer was made.

"I'm not a booker, I'm a seller," states Bressler. "My reputation is based on selling people who are competent both personally and professionally. I look for somebody who has the ability to take ideas and express them visually."

Not all below-the-line talent needs to have an agent. It is a good idea, however, for key crew members and department heads. "They need it for both the PR function and the procuring function, finding that job for them with other people that they haven't worked with," notes Bressler.

When crewing a film, most producers look at a person's credits to determine if she should be considered for a particular position. This sometimes makes it difficult for newcomers who may be very talented but do not yet have the requisite notable credits on their résumé. It's the job of the agent to get his clients introduced. "A lot of those people would never have changed their [careers] if they hadn't had representation that went out and fought for them and got them noticed by people who were credit whores," says Bressler.

Below-the-line agents work with people who employ their craft on projects that are being made, and those people get paid every week. "It's a much more satisfying business in that sense than in representing writers," notes Bressler. "The very nature of the below-the-line business is you work a week, you get paid a week. There's no worrying about projects that are not being made because the below-the-line person only goes to work when the project is greenlighted."

BECOMING AN AGENT

"To become an agent, you have to go through probably the most grueling Hollywood boot camp there is," says Debbie Deuble. "Anybody will tell you agency pay is the lowest of the low. When I moved here with my big fancy college degree, I made less money as an agent trainee than I had been collecting from unemployment. And what do you do with your education and your knowledge of writers and directors? You make a lot of [photo]copies. You learn how to put script covers on at the speed of sound. But you have to do it."

Angela Cheng agrees. "Agencies are notorious for really long hours and really bad pay, so the attrition rate is pretty high. Agencies think that if you're going to stick it out and you're going to endure the abuse and the hours, it will pay off down the road."

It certainly paid off for Cheng and Deuble. Both women began their industry careers as assistants to other agents. This is probably the quickest way to work your way up to becoming an agent, and it is the only way at smaller agencies, which don't have a trainee program. At the larger agencies, trainee programs are key to becoming an agent. In fact, it's the only way to become an agent at most of the bigger companies.

Having an agency background is a great way to jump into a career in most other above-the-line or executive jobs in Hollywood. For those who do want to become agents, it's the only place to learn. Cheng remembers, "Ron Bernstein [a veteran literary agent at The Gersh Agency] was a really terrific mentor. It wasn't ever about stopping in the middle of the day to say, what have we learned? It was more about my being able to keep up with him, really a baptism by fire. It was about being really aggressive, reading everything that wasn't nailed down shut, and asking questions about things I didn't understand without having to stop him from his flow of work."

Deuble adds, "Within two months of working on an agent's desk [Hollywood talk for being an agent's assistant] in a literary department, you will know the name of every production company in Hollywood. By answering the phone, you learn everybody's name."

For Cheng, the most important attribute in an assistant is the ability to read and cover scripts. "Be able to engage in a meaningful conversation about the material," she says. "If I need a secondary opinion, I need to be able to turn to an assistant and say, take a look at this."

Working at an agency is not a nine-to-five job. The hours are more like eight to eight, with scripts to read at night and on the weekend. As Deuble says, "The lows are very low, but the highs are very high. When you start out, and you're making nothing, and you're going home with a hundred paper cuts on your fingers every single day, and your eyes are crossing from reading so much, and you're looking at your $250 per week paycheck, life sucks. But ten years from now, when you're setting up a deal and you're making a $200,000 commission, life is good. There's big, big money to be had, and there's enough for everybody."

Joel Dean took a different path. He began his career years ago as a trainee with the William Morris Agency. Wanting any "in" to the film business, he took the first opportunity available. "To me the initial attraction was the glamour," he recalls. "I didn't think about the *business* part of it. I only thought about the *show*."

After a few months of doing chores like cleaning the bathrooms and delivering packages, Dean began to have second thoughts. "I thought, *What the f*** am I doing?* I'm a college graduate and I just finished my chores in the men's room changing the toilet paper and cleaning the soap dishes. [But I did it] because my eye was on the show. I was still fantasizing."

"The agent trainee program really is like a graduate school," notes Deuble. "It's a glorified internship with some lunch money." In fact, because the pay is so notoriously low, it's not a job that everyone can do. Many people pass up this opportunity completely because they can't support themselves on the menial salary. If you don't have money saved up or someone helping to support you, or if you have your own family to support, it may not be financially viable to be an agent trainee. Generally, it's a great job for someone fresh out of college or someone with little financial liability.

Many concur that an agency is a great place to start no matter what film career you want to pursue. But how do you determine whether you should start as a trainee or as an assistant? As a rule, if you know for certain that you want to become an agent, enter a trainee program immediately. If you just want to gain experience to learn about the business and to get an overview of the industry, and you're not yet sure whether you want to become an agent further down the line, get a job as an assistant.

The larger agencies have the best trainee programs and provide the most opportunities. There's also a certain degree of prestige that comes with a trainee program at one of the bigger agencies. Because competition is fierce to win these positions, just getting in is a notable accomplishment.

At the bigger agencies, everything you do is preparing you to become an agent. You may start off doing menial tasks. Eventually you will be promoted to a desk, which means you will work as an assistant. Don't feel that you've wasted two years of your life when you could have started out at a desk. Those who began as an assistant instead of a trainee will not be promoted to an agent within the larger firms.

The trainee programs at the smaller agencies work a little differently. It's very possible to start as an assistant at a smaller agency and be promoted to full agent without ever being in a trainee program at all. You could even start as an agent's assistant at one of the bigger agencies and move from there to become an agent at a smaller agency. What it ultimately comes down to is how far up the ladder you want to get in the Hollywood game. Do you want to be a *player*, or do you just want to play?

MANAGEMENT FIRMS

In 1975, an agent named Michael Ovitz threw the industry for a loop when he and a small group of his colleagues left the William Morris Agency to co-found a new agency, which they named Creative Artists Agency (CAA). Within a few years, with Ovitz as chairman, CAA became the most powerful talent agency in Hollywood, and Ovitz became one of Tinseltown's most influential players. He literally redefined the agency business and Hollywood.

As this book was being written, Ovitz had founded a new company, this time a management firm called Artists Management Group (AMG), which is sure once again to alter the way business is done in Hollywood. Already the company's client roster includes Claire Danes, Cameron Diaz, Leonardo DiCaprio, Matt Dillon, Samuel L. Jackson, Robin Williams, writer/director Ted Demme, and directors Penny Marshall and Martin Scorsese. The new role and importance of managers in Hollywood has been reaffirmed by Ovitz.

Managers have always been in existence. In recent years, however, they have taken on an increasingly important role in almost every aspect of making a film. Today there are management firms that are as powerful as the biggest agencies. The role of the manager has grown far beyond that of merely advising talent. Many managers now also develop and produce their client's material and/or material for their clients. As a result, both the earning potential and career opportunities for a manager far exceed those of an agent. In fact, by California statute, per the State Labor Commission, agents are legally unable to simultaneously produce.

Today is a very exciting time for managers in Hollywood. Many are making the jump from agent to manager, and many producers are opening up their own management divisions. Of course, with any major change there are bound to be problems. For example, not too long ago, actor Garry Shandling filed a $100 million lawsuit against his former manager, Brad Grey, alleging he failed to properly protect Shandling's professional interests. While the case has since been resolved, this and other high-profile lawsuits may set precedents for how managers handle their different professional roles in the future.

Some of you may be excited about the prospects of a career in management and getting in while the profession is still defining itself. Others may be confused just trying to distinguish the difference between an agent and a manager. This section outlines these differences, and also clarifies how the two entities work together.

TALENT MANAGERS

In the most general terms, managers serve talent in an advisory capacity and counsel them on career decisions. Managers are not making the deals, but rather overseeing them, making sure the clients are getting what they want and that their interests are protected. A manager works in conjunction with the other handlers to take care of the clients, advising them on decisions that will affect their long-term careers.

"You'll read scripts and say, 'This is a role you should go up for, and here's why; or this is a role you shouldn't go up for, and here's why,'" explains manager Michael Valeo. For example, Valeo suggests, "If you are a classy actor with a good reputation, you don't want to do this B-movie where you flash your [privates]. Our job is to look at the client's whole career. If there's a piece of it that's not working, part of our job is to fix the problem." This may mean helping an actor switch agencies if there is a problem with the existing one. In the case of a new actor, the manager may place him with his very first agent. For managers who work to develop new talent, they may advise him on everything from which classes to take to what outfit he should wear to an audition.

LITERARY MANAGERS

Literary managers work in much the same capacity as talent managers. "Instead of which role you should take, it's which movie you should direct," says Valeo. "Do you want to direct an episode of *ER*, or do you want to keep directing features? Do you want to write on spec, or do you want to try and get a hired job as a writer?"

The players are a bit different in the world of literary management. Instead of dealing with casting directors, they're dealing with development executives. Regardless, the primary functions remain the same. It's still about advising people on their careers and trying to create opportunities for them.

In addition to their traditional managerial duties, literary managers often play a role similar to that of the development executive. They work very closely with writer clients to help them develop their screenplays, sometimes working through several different drafts until a script is the strongest it can be. They also can be a great sounding board for their clients in helping them determine what to write and what the marketplace is currently buying.

Like their agent counterparts, managers find and sign clients in a variety of ways. They might spot someone in a movie who they think is great, and find out if that actor has a manager. "If I find out an actor is represented by [an agent], and we have a relationship with that agency, I can just pick up the phone and call and ask who this person's manager is," Valeo states. "If they don't have one, then I'll say that I'd love to get into business [with them]. Maybe you know their lawyer. Maybe you know their publicist. Maybe you know the producer of the movie they're working on at the time, and you can get to them that way. You just track them down, find out who's in their life, and see how you can get in there too. Tell them that you are interested and passionate about them."

Sometimes talent seeks out managers based on knowing their reputation. "You'll go to a set to visit one of your other clients and you'll meet someone else and hit it off," Valeo says. But most often the connection comes from referrals from agents, the same way managers refer clients to agencies.

BECOMING A MANAGER

Starting out in the management business is similar to beginning a career at an agency. That is, you start on a desk or in the mailroom at an existing management firm and work your way up the ladder. However, whereas agents are franchised and need to be approved by SAG, there are no such regulations on management at this time. What this means is, literally, almost anybody can hang a sign on his door and call himself a manager. All you need to start are actors or other talent to represent.

"The one thing about Hollywood is that there are no rules and there are no clear paths. That's a given," notes Valeo. "If you wanted to, you could go down to Melrose Avenue and start signing people up and call yourself a manager. I'm not sure you'd get your calls returned, but you could certainly start a company out of your bedroom."

Valeo took a more practical approach, starting as an assistant to veteran manager Delores Robinson. Because he was at the right place at the right time, he became a manager within three months. "I think more often than not, you're going to spend a couple of years as an assistant paying your dues. I just sort of had an innate sense for a lot of it and my instincts tended to be right." In other words, he got lucky.

"Don't ever be embarrassed to ask a question, because it's so much better to ask a question and learn the answer than to do something wrong," Valeo advises. "If I didn't know something, I would ask for help. I would listen to a lot of people, and I just picked it up very fast."

AGENTS-TURNED-MANAGERS

Managers typically handle a much smaller group of clients than agents do, and as a result they share a much closer personal relationship with those clients. However, with the growing number of managers in the industry and the onslaught of large management conglomerates, many feel that this unique relationship may be in jeopardy.

"The agent's mentality is to get as many appointments as he possibly can for all of his clients and get them as many jobs as he can," assesses Valeo. "Managers will look more at the long term and say, well, it would be nice if you made this movie for a million dollars, but maybe that's not the best move. Maybe we should make this littler movie for $300,000 because it will lead to the next movie for $5 million. Theoretically, we think more about each person because we have fewer people to think about and to pay attention to."

Legally, per the California State Labor Commission, managers are not allowed to solicit or procure work for their clients, only to advise on work procured by other people. This too is a fine line that's not always easily enforceable.

"The whole idea is probably that you can't be owning the product and the actor you're trying to sell into the product," says Valeo. "If we were able both to get jobs for our clients and to produce, there potentially would be a conflict of interest."

Thus begins the big debate. Established producers are a bit annoyed at the managers who invade their turf by attaching themselves as producers to their clients' projects. Studio execs are perturbed that now, in order to secure an actor, they also have to pay the actor's manager a producing fee. More and more agents are abandoning ship to become managers because the opportunities are so much greater.

"I think the reason most agents are becoming managers is because they want to be producers," says Valeo. "It becomes much more about what the client can do for my producing career than what I can do for the client's career. I think that's a very dangerous trend because it's not the point of personal management. The only reason personal managers should be producing is if it's 100 percent to service the needs of and protect the client in a given situation—not to advance the manager's own career. My job is not to produce movies. My job is to guide a career. If I want to be a producer, I should go be a producer.

"Jerry Weintraub once said to Delores [Robinson], 'Yeah, I made a lot of money as a manager,' and Jerry was a very successful manager, but it's nothing compared to what I make as a producer. Ten percent of a back end is not a back end. You can't ever compete with that if you're truly successful as a producer. There really is more money. The way agents get more money is by packaging. But most often that's going to a company, not an individual, whereas in management companies, since they tend to be smaller, the individual managers see more of the profits."

In today's Hollywood, with managers taking on a more prominent role, the attrition rate at the agencies has slowly begun to increase. The scenario emerging is that managers can do everything agents can do and more, plus they have the potential to make a lot more income. Whether this is good for the future of management remains to be seen. "I think part of the problem is that a lot of agents are becoming managers now and are bringing the agent mentality into the management world," notes Valeo.

The future is still unknown. We can only watch the effect Michael Ovitz and his Artists Management Group have on the way business is done in the film industry. This is one Hollywood story with an unpredictable ending.

PUBLICISTS

For the personal publicist, the product being sold to the media is an actor or filmmaker. Jimmy Dobson, publicist and owner of Indie PR, represents actor Jared Harris, who stars in the Miramax release *B. Monkey* (1999). It was Dobson's goal to generate press for Harris when the film was released. In contrast, the goal of the studio publicity department was to get press for the overall production.

Although it seems that each objective would help the other, it's really more a case of competition than complement. "Often you come at odds with the studio," explains Dobson. "I rarely tell the studio my plans with the actor because they tend to piggyback their people on top of your actor's story, which lessens the impact of your actor's story."

The upside of this competitive attitude is that two separate publicity units are working just as hard on different story angles, which ultimately will benefit the movie and its players. For the personal publicist who is hired by the actor, however, the primary goal is to make sure that the actor is the one in the spotlight.

Dobson meets most of the people he signs through their other handlers. Over the years he has represented such performers as Roseanne, Bill Paxton, Diane Ladd, and Will Smith. But these days he prefers to work with filmmakers and the films themselves. "Representing a personality takes so much energy out of you. I enjoy working with films and filmmakers more because you can actually put together a project, then three months later complete the project and see the results."

Dobson believes that in today's Hollywood it is necessary for moviemakers to have publicists because there are so many publications and outlets that filmmakers would never have the opportunity to be a part of unless a publicist is involved. "It's all about educating the media about who that filmmaker is," he says.

"One of my clients, Jonathan Nossiter, directed a movie called *Sunday* [1997], which went on to win the Sundance Film Festival," reveals Dobson. "During the Sundance Film Festival, he hired me because he felt he was not getting any press and not getting any attention. We immediately set up introductions with him and the media. They started interviewing him. They started actually seeing the film through our introductions. We'd actually take a critic like Roger Ebert and make him sit and watch the film so that we could get a [potential] thumbs-up from him. The film went on to win, which really established the director as a leading force."

BECOMING A PUBLICIST

"I ran a full page in *Variety* saying, 'Young, talented, aggressive individual seeks any position in the entertainment industry,' and I got two phone calls back," Dobson recalls. "One of them was a talent agency that hired me as a trainee, and six months later I became an agent. [A few years later,] I left because I was having more fun going to celebrity golf tournaments with Cybill Shepherd, and I had decided that's what PR people do, so I took all of the [actors I represented] as my clients and opened up my own PR firm and just started building the firm."

Dobson's may sound like the typical success story, but the best way to learn public relations is to actually intern in a PR firm. "You have to be a natural salesperson, and you have to be good at talking," Dobson notes. "You have to be good at schmoozing and mingling with new people. If you're good at that, you'll be a good publicist."

He advises taking journalism classes to understand how journalists work, and taking public relations classes to learn the elements of formulating and writing press releases. Wannabe publicists should provide sample press releases as a selling tool in the same fashion as a director utilizes a reel.

ENTERTAINMENT ATTORNEYS

Nowadays, when an above-the-line player achieves a certain level of success, an additional handler is added to her growing team. This person is the entertainment attorney. The lawyer takes the deal that the agent has structured and makes it real by examining all of the detailed points, making sure that the client is protected and that she's receiving what she really needs. Attorneys try to leverage and get the client even more with each successive deal because of the precedent system that exists in Hollywood.

"Acting agreements are employment agreements," says David Steinberg, an attorney who left the world of business and legal affairs behind to open up his own practice, David Steinberg & Associates. "If you are an inventor working for Bell Labs and Bell wants to own what you invent, it's the same thing as my doing an acting agreement for Sharon Stone and the production owning the results of her services.

"People on the talent side have to be out there and going to screenings and constantly networking and doing a lot of the schmoozing. My clients all come to me," says Steinberg, who prefers to work on individual productions rather than for individual clients. "With a lot of these production jobs and bond jobs, you have to be approved not only by your client, but by the other side. So there's a relatively small community of people who do what I do."

There's actually a lot more work out there for entertainment attorneys other than representing actors or other individuals. With all of the independent films being made today, the scope of opportunities includes production finance, completion guarantees, distribution work, and most commonly, production counsel, which represents the production entity in every aspect of making the movie. Depending on when the attorney comes on to a screen project, production counsel chores can include everything from acquiring the rights to the book and going through the entire development process once a film is greenlighted, to handling contracts on casting and locations.

In Hollywood, lawyers tend to fall relatively low on the totem pole until you need one, and then they're placed really high. "Everybody complains that you need a lawyer at every step, but whenever anything goes wrong, they're the first person everybody turns to," says Steinberg. "I think in some ways it's symptomatic of American society right now being very litigious and legal oriented. Particularly because these are big investments in each individual feature, and at the end of the day, an intangible product. It's not like I can really hold on to something. Lawyers are involved and are important and can play either an obstructionist or facilitating role. You're sometimes asked to do both."

PERSONAL ASSISTANTS

The absolute bottom rung on the Hollywood handler food chain is the personal assistant. This person works for a piece of talent, usually an actor or director, and his sole mission is to make that person's life easier. The demands of making a film are extremely difficult for an actor or director. There is so much at stake and so many things to consider that personal assistants are needed to alleviate some of the stress associated with making a movie. This position might cover work-related duties like scheduling appointments and going over dialogue, to personal duties like grocery shopping and walking the dog.

Yvette Taylor, vice president of production at All Girl Productions, worked as a personal assistant to director Terry Gilliam on *The Fisher King*

(1991) when she was first starting out. "My job duties were everything. I was literally setting meetings, attending meetings, and helping him in every aspect of pre-production, while at the same time finding him a house to live in. I was out at six o'clock in the morning meeting the real estate agent to look at houses. Then at nine o'clock there's a production meeting. At times it was like being a middleman. You want to try to cushion everything for them, including their personal lives, in an effort to make every aspect of their life easier because they have so much going on."

Campbell Katz started out as actor-writer-director Albert Brooks's assistant. "I used to have to transcribe his dreams," Katz details. "He would tape-record them and have me type them up." Katz also used to cook him turkey. "We had a kitchen in the office, and there was a special way that he liked them," says Katz. "He'd make me so mad, I'd take a knife and stab the turkey before I served it to him."

These positions generally are found on a referral basis only. Because of the celebrity factor involved, good references are the best credential to obtaining this type of job. There's no definitive career path that emanates from a job like this. Some people love the close interaction with a star and go from movie to movie as a personal assistant, while others springboard the position into an incredible opportunity.

Producer Bonnie Bruckheimer was working as an assistant to the producer on *The Rose* (1979) when she first met Bette Midler. Soon thereafter, Midler asked Bruckheimer to work as her assistant. "I had never worked for a star or an actor before, only producers and directors," recalls Bruckheimer. "But I was fascinated by her because she's such a huge talent."

Bruckheimer agreed to be Midler's assistant. Because the star did not have a manager or anyone else handling her business other than her lawyer, Bruckheimer did much more than an ordinary assistant would do. "Obviously I'd be booking appointments and doing telephones, but I gradually did more and more," she says. "We became a team and worked on everything that she did together.

"I learned a lot from Bette about business and never giving up," says Bruckheimer. "I think I gained a lot of self-confidence from working with her. I realized how well we were doing and that I could do anything I set my mind to. As a child, I was never taught that a woman could be anything she wanted. I was told you'd better learn how to type. I didn't have life lessons that helped me in my career. She had a lot to do with showing me I could be successful at whatever I tried." Bruckheimer has been Midler's partner at All Girl Productions for more than twelve years.

PART FIVE

THAT'S A WRAP

18

You Can Always Eat Lunch in This Town Again

Far from there being one answer, there's probably not even ten answers to any of these questions about how you break in.

MARSHALL HERSKOVITZ, director

No matter which career in film you pursue, having a complete overview of the motion picture industry puts you ahead of the pack. Knowing not only about the position that interests you, but also about how it interacts with other professions in Hollywood, allows for a more complete understanding of the movie business as a whole.

My advice now is to go out and do it! One point that's been reiterated by the experts in this book is that there is no one way to climb the Hollywood ladder. Forge ahead and carve out your own path. To quote from one of my favorite movies, *Dead Poets Society* (1989), written by Tom Schulman, *Carpe diem*—seize the day. Once you've made it, have your person call my person. We'll do lunch.

I will leave you with helpful advice from today's working industry professionals.

I think one of the best pieces of advice I ever got was when a line producer said to me, "I hired you to help me win. That's your job description." Whatever you can do to make their life easier and help them win, that's what you do.

—KRISTIEANNE GROELINGER,
director of production, Jerry Bruckheimer Films

I think you have to be absolutely crazy and possessed about what you want to be in this business. You have to love it. You have to think and sleep and breathe it twenty-four hours a day.

—JOHN CAGLIONE JR., makeup artist

No matter what job you're doing, watch everyone and learn their job as well. Don't say, because I'm going to be a producer, I don't need to know what a script supervisor does, because that's the wrong attitude. I think that that's a very important way to learn and move up.

—BONNIE BRUCKHEIMER, producer

Do your homework. When you're talking to a company, know what their business is. If what you want to do is make movies with Peter Greenaway [*The Pillow Book*], don't go interview at Paramount. Paramount is not in the business of making little art movies. Also, be honest. If that's what you want to do, there is a place to do that. Don't tell people things they want to hear. One of the most valuable things people have is a good, informed opinion. That's currency.

—JONATHAN KING, president of production,
Laurence Mark Productions

Don't talk when you're starting out. You'll learn more from everyone else than from yourself.

—DAVID KATZ, assistant director

As sick and cliché as it sounds, it really is all about relationships and nepotism. It's all about being out there and open to what's possible, and being flexible. You have to deal with a lot of attitude

and a lot of personalities, and if you can do that and you perse-
vere, I think most people do eventually make it.

—DAVID STEINBERG, entertainment attorney

Everybody wants to be in this business. So if you really want to
be successful, it has to be the only thing you care about and it
has to be your whole life, at least until you prove yourself. When
you're starting out, you have to put in those twelve-hour days
and do it with a smile on your face, at least until you get noticed.

—MICHAEL VALEO, manager

Get to know as many people as possible in Hollywood, without
using them. Get to know them as human beings and get to know
them as friends, because if you're a friend, people will help you
out. But when they sense that you're using them for an opportunity, they'll turn away from you. So get to know as many people as you can socially. When they're my friend, I want to help
them because I care about them.

—JIMMY DOBSON, publicist

The Always/Never Rules

ALWAYS cover your ass! This rule applies to everyone, whether you're a PA, an assistant, a producer. Check everything. Double-check everything. Triple-check everything. And always get the
name of the person you spoke to, or a confirmation number, whenever possible.

NEVER assume. Assumption is the mother of all f*** ups.

NEVER trust anyone in this business as far as you can see them with your eyes closed. Of course,
there are exceptions to this rule, but very few. Just be smart.

NEVER put all of your eggs in one basket. Don't sit around waiting for that *one* person to make
that *one* call about that *one* job. Try to create new possibilities for yourself every day, whether
it's calling production companies in the *Creative Directory* to ask about job openings, or putting
yourself in the proper social situation to meet people who may know of a production or company who is looking for someone with your qualifications.

ALWAYS pay attention to everything that is going on around you at all times. You can learn a lot
by observing the mistakes and triumphs of others.

—Yvette Taylor, vice president of production, All Girl Productions

Every time I'd go to an interview, I'd make sure I wouldn't leave that interview without at least four or five more names to call. I'd always say, please, who do you recommend I can talk to?

—GARY WISSNER, production designer

I think nice goes a long way, but what people respond to in any business, I think, is passion and focus. Is this person taking himself and his vision seriously? You can just see it in somebody's eyes. People are willing to follow anyone who seems to really believe what they're saying.

—JON TURTELTAUB, director

Be careful who you sleep with out here, because you're going to be surrounded by these people for a very long time.

—DEBBIE DEUBLE, agent

Integrity works, even in a town where it's not always the most admired value.

—PAULINE CYMET, co-owner,
The Right Connections Personnel Service

Appendix A
Resources

ENTERTAINMENT DIRECTORIES

Hollywood Agents & Managers Directory
Hollywood Creative Directory
(310) 315-4815
www.hcdonline.com

Hollywood Reporter Blu-Book
(323) 525-2150
secure.telescan.com/blubook.asp

The Industry Labor Guide
(818) 995-4008
www.entertainmentpublisher.com

LA 411
(323) 460-6304
www.la411.com

Pacific Coast Studio Directory
(800) 722-5667
www.studio-directory.com

Paymaster
(818) 955-6000
www.ep-services.com

ENTERTAINMENT TEMP AGENCIES

All Star Agency
(310) 271-5217

Apple One Employment Services
(818) 247-2991

Friedman Personnel Agency
(310) 550-1002

London Personnel Agency
(818) 243-8100

Our Gang Agency, Inc.
(323) 653-4381

The Right Connections
(310) 657-3700

FILM FESTIVALS

AFI Los Angeles International Film Festival
2021 N. Western Ave.
Los Angeles, CA 90027-1657
(323) 856-7707
(323) 462-4049 fax
www.afifest.com

Slamdance Film Festival
6381 Hollywood Blvd., Ste. 520
Los Angeles, CA 90028-6311
(323) 466-1786
(323) 466-1784 fax
www.slamdance.com

Sundance Film Festival
307 W. 200 South, Ste. 5002
Salt Lake City, UT 84101-1268
(801) 322-4033
www.sundance.org/festival

FILM SCHOOLS

American Film Institute
2021 N. Western Ave.
Los Angeles, CA 90027-1657
(323) 856-7600
www.afionline.org

Assistant Directors Training Program
15260 Ventura Blvd., Ste. 1200-A
Sherman Oaks, CA 91403-5347
(818) 386-2545
www.dgptp.org

Northwestern University Department of Radio, Television, and Film
Evanston, IL 60201
(847) 491-7315

Tisch School of the Arts, New York University
721 Broadway, 8th Floor
New York, NY 10003-6807
(212) 998-1918
www.nyu.edu/tisch/filmtv.html

UCLA School of Film and Television, c/o Student Services
P.O. Box 951622, UCLA
Los Angeles, CA 90095-1622
(310) 825-5761

USC School of Cinema-Television
Garden Terrace 106, University Park
Los Angeles, CA 90089-2211
(213) 740-2911
www-cntv.usc.edu/

LOS ANGELES RESOURCES

LA Weekly
(818) 545-0396
www.laweekly.com

Los Angeles Convention and Visitors Bureau
633 W. 5th St., Ste. 6000
Los Angeles, CA 90071-2088
(213) 624-7300
(213) 624-9746 fax
www.lacvb.com

Los Angeles Magazine
(800) 876-5222
www.lamag.com

Los Angeles Times
(310) 314-1218
www.latimes.com

Thomas Bros. Maps
(800) 899-MAPS (6277) (West Coast)
(888) WE-MAP-DC (936-2732) (East Coast)
www.thomasguide.com

Yahoo Los Angeles
dir.yahoo.com/Regional/U_S__States/
California/Metropolitan_Areas/
Los_Angeles_Metro/

MAGAZINES

American Cinematographer
(323) 969-4344
www.cinematographer.com

Back Stage West
(323) 525-2356
www.backstage.com

Cinefex
(909) 781-1917
www.cinefex.com

Creative Screenwriting
(323) 957-1405
www.creativescreenwriting.com

Daily Variety
(818) 487-4554
www.variety.com

DGA Magazine
(310) 289-2000, x5306
www.dga.org/magazine/magazine_index.htm

Entertainment Employment Journal
(818) 920-0060
www.eej.com

Fade In
(310) 275-0287
www.fadeinmag.com

Film & Video
(800) 777-5006
www.kipinet.com/film

Film Comment
(800) 783-4903

Film Music Magazine
(818) 729-9500
www.filmmusicmag.com

Hollywood Reporter
(323) 525-2150
www.hollywoodreporter.com

International Photographer
(323) 876-0160
cameramag@aol.com

Location Update
(818) 785-6362
www.cineweb.com

Locations
Association of Film Commissioners International
(323) 462-6092
www.afci.org

Millimeter
(800) 441-0294
www.millimeter.com

Movieline
(800) 521-1966
www.movielinemag.com

Moviemaker Magazine
(310) 234-9234
www.moviemaker.com

Premiere
(800) 289-2489
www.premiere.com

Scenario
(800) 222-2654
www.scenariomag.com

Scr(i)pt
(888) 287-0932
scriptmg@erols.com

Written By
(323) 782-4522
www.wga.org/WrittenBY

ORGANIZATIONS

Academy of Motion Picture Arts & Sciences
(310) 247-3000
www.oscar.com

Academy of Science Fiction, Fantasy & Horror Films
(323) 752-5811

Academy of Television Arts & Sciences
(818) 754-2800
www.emmys.org

Alliance of Motion Picture & TV Producers
(818) 995-3600

American Cinema Editors
(323) 850-2900
www.theaces.org

American Film Institute
(323) 856-7600
www.afionline.org

American Society of Cinematographers
(323) 969-4333
www.cinematographer.com

American Society of Composers, Authors & Publishers
(323) 883-1000
www.ascap.com

Assistant Directors Training Program
(818) 386-2545
www.dgptp.org

Association of Film Commissioners International
(323) 462-6092
www.afci.org

Association of Independent Commercial Producers
(323) 960-4763
www.aicp.com

Association of Talent Agents
(310) 274-0628
agentassoc@aol.com

Casting Society of America
(323) 463-1925

Conference of Personal Managers, Inc.
(310) 275-2456
www.cybershowbiz.com/ncopm

Greater Los Angeles Press Club
(323) 469-8180

Hollywood Arts Council
(323) 462-2355

Hollywood Foreign Press Association
(310) 657-1731
www.goldenglobes.org

Independent Feature Project/West
(310) 475-4379
www.ifp.org

International Association of Audio/Visual Communicators
(619) 461-1600

Motion Picture Association of America
(818) 995-6600
www.mpaa.org

Music Video Production Association
(323) 469-9494
www.mvpa.com

National Academy of Recording Arts & Sciences
(310) 392-3777
www.grammy.com

Production Assistants Association
(310) 659-7416

Screen Composers of America
(323) 876-6040

Set Decorators Society of America
(310) 289-1959
www.setdecorators.org

Women in Film
(323) 463-6040
www.wif.org

Women in Show Business
(310) 271-3415

SOFTWARE

Budgeting/Finance/Accounting
FilmProfit
www.filmprofit.com

Industry Labor Guide
www.laborguide.com

Movie Magic Budgeting
www.screenplay.com

Movie Magic Labor Rates
www.screenplay.com

Reference
MovieBuff
www.moviebuffonline.com

Scheduling
Movie Magic Scheduling
www.screenplay.com

Screenwriting
Final Draft
www.finaldraft.com

Movie Magic Screenwriter
www.screenplay.com

ScriptThing
www.scriptthing.com

Scriptware
www.scriptware.com

Story Planning
Dramatica
www.dramatica.com

Plots Unlimited
www.ashleywilde.com

Storybuilder
www.svsoft.com/svsoft/

Story Craft
www.writerspage.com

UNIONS

Key to Acronyms
AFL: American Federation of Labor
AFM: American Federation of Musicians
CIO: Congress of Industrial Organizations
IATSE: International Alliance of Theatrical Stage Employees
IBEW: International Brotherhood of Electrical Workers
IBT: International Brotherhood of Teamsters
MPMO: Motion Picture Machine Operators

Affiliated Property Craftsmen
Local 44, IATSE, AFL
(818) 769-2500

Broadcast TV Recording Engineers
Local 45, IBEW
(323) 851-5515

Costume Designers Guild
Local 892
(818) 905-1557

Directors Guild of America
(310) 289-2000

Electricians
IBEW Local 40, AFL-CIO
(818) 762-4239

International Photographers Guild
Local 600, IATSE
(323) 876-0160

International Sound Technicians/Cinetech/TV Engineers
Local 695, IATSE, MPMO, AFL
(818) 985-9204

Makeup Artists and Hairstylists
Local 706, IATSE/MPMO of US and Canada
(818) 984-1700

Motion Picture Costumers
Local 705, IATSE, MPMO, AFL
(323) 851-0220

Motion Picture Crafts Services
Local 727, IATSE
(818) 385-1950

Motion Picture Editors Guild
Local 776, IATSE
(323) 876-4770

Motion Picture Illustrators and Matte Artists
Local 790, IATSE
(818) 784-6555

Motion Picture Set Painters
Local 729, IATSE, AFL
(818) 842-7729

Motion Picture Studio Grips
Local 80, IATSE, AFL
(323) 931-1419

Musicians Union
Local 47, AFM
(323) 462-2161

Ornamental Plaster, Model and Sculpting
Local 755, IATSE, AFL-CIO
(818) 379-9711

Producers Guild of America
(310) 557-0807

Production Accountants
Local 717, IATSE
(818) 906-9986

Production Office Coordinators
Local 717, IATSE
(818) 906-9986

Publicists Guild of America
Local 818, IATSE and MPMO, AFL
(818) 905-1541

Scenic, Title and Graphic Artists
Local 816, IATSE, AFL-CIO
(818) 906-7822

Script Supervisors
Local 871, IATSE
(818) 995-6195

Set Designers and Model Makers
Local 847, IATSE
(818) 784-6555

Society of Motion Picture and TV Art Directors
Local 876, IATSE
(818) 762-9995

Sound Construction Installation and Maintenance Technicians
Local 40, IBEW, AFL-CIO
(818) 762-4239

Story Analysts
Local 854, IATSE
(323) 801-2201

Studio Electrical Lighting Technicians
Local 728 IATSE, MPMO, AFL-CIO
(818) 891-0728

Studio Transportation Drivers
Local 399, IBT
(818) 985-7374

Theatrical Wardrobe Attendants
Local 768, IATSE
(818) 789-8735

Writers Guild of America West
(323) 951-4000

WEB SITES

Audio and Sound Services
Architecture and Acoustics Studio 440
www.studio440.com

Bang Zoom Kapow! Weddington Prods.
www.weddington.com

Hollywood Recording Services
www.hrsaudio.com

Location Sound Corp.
www.locationsound.com

Outlaw Sound
www.outlawsound.com

Remote Film Sound
www.remotefilm.com

Rumbo Recorders Recording Studio
www.pobox.com/~rumbo/

Skywalker Sound
www.ldlhr.com

Soundelux Online
www.soundelux.com

Voice of the Arts
www.voiceofthearts.com

World Studio Group
www.worldstudio.com

Crew and Service Directories
CineWEB
www.cineweb.com

The Crew Net
www.crew-net.com

Entertainment Directory
www.edweb.com

Film Folks
www.filmfolks.com

Hollywood 911
www.hollywood-911.com

MAX Film Pro
www.maxfilmpro.com

Producer's Source
www.producers-source.com

Directories and Databases
Internet Movie Database
www.us.imdb.com

Lone Eagle: Entertainment Industry Resource
www.loneeagle.com

Moviebuff Online
www.moviebuffonline.com

UCLA Film and Television Archive
www.cinema.ucla.edu

Employment Resources
Brad Marks International
www.bradmarks.com

The Broadcast Training Program
www.webcom.com/mibtp

Entertainment Recruiting Network
www.showbizjobs.com

Film, TV, and Commercial Employment Network
www.employnow.com

The Maslow Media Group
www.maslowmedia.com

Entertainment Industry Data
Alexander & Associates
www.alexassoc.com

Entertainment Data
www.entdata.com

PKBaseline
www.pkbaseline.com

Entertainment Industry Resources
Cyphon
www.cyphon.com

Entertainment Industry Development Corp.
www.eidc.com

FilmProfit
www.filmprofit.com

Producer Link
www.producerlink.com

Producer's Source
www.producers-source.com

Equipment Sales and Rental
Cinelease
www.cinelease.com

Mole Richardson Moletown
www.mole.com

Otto Nemenz International
www.ottonemenz.com

WESCAM
www.wescam.com

Expendables and Supplies
Fuji Film
www.fujifilm.com

Kodak
www.kodak.com

Film Studios and Distributors
Dimension Films
www.dimensionfilms.com

Fine Line Features
www.flf.com

First Look Pictures/Overseas Filmgroup
www.flp.com or www.ofg.com

Good Machine
www.goodmachine.com

Gramercy
www.reellife.com

Metro-Goldwyn-Mayer
www.mgmua.com

Miramax Films
www.miramax.com

New Line Cinema
www.newline.com

New Regency Productions
www.newregency.com

October Films
www.octoberfilms.com

Paramount Studios
www.paramount.com

The Shooting Gallery
www.shootinggallery.com

Sony Classics
www.spe.sony.com/classics

Sony Pictures Entertainment
www.spe.sony.com

Strand Releasing
www.strandrel.com

Trimark Entertainment
www.trimarkpictures.com

Twentieth Century-Fox
www.foxmovies.com

Twentieth Century-Fox Searchlight
www.foxsearchlight.com

Universal Studios
www.universalstudios.com

Walt Disney
www.disney.com

Warner Bros.
www.warnerbros.com

Film-Related Information Resources
Ain't It Cool News
www.aint-it-cool-news.com
All Movie
www.allmovie.com

@LA Entertainment Industry services database
www.at-la.com/@la-film

CineMedia Entertainment Directory
afi.cinemedia.org

Entertainment Asylum
www.asylum.com

E! Online
www.eonline.com

Film.com
www.film.com

FilmBiz Resource Guide
www.filmbiz.com

Hollywood Access Directory
www.hollywoodnetwork.com/hn/directory/dirsearch/tview.html

Hollywood Online
www.hollywood.com

HollywoodNet News
www.hollywoodnet.com

IndieWIRE
www.indiewire.com

In-Hollywood
www.inhollywood.com

Internet Movie Database
www.us.imdb.com

MovieFone MovieLink
www.moviefone.com

Mr. Showbiz
www.mrshowbiz.com

Roger Ebert & the Movies
tvplex.go.com/buenavista/siskelandebert

Showbiz Data Entertainment Search Engine
www.showbizdata.com

Spectracom Global Media Links
www.spectracom.com/globalmedia/database.html

Worldwide Production Source
www.wpsource.com

Legal Services
All Law
www.alllaw.com

de Forest Research Associates
www.deforestresearch.com

Entertainment Law Resources
www.laig.com/law/entlaw/index.html

Entertainment, Multimedia and Intellectual Property Law and Business
Network
www.medialawyer.com

Lighting Equipment and Services
Acey Decy Lighting
www.aceydecy.com

Angstrom Stage Lighting
www.angstromlighting.com

Media Lighting and Supply
www.medialighting.com

Strand Lighting
www.strandlight.com

Post-Production Services
Avid
www.avid.com

Crest National Digital Media Complex
www.crestnational.com

Encore Video Hollywood
www.encorevideo.com

Hollywood Digital
www.hollydig.com

Novocom
www.novo.com

POP
www.popstudios.com

Runway Non-Linear
www.runway.com

Sunset Post
www.sunsetpost.com

Video Media
www.wizvax.net/videocen/index.html

Professional Resources
Entertainment Industry Development Corporation
www.epg.org

Hollywood Network
www.hollywoodnetwork.com

Movie Pubs
home.mecfilms.com/moviepubs

Runway
www.runway.com

Silicon Studio Los Angeles
www.sgi.com/studiotraining

Visual Effects Resource Center
www.visualfx.com

Promotion and Marketing Services
Creation Entertainment
www.creationent.com

Creative Productions
www.creativeproductions.com

Deja Vu Design
www.dejavudesign.com

Echo Images
www.echoink.net

Props and Prop Rentals
Promo & Props Co.
www.promoandprops.com

Scripts and Screenwriting
Author Link
www.authorlink.com

Drew's Script-O-Rama
www.script-o-rama.com

GreatScripts.com
www.greatscripts.com

Hollywood Lit Sales
www.hollywoodlitsales.com

Internet Screenwriters Network
www.hollywoodnet.com/scriptindex.html

Megahit Screenplays
www.megahitmovies.com

MovieBytes
www.moviebytes.com

The Pitch
www.zyworld.com/pitch

Robert McKee's Story Structure
www.mckeestory.com

Sapex Scripts Services U.K.
www.sapex.demon.co.uk

Screen Connect
www.screenconnect.com

Screenwriters Online
www.screenwriter.com/insider/news.html

Screenwriter's Resource
www.screenwriting.com

The Screenwriting Center
www.clearstream.com

The Spec Script Library
www.thesource.com.au/scriptservice/

The Writers' Computer Store
www.writerscomputer.com

Set Design and Construction
Asylum Design Works
www.asylumdesignworks.com

Special Effects and Animation Services
Chiodo Bros. Productions
www.chiodobros.com

Click 3X
www.click3X.com/index.html

Dan Krech Productions
www.dkp.com

Dream Theater
www.dreamtheater.com

Engram Digital Productions
www.engramdigital.com

Image Creators
www.flash.net/~creators

Image G
www.imageg.com

Novocom
www.novo.com

Pinnacle Efx
www.pinnaclestudios.com

Pixar Animation Studio
www.pixar.com

Special Effects: Practical and Mechanical
Bodytech
www.bodytek.com

Cinnabar
www.cinnabar.com

FX Rentals & Design
www.loop.com/~fxrentals

Special Effects Supply
www.fxsupply.com

Special Effects Unlimited
www.specialefxunltd.com

Special Effects Services
BUF Compagnie
www.buf.fr

Cinesite
www.cinesite.com

Digital Domain
www.d2.com

EAI
www.eai.com

Foundation Imaging
www.foundation-i.com

House of Moves
www.moves.com

Industrial Light & Magic
www.ldlhr.com

Kleiser-Walczak Construction Company
www.kwcc.com

Lamb & Co
www.lamb.com

Matte World Digital
www.matteworld.com

Medialab
www.medialab3d.com

MetroLight Studios
www.metrolight.com

Pacific Data Images
www.pdi.com

Pittard Sullivan
www.pittardsullivan.com

Rhythm & Hues Studios
www.rhythm.com

Sony Pictures Imageworks
www.spiw.com

Stan Winston Studios
www.swfx.com

Vision Crew Unlimited
www.visioncrew.com

Stock Footage
Archive Films/Archive Photos
www.archivefilms.com

BBC Library Sales
www.bbcfootage.com

Footage.Net
www.footage.net

MPI Media Group
www.mpimedia.com

Puritano Media Group
www.puritano.com

Videotape Library
www.videotapelibrary.com

Title Services
Scarlet Letters
www.ciagroup.com/sl.html

Transportation
Entertainment Transportation Network
www.etninc.com

Appendix B

Guild/Union Minimum Payments

All salaries listed are union scale rates as of January 1999 unless otherwise specified. Because rates change periodically, consult the appropriate union or guild for the most up-to-date information. There is no difference between a union and a guild.

Above-the-Line

Director

Budget less than $500,000	$6,862/week
Between $500,000 and $1.5 million	$7,799/week
Greater than $1.5 million	$10,919/week

Producer

The pay rate for a producer is not determined by any guild. It can vary immensely according to the type of producer and the budget of the particular film. Generally, producer salaries are set by precedent. Once a producer is paid a certain amount of money for one movie, his fee on the next project will be at least as much as the last fee, and probably greater. On average, a producer might make anywhere from $100,000 to $1 million in addition to net points (a percentage of the net profit, which is equal to box-office grosses minus any expenses such as print and advertising costs).

Writer

	Low Budget (< $2.5 million)	High Budget (> $2.5 million)
Original screenplay, including treatment	$43,952	$82,444
Original screenplay, excluding treatment or sale of non-original screenplay	$29,536	$60,456
Non-original screenplay, including treatment	$38,466	$71,531
Non-original screenplay, excluding treatment or sale of non-original screenplay	$24,036	$49,464
Additional compensation for story included in screenplay	$5,500	$10,992
Story or treatment	$14,423	$21,988
Original story or treatment	$19,917	$32,980
First draft screenplay	$17,310	$32,980
Final draft screenplay	$11,536	$21,988
Rewrite of screenplay	$14,423	$21,988
Polish of screenplay	$7,215	$10,922

BELOW-THE-LINE

In the following list, studio refers to a situation where shooting occurs within the confines of a sound stage, most likely on a studio lot. Location refers to any filming outside a sound stage and away from the studio lot.

Additional second assistant director	$1,144/week studio salary
	$1,601/week location salary
Apprentice editor	$882.62/week
Apprentice publicist	$828.84/week
Art department coordinator	$875.50/week
Assistant art director	$1,714.17/week
Assistant costume designer	$1,331.80/week
Assistant editor*	$1,188.59/week
Assistant location manager	$763/week
Assistant production accountant	$1,101.39/week
Assistant production coordinator	$671.57/week
Assistant propmaster	$25.27/hour
Best boy	$1,549.22/week
Boom operator	$31.07/hour
Camera operator	$1,630.70/week
Costume department production supervisor	$1,568.64/week
Costume designer	$1,631.04/week
Costumer	$1,321.96/week
Craft services foreperson	$1,236.94/week
Director of photography	$2,590.42/week
Editor (starts at)	$1,617.86/week
Electrician	$24.85/hour
Film loader	$23.45/hour
First assistant camera person	$1,288.88/week
First assistant director	$2,963/week studio salary
	$4,145/week location salary
Gaffer	$1,722.30/week
Grip (starts at)	$24.72/hour
Hair department head	$1,988.06/week
Hairstylist	$1,297.69–$1,466.17/week
Junior storyboard artist	$1,431.93/week
Key costumer	$1,461.49/week
Key grip	$1,722.30/week
Leadman	$1,324.51/week
Location manager	$1,977/week
Makeup artist	$1,435.74–$1,689.09/week

Makeup department head	$1,988.06/week
Music editor	$1,490.27/week
On-set dresser	$23.61/hour
Playback operator	$26.64/hour
Production accountant	$1,985.99/week
Production coordinator	$1,154.27/week
Production sound mixer	$46.06/hour
Propmaker foreman	$1,548.62/week
Propmaster	$28.62/hour
Second assistant camera person	$1,188.26/week
Second assistant director	$1,986/week studio salary
	$2,775/week location salary
Second second assistant director	$1,874/week studio salary
	$2,621/week location salary
Senior publicist	$1,540.17/week
Senior set designer	$1,151.77/week
Senior set model builder	$1,151.77/week
Senior storyboard artist	$1,603/week
Set carpenter	$25.28/hour
Set decorator	$1,757.32/week
Set dresser/swing gang worker	$23.61/hour
Sound editor	$1,490.27/week
Sound mixer	$46.06/hour
Sound utility	$27.75/hour
Special effects foreman**	$1,548.62/week
Still photographer	$1,326.92/week
Unit production manager	$3,118/week studio salary
	$4,366/week location salary
Wardrobe supervisor	$1,524.80/week

*The union does not differentiate between first and second assistant editor. Obviously, a first assistant will be paid a higher rate than a second assistant.
**There is no union category for visual effects.

The union does not differentiate between production designer and art director. Because most PDs are senior-level art directors, they will be paid a higher rate than an art director. Scale for this position is determined by months of experience.

First six months in industry	$1,873.26/week
Second six months	$2,084.82/week
After one year	$2,290.16/week

Minimum salary for a script supervisor is determined by length of experience in the industry.

First year	$1,277.28/week
Second year	$1,345.27/week
Third year and after	$1,423.54/week

Union readers are paid hourly depending on length of experience. Minimum salary ranges from $21.72/hour for less than six months experience to $26.31/hour for more than fifty-five months experience. (Nonunion readers generally are paid $30–50 per script; $60–80 per book.)

Production Fees
Certain craft positions also get a production fee. A production fee is money on top of the normal salary, and it is a union-specified payment.

First assistant director	$548/week studio production fee
	$675/week location production fee
Second assistant director	$418/week studio production fee
	$548/week location production fee
Unit production manager	$675/week studio production fee
	$806/week location production fee

Glossary

Above-the-line: Collectively refers to creative talent: actors, directors, producers, and writers. Also, the part of the budget that includes costs and fees associated with this division of talent.

Acquisition: A project purchased by a studio or distributor in either packaged or finished form. Often the production is financed through acquisition funds.

Agent: A handler who represents above- or below-the-line talent. His primary function is to secure work for his clients.

Art director: The person who executes the vision of the production designer in creating the look of the film.

Assistant director: The crew member responsible for delegating the director's instructions and making sure the cast and crew are in their required positions at the right time.

Attachment: A piece of talent that has committed to being in a film.

Avid: A name-brand, Macintosh-based, nonlinear digital editing system.

Back end: Deferred payment of fees and/or percentage of net profits paid to certain above-the-line players once a film turns a profit.

Below-the-line: Collectively refers to all workers on a film crew that are not considered above-the-line creative talent. Also, the part of the budget that includes costs and fees associated with these workers.

Best boy: Right-hand person to a gaffer or key grip.

Blue screen: Literally, a blue backdrop that, when filmed upon, can be digitally replaced by alternate background footage. For example, an actor playing Superman is shot flying against a blue screen, and the shot is then transposed into an aerial view of Metropolis.

Boom: A large, pole-shaped mount that positions a microphone directly over an actor on set so that the sound mixer can record her dialogue.

Breakdown: The process of reading through a script and pulling out critical information needed by each department to do their job. For example, the property master breaks down all the needed props; a costume designer counts the number of changes per character.

B-roll: Used in the context of this book, B-roll refers to footage of the actual film being made. Generally, the B-roll might be included as part of the EPK.

Call sheet: Daily report that lists the time the cast and crew are to arrive on set.

Callback: A subsequent audition for an actor being considered for a role in a film.

Camera package: All equipment used on a shoot relating to the camera.

Cast: (n.) The actors in a film. (v.) To select actors to portray characters in a film.

Casting director: The person responsible for selecting lead and supporting actors for a film.

Cinematographer: The person responsible for conceptualizing the camera and lighting design to achieve the director's vision, then capturing that vision on film.

Composer: The person who writes the instrumental score for a film.

Continuity: Ensuring that actors, props, lighting, and other elements remain the same from shot to shot within a scene.

Costumer: The person responsible for dressing the actors and overseeing the continuity of the costumes on set.

Coverage: (1) The process by which multiple camera setups and angles are filmed to ensure that the editor has sufficient footage to cut together a complete sequence. (2) Synopsis and analysis of a script for purposes of development.

Craft services: Crew members responsible for feeding the cast and crew in between meals on set.

Crane: A large device on which the camera is mounted that is used to capture large, sweeping movement, high and low angles, and other specialized shots.

Dailies: The day's footage screened by the department heads at the end of the following production day.

Development: The process of perfecting a film script so that it is ready to shoot.

Digital effects: Special movie effects generated by a computer.

Director: The primary creative and artistic force behind a film. In charge of actors' performances on camera and determining the overall look and feel of the film.

Director of photography: See Cinematographer.

Dissolve: An effect between two shots in which one fades out as the other fades in.

Distribution: The process by which prints of a film are sent to theaters for exhibition.

Dolly: A piece of equipment on which the camera is mounted in order to achieve smooth motion in any direction.

Dubbing: The addition of sound onto a picture.

Editor: The person responsible for creating a successful narrative by joining together the separate shots of film.

Effects: Sounds or images specially designed and executed to heighten or enhance a scene.

Electronic press kit: Video footage consisting of interviews with the cast and creative team, as well as behind-the-scenes footage. EPKs are sent to visual media outlets to assist in publicizing a movie.

Exhibition: A commercial presentation of a film for the public.

Extras: Background actors who do not have any lines of dialogue.

Fades: An optical effect in which a shot gradually goes to black or emerges from black to picture.

Feature: A full-length motion picture.

Film commission: City, state, or country offices set up to entice filming in their community, and to assist in filming activity within that community.

Film stock: The raw material used to record photographic images.

Financier: An independent party that provides the funding for a motion picture.

First-look deal: The most common arrangement between a studio and a production company in which the studio provides all overhead expenses in exchange for a "first look" at viable material from the production company.

Flag: The act of placing a piece of cloth or metal in front of a light to diffuse the light's effect.

Foley: Post-production process by which certain sounds within a motion picture are created by first watching the scene, then simulating effects to match the onscreen action.

Footage: Film that has been run through a camera and now contains an image.

Gaffer: The person responsible for lighting a scene as directed by the cinematographer. Also known as chief electrician.

Greenlight: Term used by studio indicating they have decided to put a development project into production.

Grip: The person responsible for the general maintenance and rigging on a film set.

Guild: See Union.

High concept: An easily expressed, extremely commercial idea. For example, a lawyer who cannot lie (*Liar, Liar*) or a singing nun (*Sister Act*).

Hot sheet: A hot-cost report that reveals the actual cost of one production day.

Independent film: A film financed without the assistance or creative input of a major studio.

Key crew: Department heads within a film crew.

Labels: Separate movie divisions within the same studio that loosely define the product they release.

Lead: The main role in a film.

Leadman: The person who manages the crew of swing gang and set dressers.

Lightworks: A name-brand, DOS-based, nonlinear digital editing system.

Limited release: Distribution strategy that starts a film's exhibition in a small number of theaters to test the audience response.

Literary: General term referring to writers, directors, and sometimes producers.

Location manager: The person responsible for finding and attaining sites for shooting the film.

Looping: Post-production process by which actors redub inaudible production dialogue.

Marketing campaign: A plan to promote and publicize an upcoming feature.

Material: General term used to describe a screenplay or manuscript.

Matte painting: Artwork of a backdrop or landscape that is inserted behind the filmed action during post-production.

Mixing: The process of integrating all the various soundtracks of a film into one.

Montage: An editing style that utilizes a rapid succession of separate shots within a film, usually related and combined, to convey the passage of time.

Narrative: A story.

Net profit: Contractual payment to certain above-the-line players equal to a percentage of profits, minus expenses for such things as prints and advertising.

Networking: Making contacts within the industry that will be beneficial to launching or helping a career in Hollywood.

Non-pro: A person who does not work in the film business.

On location: Shooting that takes place outside of a sound stage and away from a studio.

On-set: Where filming takes place.

One-sheet: A movie poster (just over 2 x 3 feet) used for advertising purposes.

Opening: A film's commercial debut.

Option: To take a project off the market for a specified period of time by paying a deposit against a set purchase price when the film is set up.

Overhead: The operating costs of running a production company, including rent, employees' salaries, and entertainment expenses.

Package: General term used when two or more elements are attached to a project, such as a director and star.

Perks: Nonmonetary considerations given to above-the-line players, mostly stars, such as star requests, personal trainers, personal chefs, and extra airline tickets.

Pitch: To verbally present an idea or story to a production company or studio.

Point of view (POV): The subjective angle from which a story is told.

Polish: A slight rewrite of a screenplay.

Post-production: The final phase of the filmmaking process. It includes everything that is done to a film after shooting is completed.

Pre-dub: Cleaning, editing, and preparing of all soundtracks for the final mix.

Pre-production: Everything that takes place before filming commences.

Pre-selling: A method of raising financing for an independent film by selling distribution rights to various territories before a film is made.

Press junkets: A planned publicity opportunity during which journalists screen a movie and then conduct short interviews with the film's actors and director on a one-on-one basis.

Press kit: A package containing photographs, a synopsis of the movie, detailed production notes, and biographies of the cast and filmmakers, which is sent to the print media in connection with promoting a movie.

Principal photography: The actual filming period.

Producer: The person who is ultimately responsible for the success or failure of a film, and the person who generally oversees a project from initial concept to release.

Product placement: The strategic placement of name-brand products within a film.

Production: General term to describe the actual filming of a movie, or the movie being filmed.

Production assistant: An entry-level gofer who works on a film set or in a production office.

Production company: A firm that develops and produces films.

Production coordinator: The person who runs the production office.

Production designer: The person responsible for the overall look of the picture as it pertains to form, color, and texture.

Production manager: The person responsible for supervising and coordinating all of the technical and administrative details of a production.

Production report: A daily report listing actual hours worked, total footage shot, and other information about each production day.

Production sound: Dialogue and some effects that are recorded during production.

Promotions: The creation of specific product to market a film.

Props: Any item that moves or is handled by an actor, or is identified in a script but not handled.

Publicity: The process of generating media coverage without paying for ads.

Pulling focus: The process by which the assistant camera operator moves the lens during filming to adjust for movement between the camera and the subject without losing a sharp image.

Query letter: An unsolicited letter used to introduce a writer's screenplay to a producer or agent.

Reader: A person who reads scripts and writes coverage.

Reading: An audition in which actors read from a script for the director or producer.

Reel: A visual résumé on video used by directors, cinematographers, and others that contains samples of their work.

Rough cut: Version of a film-in-progress that is put together after the editor's initial assembly and prior to a fine cut. The rough cut is generally fat (i.e., on the long side).

Runner: Production assistant whose primary duty is to run errands for the production.

Sample: A script used to attain writing assignments.

Scene: A segment of the script using only one location or a particular character, ending only in a change of location, time, or space.

Score: A film's musical composition.

Screenplay: A script intended for motion picture production.

Screenwriting: Writing characters, dialogue, and situations specifically meant to be enacted on film.

Scrim: A type of diffusion placed in front of light to soften shadows and harshness.

Script: See Screenplay.

Script supervisor: The person responsible for keeping track of which scenes have been covered, along with any deviations in the script, dialogue, or continuity.

Set: An area used for filming.

Set up: A particular camera and lighting plan relating to a certain scene or shot.

Shooting schedule: A detailed schedule of shooting days, times, cast and crew needs, and location changes.

Shooting script: The final version of the script when production begins.

Shop: To present a project to various financing entities for potential purchase or option.

Sides: Pages of a script that actors read at an audition.

Sound effects: Sounds added during post-production that do not include dialogue, music, or narration.

Spec script: A script written but not commissioned, that is used to sell to potential buyers once it has been finished.

Stand-in: A person other than the actor, who is used to block and light a scene that involves that actor.

Star request: Generally a specific hair, makeup, or wardrobe person demanded by a lead actor.

Storyboard: Illustrations depicting a sequence of events to help the director and key crew visualize a scene.

Studio: A company that produces, finances, and distributes films. The larger studios house sound stages and other filmmaking facilities.

Stunt coordinator: The person responsible for making sure that stunts are safely choreographed and executed.

Subsidiary rights: Ancillary rights, such as film or television rights, for a piece of material.

Swing gang: Members of the art department that do the lifting, moving, and rigging on the set. Also called set dressers.

Sync sound: Sound—mainly dialogue—that is matched to the picture.

Talent: A creative player, generally an actor, director, or writer.

Talent deals: Contracts and agreements with talent that secure their services for use on a production.

Territory: (1) A separate country or location that exhibits films. (2) A studio or buyer that has the financial ability to option or purchase material.

Time code: Coding that is permanently attached to specific frames of film for reference and editing purposes.

Trades: Daily and weekly industry magazines that cover the film business. The *Hollywood Reporter* and *Daily Variety* are the major ones in Hollywood.

Treatment: A synopsis of a screenplay that gives the reader a general understanding of the story line, plot elements, and characters in order to generate interest in the script.

Turnaround: The period in which a studio decides not to proceed with the production of a film, and the rights revert back to the owner of that material so it can be set up elsewhere.

Union: An organization created to protect the rights of its members in various occupations.

Union scale: The minimum wage that a member of a union can be paid for a given position.

Video playback: The video that is available to the director and crew as a source of immediate feedback before the film actually can be processed.

Visual effects: Effects created for the visual portion of a film in order to enhance an image, create something that was not originally there, or create an element that would be dangerous or impossible to film live.

Weekend read: The material read by studio executives over the weekend that will be discussed in a meeting early the following week. The read typically consists of scripts that some executives have read and liked.

Wide release: Refers to a film exhibited to a large number of theaters in many markets across the country and world.

BIBLIOGRAPHY

INTERVIEWS

Bressler, Carl (in person) 8/30/98

Britt, Amy McIntyre (in person) 7/22/98

Bronson, Tom (by phone) 1/4/99

Bruckheimer, Bonnie (in person) 12/10/98

Caglione, John, Jr. (by phone) 12/18/98

Cannold, Craig (in person) 10/22/98

Cheng, Angela (in person) 7/20/98

Dean, Joel (in person) 8/31/98

Deuble, Debbie (in person) 8/5/98

Dobson, Jimmy (in person) 9/29/98

Ferrin, Ingrid (by phone) 12/29/98

Garrick, Tim (by phone) 1/15/99

Green, Michael (by phone) 1/21/99

Groelinger, KristieAnne (in person) 8/11/98

Herskvitz, Marshall (in person) 2/18/99

Hill, Debra (in person) 2/8/99

Indig, Mark (in person) 10/27/98

Kaplan, Christian (in person) 10/16/98

Katz, David (in person) 11/16/98

Katz, Marty (by phone) 12/29/98

Katz, Stephen M. (by phone) 1/29/99

King, Jonathan (by phone) 1/13/99

Lambert, Mary (by phone) 1/14/99)

Martin, Maggie (in person) 10/14/98

May, Karon (by phone) 12/18/98

McAlister, Micheal (by phone) 12/23/98

McNabb, Mark (in person) 12/7/98

Mink, Bruce (in person) 9/17/98

Nelson, Andy (in person) 1/28/99

Ottman, John (in person) 9/29/98

Pitchford, Dean (in person) 11/17/98

Ramos, Robert (in person) 1/14/99

Shuman, Ira (by phone) 1/28/99

Skweres, Mary Ann (by phone) 1/5/99

Steinberg, David (in person) 9/15/98

Taylor, Yvette (in person) 12/10/98

Turteltaub, Jon (in person) 2/4/99

Valeo, Michael (in person) 8/6/98

Wissner, Gary (in person) 10/5/98

Yost, Daniel (in person) 8/27/98

MAGAZINES AND NEWSPAPERS

Blair, Ian. "Sync Up." *Film & Video*, August 1998, pp. 37–39.

Carver, Benedict, Dan Cox, Andrew Hindes, Paul Karon, Nick Madigan, Chris Petrikin, Monica Roman, and Ben Fritz. "Facts on Pacts." *Daily Variety*, June 22, 1998, p. 14.

Cox, Dan, and Chris Petrikin. "H'wood Script Story: Art Imitates Art." *Daily Variety*, July 22, 1997, pp. 1, 19.

Ferrante, Anthony C. "Breaking into the Business and Staying There." *Scr(i)pt*, March/April 1997, pp. 16–18.

Gerstein, Marvin. "Sound . . . Stepchild or Sibling." *Ross Reports TV/Film*, August 1998, pp. 4–6.

Higgins, Bill. "Studios Catering to Mood for Food." *Daily Variety*, October 4, 1998, pp. 9, 14.

Kim, John. "What Is Hollywood Thinking?" *Scr(i)pt*, vol. 4, no. 4, 1996, pp. 32–36, 55.

Luethje, Christine. "The Big Picture." *Film Music*, July 1998, p. 31.

Miller, Christina. "Reader's Pet Peeves." *Scr(i)pt*, March/April 1997, pp. 10–13.

Morris, Sheryl A. "Pitching to Hollywood." *Scr(i)pt*, November/December 1996, pp. 24–27.

Strauss, Alix. "Schmoozing Without Losing: The Arts of Networking." *Scr(i)pt*, November/December 1996, pp. 34–36.

Suppa, Ron. "Literary Management." *Creative Screenwriting*, Fall 1997, pp. 73–75.

_____. "Protecting Your Work." *Creative Screenwriting*, vol. 3, no. 4, 1996, pp. 35–37.

Trapp, Joanna K. "The Absolute Best Deal." *Men's Health*, July/August 1998, p. 92.

Willis, Holly. "The Script Supervisor." *Scr(i)pt*, vol. 4, no. 5, 1996, pp. 44–45.

BOOKS

Ames, Christopher. *Movies About the Movies: Hollywood Reflected*. Lexington, KY: University Press of Kentucky, 1998.

Brown, Blain. *Motion Picture and Video Lighting*. Newton, MA: Focal Press, 1996.

Buzzell, Linda. *How to Make It in Hollywood*. New York: HarperPerennial, 1996.

Connors, Martin, and James Craddock, eds. *VideoHound's Golden Movie Retriever 1999*. Detroit, MI: Visible Ink Press, 1999.

Fitzsimmons, April. *Breaking & Entering*. Los Angeles: Lone Eagle, 1997.

Giannetti, Louis. *Understanding Movies*. Englewood Cliffs, NJ: Prentice Hall, 1987.

Givens, Bill. *Film Flubs: Memorable Movie Mistakes*. Secaucus, NJ: Citadel Press/Carol Publishing Group, 1999.

Gottlieb-Walker, Kim, ed. *Setiquette*. Los Angeles: International Photographers Guild, 1997.

Katz, Ephraim. *The Film Encyclopedia*. (3rd ed., Fred Klein and Ronald Dean Nolan, eds.) New York: HarperPerennial, 1998.

Litwak, Mark. *Reel Power*. New York: Plume, 1986.

Lumet, Sidney. *Making Movies*. New York: Vintage, 1996.

Maltin, Leonard, ed. *Leonard Maltin's 1999 Movie & Video Guide*. New York: Plume, 1998.

_____. *The Whole Film Sourcebook*. New York: New American Library, 1983.

McAlister, Michael J. *The Language of Visual Effects*. Los Angeles: Lone Eagle, 1993.

Penney, Edmund F. *The Facts on File Dictionary of Film and Broadcast Terms*. New York: Facts on File, 1991.

Resnik, Gail, and Scott Trost. *All You Need to Know About the Movie and TV Business*. New York: Simon & Schuster, Inc., 1996.

Squire, Jason E., ed. *The Movie Business Book*. New York: Simon & Schuster, 1983.

Taub, Eric. *Gaffers, Grips, and Best Boys*. New York: St. Martin's Press, 1987.

Uva, Michael G., and Sabrina Uva. *The Grip Book*. Woburn, MA: Focal Press, 1997.

WEB SITES

Internet Movie Database: us.imdb.com

Mr. Showbiz: www.mrshowbiz.com

INDEX

ABOUT THE AUTHOR

Frederick Levy is vice president of development and production at Marty Katz Productions. Since joining the company in 1994, he has been involved in such films as *Man of the House* (1995), starring Chevy Chase, for Walt Disney Pictures; *Mr. Wrong* (1996), starring Ellen DeGeneres, for Touchstone Pictures; *Titanic* (1997), starring Leonardo DiCaprio, for Paramount Pictures and Twentieth Century-Fox; and *Reindeer Games* (2000), starring Ben Affleck, for Dimension Films.

Levy began his Hollywood career as a studio guide at Universal Studios Hollywood. Soon thereafter he started working in television as a guest coordinator on more than a dozen game shows, including *Love Connection*. He also worked in professional radio as producer of *The Morning Magazine* on KWNK, Los Angeles, and the syndicated *Then & Now* and *The Celebrity DJ Party*, both of which he created. Born in Stoughton, Massachusetts, he is a graduate of USC, where he majored in business—not film. *Hollywood 101: The Film Industry* is his first book.

Correspondence to the author can be sent in care of this publisher or directly by e-mail to author@hollywood-101.com. Readers can visit his Web site at www.hollywood-101.com.